# MADAME

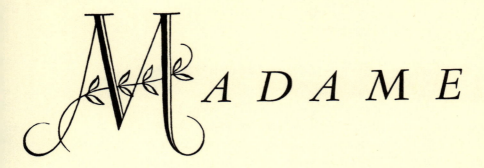

# MADAME

AN INTIMATE BIOGRAPHY OF

## HELENA RUBINSTEIN

### PATRICK O'HIGGINS

NEW YORK / THE VIKING PRESS

First published in 1971 by The Viking Press, Inc
625 Madison Avenue, New York, N.Y. 10022

Published simultaneously in Canada by
The Macmillan Company of Canada Limited

SBN 670-44530-4
Library of Congress catalog card number: 71-147394

Printed in U.S.A.


ACKNOWLEDGMENT

*Vogue* photographs Copyright © 1937, 1938, 1965, 1966
by The Condé Nast Publications Inc.

Sixth printing October 1971

*To Mala Rubinstein Silson and to all my friends in the Helena Rubinstein offices and factories throughout the world.*

# Contents

⚜ ⚜

*Illustrations follow pages 14, 42, 80, 126, 180, 228, 262*

# MADAME

# "Remember, I'm Your Friend ..."

I first remember her zooming down Madison Avenue on a bright October morning. Her short legs and tiny feet propelled the compact bulk of her body at such speed that it seemed a miracle she managed to keep her balance.

I had to move sharply as I amused myself tacking behind her through the crowds swarming to work. She darted along with the impulsive steps of a sandpiper, looking neither left nor right.

What had first caught my eye were her fantastic clothes. She wore a black bowler hat similar to those sported by Bolivian Indians; her body was tightly packed into a belted fur coat of what looked like a jigsaw puzzle of a thousand mink tails; elegantly buckled suède shoes rounded out her outfit.

We seemed to favor the same morning walk—the sunny side of the avenue. Now a red light, on the northwest corner of Fifty-fifth Street, halted her onward rush.

Sidling up, I cautiously looked down at her profile. Her jaunty hat was firmly anchored on a small head; her blue-black hair, drawn in a tight, glossy chignon, dramatized the imperial line of a commanding nose curving over a flaring nostril. Her mouth, a flash of crimson, was set over a strong jawbone. She gazed with concentrated fury at the offending light.

As we stood side by side one of her feet hammered an impatient tattoo on the asphalt pavement. It was then I noticed that she clutched a luxurious crocodile bag in one hand, a brown paper one in the other.

The street light changed to green. She shot off again, almost toppling over in her haste.

I now saw a familiar figure coming up the avenue toward us. He waved ecstatically. His pink moon face was aglow with enthusiasm. This was Federico Pallavicini, my colleague on the new magazine, *Flair,* where I worked as "Travel Editor" and where he filled the dual occupation of confidant and personal art adviser to our editor, Fleur Cowles.

Pallavicini had just recently been imported from Italy by the lady. His aristocratic manners, ebullience, and spicy gossip not only cheered *Flair*'s staff, but everyone with whom he came into contact in the heterogeneous group then known as "Café Society." This seemed to include just about anyone in New York whose name appeared more than once a month in Cholly Knickerbocker's daily gossip column, in the *Journal American.*

I now realized that Pallavicini wasn't waving at me but at the formidable figure with the paper bag some three steps ahead. She was forced to grind to a sudden stop as he danced a welcoming jig in her path. I almost collided with her.

Pallavicini indicated, with a flick of his pale blue eyes, that I was to stand by for introductions while, with delirious Italian enthusiasm, he greeted her in a goulash of four languages: "*Ah, très chère Madame! Délicieuse Princesse!* What a pleasure . . . *quelle joie! Meine gnädige Frau . . . guardate come è bella!*"

She stood rock-still, frowning slightly, as he cooed away, voicing his pleasure in the morning sunlight, Carol Channing, Monsignor Fulton Sheen, *and* her hat.

The year was 1950. Carol Channing was filling the Ziegfeld Theatre to the rafters in *Gentlemen Prefer Blondes*; while Monsignor Sheen mesmerized a new TV public with fiery eyes and sublime dogma.

I continued to hover in the wings until Pallavicini, with a sweep of his hands, introduced us with so many qualifying clauses that I failed to catch her name.

:[ 4 ]:

Unable to give me her right hand, due to the paper bag, she bobbed her head in curt acknowledgment. I was immediately conscious that in one swift glance a pair of button brown eyes had assessed my clothes, calculated my age, probably knew I had an overdraft at the bank.

She said nothing, turned on her heels, and trotted briskly west on Fifty-second Street. Two colossal diamonds, hanging from her ear-lobes, caught the sun as she disappeared.

"Who is she?" I asked Pallavicini who was still bent over double in the last of a series of farewell salaams.

"The Princess!" His voice was like a snake charmer's flute. "*Quelle originale!* She introduce African art to Picasso, the Polish sculptor Nadelman to America, Dali to dollars. The Princess . . . aah!" He sputtered in an effort to find the correct image in fractured English: "Is . . . the Sarah Bernhardt *de la beauté!*"

I hadn't the foggiest idea what he was talking about. When we reached the *Flair* offices I went to my travel editor's cubbyhole while Pallavicini, humming an aria from *Der Rosenkavalier*, danced into Mrs. Cowles' private powder room to paint the finishing touches on a trellis of full-blown roses. Fleur Cowles was dotty for roses.

With the recent launching of *Flair*, Mrs. Cowles had reached the zenith of her editorial career. She had married, some three years pre-viously, the millionaire publisher Gardner Cowles, who owned news-papers, radio stations, and a vast communications empire headed by *Look* magazine.

Fleur was a brilliant editor. Her light touch helped to transform *Look* from a depressing journal for Midwestern housewives into a national publication of taste, visual impact, and political influence. Her husband rewarded her efforts by giving her a magazine all her own. She christened it *Flair*, and gaily declared during one of many press conferences to herald its launching: "Without *Flair* the world's flat! Besides, *Flair* rhymes with Fleur." In point of fact, her actual name was reputedly Flora.

*Flair*'s editorial content gluttonously embraced the arts, fashion, travel, and literature; the first issue of this ambitious smorgasbord appeared gift-wrapped in a firehouse-red cover with a gaping hole in the center. Through this aperture a second cover was teasingly visible.

Soon these covers, although a costly gimmick, were celebrated as a national joke. *The New Yorker* caricatured them. They were gossiped about by Walter Winchell, Leonard Lyons, and Dorothy Kilgallen who quoted Gary Cooper's laconic remark: "I spent half an hour fishing Fleur out of the tub!"

That morning, after my encounter with Pallavicini and the lady with the paper bag, I was summoned to a general "Think" meeting in Mrs. Cowles' office. She was seated behind her vast kidney-shaped maplewood desk. Her back was to the light. She wore, as usual, harlequin sunglasses.

Fleur worked with a bookkeeper's concentration until she sensed her entire staff was present; then she announced dramatically, stroking her ash blond hair: "*Flair* will dedicate a whole issue to the rose in April. The rose represents to me all that is beautiful, tender, feminine. My good friend Katherine Anne Porter . . ." she paused to let this information impress us. "My good friend Katherine Anne Porter has written a touching, sensitive, *brilliantly sublime* introduction for our Rose Issue. Let me read to you the opening paragraph . . . 'The first rose was small as the palm of a small child's hand, with five petals in full bloom, the color red or white, perhaps even pink, and maybe sometimes streaked . . .' "

We, the staff, now competed to add a few sprigs of our own.

"A rose is a rose is a rose . . ."

"Roses printed on Kleenex could be *delicious* . . ."

"Mainbocher will surely go mad for roses . . . when he hears!"

Pallavicini's offering was accompanied by rich pantomime. "Fleur, darlink! Surely lilies for Easter is less corny? The Virgin Mary, Cardinal Spellman, and Saks all love them!"

Fleur snapped: "Thank you, Federico. But the subject is roses!"

As the meeting adjourned Mrs. Cowles held up a carefully manicured hand decorated with a single huge uncut emerald. "Mike and I . . ." she said using her social voice, "will be giving a cocktail party tomorrow night to announce the Rose Issue to a few very special, dear friends. I know I can depend on all of you to be there!"

This was the first time I had been invited to Fleur's town house in the East Sixties. When I arrived on the following evening I was agog with curiosity since Pallavicini, over a quick lunch at Hamburger Heaven, had already filled me in on the décor, "*Très* Fleur, she mix all the Louis with all the Georges . . . Mexican paper flowers with fresh green leaves . . . Renoir with her own paintings. *Quelle salade!*"

Although half an hour early, several of my junior colleagues were already hovering uncertainly in the hallway combing their hair, examining make-up, exchanging hushed small talk. Taking charge, a curvy French maid now led us up a sumptuous winding staircase carpeted in what looked like black poodle hair.

Fleur, dressed in a pink Valentina gown of rose-flowered silk, greeted us tersely on the landing. "When the guests start coming in you must help me relax them. Meantime, do have a drink. But don't budge!"

She fluttered up another flight of stairs. We stood bug-eyed, casing our surroundings. Pallavicini's description of the Cowles' house was an understatement.

I peeked into the drawing room which appeared to be as cluttered as the stalls of the Paris Flea Market, furnished with a wild mixture of antiques, contemporary pieces, bibelots, paintings—tufted Victorian sofas competed with linear steel chairs; Chinese sandstone statues were at odds with pieces of modern Italian sculpture; carved Louis Seize armoires dwarfed Empire sideboards. And on every available surface not filled with lacquer boxes, glass paperweights, and miniatures there were bouquets of huge orange, purple, and gold paper flowers, artfully bunched with real leaves, in bright opaline vases.

The walls, painted a tactful gray, were hung with Renoirs, Tamayos, de Koonings. Impressionists and abstracts abounded as did Fleur's own mystical oils of prowling tigers, carnivorous flowers, and roses.

"This is gutsy!" I thought before being summoned back by my chums at the top of the stair well.

The guests had now started arriving.

Fleur reappeared with Mike Cowles whom I had not yet met. His quiet, commanding detachment was impressive and in marked contrast to his wife, who was in constant flapping motion; throwing her arms around his broad shoulders, pacing up and down the landing. He peered from behind heavy framed glasses, gazing impassively at his guests, while Fleur flung herself at each successive arrival with the aggressiveness of a football tackle. She embraced them, rocked them, cradled them while Mike nodded absent-mindedly.

First Leonard Bernstein bounded up the staircase displaying the agility of a circus tumbler. Fleur was given a bear hug, Mike a prim nod.

Greta Garbo, wearing a sailor's navy blue peacoat, followed in Bernstein's agitated footsteps. She was like a sleepwalker. Her splendid jawbone, jutting out of a cheap scarf knotted around her head, revealed skin smoother than the marble on a new tombstone. Eyes wide and vacant, she seemed to float on flat-heeled brogues; smiled, revealing two rows of strong white teeth, pecked at Fleur's receptive cheek, and then drifted vaguely into the drawing room. On her way she summoned a passing waiter, "I want some whisky and sugar . . ."

Bernard Baruch now lumbered up, holding a hearing aid at arm's length, preceded by a grinning Carol Channing. The undulations of her hips seemed to spark him on.

"Fleur, darling!"

"Carol . . . sweet."

*"Bernie!"*

They huddled together as Noel Coward, Mr. and Mrs. William Paley, and Cary Grant awaited their turn as if standing in line for subway tokens.

An endless procession of vaguely familiar faces trooped by us, greeting their hosts, dispersing to the left and right into the drawing room and the library. There were socialites, theater people, artists. Never had I seen such a conglomeration as I stood mesmerized, with my colleagues, until Fleur charged up and ripped out a string of commands: "Shana!" addressing Shana Alexander, who shared my office and wrote scintillating copy. "Go and listen to Mr. Baruch!" She then turned to Robert Offergeld, another bright young editor much enamored with the Hollywood scene. "See what you can do with darling Greta!"

Lastly, addressing me and pointing to the library: "Patrick, cover that room!"

We all sprang to our respective posts.

The library was an austere paneled room whose bookcases at first glance seemed to be entirely lined with bound back issues of *Look*. A few guests sat chatting vaguely, thumbing through current issues of *Life,* or deciphering the signatures on silver-framed photographs decorating the piano.

I stood uncertainly in the doorway. A deep, foreign voice broke my reverie: "Young man, sit down. Speak to me!"

There, seated bolt upright and alone on a low sofa, was the lady I had followed down Madison Avenue on the previous day . . . without her brown paper bag.

She was now dressed in a tailored suit of rich magenta brocade. As I sat beside her I noticed that her shoes were stamped with twin golden crowns. My eye next caught the sparkle of carved, polished rubies—perhaps ten strands in all—pouring down her ample bosom. These matched the size and opulence of her inch-long Burgundy-colored earrings. She perked her head with the nervous impatience of a caged bird. Her jewelry dazzled me. Besides the cascading rubies, two carved emeralds glittered on each of her small, perfectly shaped hands and a huge cabochon ruby brooch glowed in her hat like an electric light bulb. This hat was similar to the oddly shaped bowler she had worn on the previous morning, only it was furry and of the same shade of magenta as her suit.

"Speak to me!" she repeated, "and tell me about the people here . . . all business?" I was fixed with a pair of ferret eyes. She didn't wait for an answer but leaned intimately toward me. "Fleur's clever, but I don't like her hors d'oeuvres. Too greasy!" And, as I anxiously examined my moist cheese puff, asked me:

"You work for Fleur? I've known her twenty years . . . she's come a long way!" She studied me, nodding and rocking.

"Where were you educated?" was her next question.

I couldn't make out her accent. It was rich, rolling, possibly Russian.

I told her that I was born in Paris, educated by Benedictine monks in England, that I had served with the Irish Guards during the war, and then emigrated to America. "Vy did you come to America?" She pronounced the "w" as a "v."

What's this to her? I wondered. It's like a third degree. I told her more: that I had inherited a bit of money from an American grandmother; also that my peripatetic parents, similarly blessed, were now living in New York.

"That's good!" she said. "Families should be close." Her lips curled slightly, a fleeting sadness clouded her granite features. I thought of faded photographs of Tzu Hsi, China's last Empress. She was a dead ringer for that mysterious, tough and forbidding autocrat.

"And what do you do for *Flair?*"

I explained my job as travel editor; reminding her that we had met briefly, on the previous day, when Pallavicini introduced us.

"He's a nice man! Talented . . . but *Flair* won't last!"

"*Flair* won't last?" I repeated. "Why?" She pulled on her gloves and checked the angle of her hat. "Too extravagant!"

Coming from her the words were deadly. I persisted. "What's wrong with *Flair?*" She dismissed the subject, shaking her head vaguely, and walked out of the room in regal slow motion. I followed as she pushed her way through the throng of guests.

"Help me find a taxi," she ordered when we reached the hallway. Carefully holding her arm I escorted her to the street. A taxi drew up. She climbed in without a second glance but, called out over her shoulder, "Don't worry about *Flair*, when it's kaput you can always come and see me."

I gaped at her tiny figure now huddled in the back of the cab. It was then I realized that I still didn't know her name. I tapped the window. She lowered it with a look of irritation.

"Excuse me! How can I come and see you when I don't even know your name?"

She now glared at me. I felt like a country bumpkin or a beggar being refused alms.

"My name is Princess Gourielli. But *for you* it may be easier to remember me as Helena Rubinstein!"

Helena Rubinstein, I thought as the cab drove off, that's a name I've seen somewhere. Before I could puzzle about it further, a large black limousine drew up depositing the current president of Columbia University, General Eisenhower. I sprang to attention and led him up the stairs in my best military fashion. Fleur was still the restless hostess. After embracing the general she seized my arm. "I hope you were nice to Helena? You certainly spent enough time with her. Will she advertise in the Rose Issue? Never mind! There's Elizabeth Arden. Go and talk horses to her."

*Flair's* Rose Issue appeared, with a rose-scented insert, as the first spring leaves were burgeoning in Central Park. This event was closely followed by several changes in the upper echelons of the staff. The quality of the magazine's paper deteriorated and the cover lost its hole. Expense accounts were closely scrutinized. Following each of these threatening events Princess Gourielli's terse warning began to haunt me. ". . . It won't last!"

One morning I was sitting in my cubbyhole laboriously composing a caption when my phone rang. An excited voice greeted mine: "This is Princess Gourielli's private secretary. Please forgive such short notice but the Princess, Madame Rubinstein, wants to know if you can lunch with her today?"

Invitations for lunch, even those extended on the same day, were pretty rare. Taken aback, I stuttered my acceptance—vividly remembering the funny little lady I had met at Fleur's and wondering how she had found out my name.

"Oh, the Princess, Madame Rubinstein, will be so happy. The Sitwells are coming. So is Salvador Dali . . . and," she added breathing heavily down the receiver, "it's an artistic luncheon. Madame Rubinstein felt you would fit in nicely. She expects you at one o'clock, at her home." I was given a Park Avenue address and then told that Pallavicini had told her who I was.

Entranced at the idea of meeting Osbert and Edith Sitwell on a double bill and seeing Dali's quivering mustache at close quarters, I rapidly wrote my caption, rushed home for a change of shirt and then ambled up Park Avenue to Sixty-fifth Street. Princess Gourielli lived in one of those mammoth apartment buildings that are a misalliance of Renaissance and pre-Wall-Street-Crash architecture. I was fifteen minutes early and decided to mark time in the lobby, a marble bastion that reminded me of the Roxy cinema. I duly announced myself to the porter on duty, a freckled Irishman, and soon learned he came from Meath, the county of my hardier forebears. After an exchange of pleasantries on the weather, the decline of amateur football, and the odds on his favorite horse for the Derby, he said, "Ah, well now, if it's to the Madame you're bound for, you might as well get up there. Lots of swells are coming for lunch. She told me so herself."

We shot up fourteen floors to the penthouse. The Irishman gave me another conniving grin as I trod on more marble and made my way through a small hall leading into a vast one. It was filled with sunlight that beamed down on a jungle of verdant potted plants.

All of the doors were open and since there was no visible bell I stood looking around me perplexed.

The plants, massed beneath three huge French windows, gave the illusion of a Douanier Rousseau painting. There were banana trees, rubber trees, azaleas, and other flora that I could not catalogue; while the furnishings—chairs, tables and sofas—were of lacy Indonesian teak, painted stark white. Occasionally, I had seen photographs of similar pieces in the pages of fashionable magazines. The caption always read, "The terrace of the Maharaja's summer palace." Marble heads decorated tall pedestals at regular intervals beneath the white walls. They looked like the busts of Roman deities as dreamed up by an ice cream company. Through an arched doorway to my left I caught a glimpse of a paneled drawing room glittering with the muted gold of many picture frames.

"Who's there?" a voice inquired, closely followed by the clatter of footsteps.

The Princess, Madame Rubinstein, appeared. She wore her usual bowler hat and a matching yellow chemise dress with balloon sleeves and a drawstring neck from which multiple strings of carved emeralds hung to the uncertain level of her waist. One small hand, decorated with a diamond the size of a bottle cap, held a piece of sausage.

"Krakowska . . . Polish sausage!" she said, chewing away. Large gypsy circles of ruby and emerald cabochons swung from her earlobes and brushed each of her well-rounded shoulders. She led me at a trot into a room some forty feet long whose walls, confirming my first hasty glance, were papered with row upon row of paintings, of all shapes and sizes, from eye level to the curve in the vaulted, stucco ceiling. There must have been more than a hundred. They were mind-boggling. Was selling paintings one of her side lines? I wondered.

"Vodka?" The Princess broke my reverie. She offered me two hunks of sausage, pointed her little finger to a bottle in a crested silver bucket and repeated: "Vodka? Good! Serve yourself! Drink! Eat!" She rolled her "r"s like a Broadway actress impersonating a Russian grand duchess.

We sat down on a small Victorian sofa covered in purple velvet, nipping vodka, munching in unison. Again I could feel her eyes piercing through me, scanning my face, my shoes, every crease in my suit.

Finally she said, "I'm glad you're early. We can chat before the others arrive. Tell me more about yourself?" She carefully raised her feet onto a footstool carved in the shape of a turtle and settled back comfortably. Her eyes never wavered from mine. Occasionally she encouraged me with another round of sausage.

Recalling my conversation with her at Fleur's cocktail party, I elaborated on my childhood, "Mother's a dynamo, Father's a mystic. My only sister's a dreamer and I'm an extrovert."

"Good!" She seemed to approve of my immediate family tree.

"In Paris, where I was born, we lived with my maternal grandfather. He was a banker."

"Aah!" She sat forward, "Have you inherited his business sense?"

"I'm afraid not."

"Never mind!" She urged me on with an upward thrust of her chin.

"When I was nine I was sent to school in England, at Downside. It's a Benedictine monastery."

The Princess's face registered disbelief.

"They wanted you to be a monk . . . so young?"

"Oh no! You see we are Irish. We are Catholics. We are expatriates. Downside caters to such hybrids."

She sat listening like a little girl to a fairy tale. Now there was warmth and wide-eyed simplicity in her eyes. I was drawn to her. I felt I could blurt out my inmost secrets.

"And then?" She prodded me in the rib cage.

I told her again about my war years when I had served with the Guards Brigade, my arrival in New York in 1948, my first job with *Town and Country*, which had preceded *Flair*.

"My two boys," she injected, "have led similar lives to yours . . . international. Both are clever—but different. I hope you will get on

:[ 13 ]:

with Horace. He's the younger . . . literary, like you. Pfft! We don't always see eye to eye."

Her voice in this sudden moment of confidence was tremulous. When she spoke Horace's name it was with sadness, yet much love.

"Do you get on with your mother?" She sat bolt upright, suddenly anxious. I reassured her that we were the best of friends.

"You live together?"

"No," I said, "for the past year I've been living in my own small apartment on West Fifty-fifth Street."

"That's good! How much rent do you pay?"

I hesitated. She leaned forward and kicked me lightly in the ankle. "Don't be ashamed. Tell me!"

Not only did I tell her that the rent was fifty dollars a month, but I described the strange appointments. "You see, it's really the master bathroom of an old converted brownstone that I've furnished with a four-poster bed, a desk, Mexican straw armchairs. . . . Very convenient, really; I only have six steps to walk from my bed to the bath."

She rocked with laughter. "That's just what I need. Must save you a lot of time! Here we have thirty-six rooms, three floors, two kitchens, and eight bathrooms. Too much for two people! Me and my husband, the Prince . . ." Since we seemed to have established such a cosy relationship I asked her if he would be joining us for lunch.

"Oh, no," she said emphatically. "The Prince hates literary people!"

There was a commotion in the hallway. Princess Gourielli gave me her hand. "Pull me up!" She then made her way to the door rushing forward in a series of tiny, hurried footsteps; arms outstretched; cooing welcoming words to a flock of guests who had arrived simultaneously.

Fascinated, I watched her greet the towering, undulating Sitwells. Sir Osbert had the dyspeptic coloring of a retired English colonel suffering from high blood pressure and chronic ennui; Doctor Edith (who was not, as yet, a Dame) wore a wimple of mud-hued brocade from which a Mother Hubbard billowed down to her angular well-shod feet. Her jewels were actually the tusks of wild animals, set in gold, studded with amethysts. She looked like a sybil but her brusque greeting reminded me of an English gym instructress.

Madame on the eve of her departure from Australia, around 1905, after she had made her first fortune.

"When I was young, I liked Spanish hats!" Connecticut, 1918.

Madame: A Cecil Beaton "portrait," circa 1938.
Beaton said: "I had to chop off four inches from her
waistline."

Both Sitwells were forced to bend nearly double over their minute hostess. A pair of cranes examining a hedgehog, I thought.

The Princess sparkled with animation. Merry and flirtatious, her eyes beamed happiness as she hopped around handing "Polish sausage," dispensing vodka, shaking her diminutive but solid frame. Any moment, I thought, she'll break into a mazurka.

No one was formally introduced. This great flurry of activity, I was to learn, was a ploy. The Princess obviously had no memory for names.

In addition to the Sitwells and a lugubrious Salvador Dali, the party consisted of two nondescript, nameless ladies; an evangelical bearded man; and a good-looking Englishman, resplendent in hairy ginger tweeds, a checked flannel shirt, old school tie. He turned out to be Scottish. "Ogilvy!" he said shaking my hand and almost knocking my shoulder out of joint. Since I knew that David Ogilvy's advertising agency was currently stirring up Madison Avenue I tactfully stalked him.

His manner was preoccupied. He kept examining the guests over a pair of tortoise-shell spectacles balanced on the tip of his nose. He epitomized the expatriate Anglo-Saxon who had memorized his role. Princess Gourielli, aware that the Polish sausage had been devoured, darted from the room. "Albert! Mathilda!" she shouted as she went.

The guests wandered around aimlessly while Dali studied his own paintings—there were many of them for him to choose from.

Dr. Sitwell instantly called everyone to heel. "I say!" she boomed out:

"Up the workers,
Use Tiz for tired feet,
And there shall be no more corns
Except the workers' wheat . . ."

We all froze speechless. "That's one of my poems," she said as we gathered around for more. Shifting voices she said: "Isn't the Princess an original? I only wish she didn't treat me like a starving *Pole*." Sir Osbert briefly shook free of his lethargy. "She's Russian, Edith!"

The bearded man, tugging his Vandyke, said quietly: "Madame Rubinstein is Polish. I should know, she's my mother!"

There was a deadly silence mercifully broken by the noisy return of our hostess, who was now accompanied by a diminutive Asiatic butler —even smaller than she—carrying an enormous platter piled high with a cornucopia of raw vegetables.

"It's-an-offer-ing-to-spring," Edith Sitwell ululated.

Nibbling a carrot, her little finger gaily cocked, the Princess pointed to the platter: "Eat, eat . . . fresh vegetables from our place in Greenwich."

After a brief communal chomp she led us pied-piper fashion across the marble hallway, through a long corridor whose walls were lined with a sparkling collection of blue china, to a walnut-paneled dining room.

There were no place cards. "You sit here. You sit there. You sit . . ." Sir Osbert miraculously landed on her right, David Ogilvy on her left.

The table was a sea of pink: pink plates, pink opaline glasses, pink ash trays, even a centerpiece of pink peonies.

"I see you approve of Miss Arden's favorite color scheme," David Ogilvy murmured to the Princess.

"Why not? Does she have a patent on pink?"

It was evident that there was no love lost between the two cosmetics tycoons. But the Princess wasn't ready to play games with Mr. Ogilvy. Her eyes flickered on Edith Sitwell's hieratic headdress. "I like your hat." She pronounced it "het."

"It's not a hat, dear Princess, but a coif."

"Pretty. Suits you!"

"It's my favorite color . . . dead Spaniard."

Meanwhile on the other side of the table Dali rattled on mixing English, French, and Spanish, trying to convey his recent experiences in New York. Sir Osbert Sitwell, after busily guzzling shrimps, now looked up at him:

"Were you not once known as Avida Dollar?"

"That name," Dali sputtered, "she brought me luck. Money rain down on me. Bad publicity sometimes better than good. Much better than none at all!"

"He's right," the Princess growled through her mouthful of shrimps.

One of the nameless ladies now became involved in a long discussion about the fall of France. Sir Osbert perked an ear, but it was sister Edith who again froze the company: "*Madame, nos ancêtres ont brulé Jeanne d'Arc!*"

Princess Gourielli let out a gull's cry. David Ogilvy tried to be a helpful interpreter:

"Doctor Sitwell has just said that her ancestors burned Joan of Arc."

"Someone had to do it!" the Princess retorted, glaring at the offending lady. Suddenly she sprang to her feet, and vanished into the pantry. A few moments later she returned triumphantly with a large pink sea shell.

"Albert forgot! Horse radish for the roast beef, for my guests of honor the Sitwells. I'm a firm believer in 'God helps those who help themselves.' "

David Ogilvy patted her hand. "Dear Madame, you've never said a truer word; and while thanking you for this excellent meal may I add that you've always lived by your pronouncements!"

She gave him an extended look. The meal proceeded without further verbal engagements, but with more pink dishes. After a towering strawberry mousse had been demolished, the Princess steered us back to the drawing room for coffee.

"I must go and buy myself some shoes." Edith Sitwell pointed to her huge feet and rose to leave. "I always do so in the Men's Department at Macy's. They treat me with such understanding!"

As the room emptied, the Princess, pointing a finger, indicated that David Ogilvy, her son, Horace, and I were to remain.

"Sit down all of you!" She turned to Mr. Ogilvy. "You should give this young man a job. He's going to need one. *Flair* won't last. I've heard that Fleur's not getting on with her husband! You can teach him your advertising methods. He can then come and work for us." David Ogilvy answered quietly: "But, dear Madame, I'm already employing six of your protégés."

"Seven's my lucky number." She tapped his knee and thrust her face in his. "Besides, he knows lots of people. Some of them might even be useful to you."

David Ogilvy politely dismissed this suggestion; the Princess held firm. "We plan to spend much more money on advertising this coming year. You'll need people. Good people. *Nice* people!"

Embarrassed, yet flattered, I rose to escape. "It's kind of you, Princess, but I'm happy where I am."

I thanked her for lunch and bowed to Mr. Ogilvy. Horace signaled good-by with two fingers. To my astonishment the Princess bustled after me and while I waited for the elevator she gently took my hand in both of hers. They were incredibly soft.

"Remember, I'm your friend. Keep in touch . . . who knows?"

Walking down Park Avenue, back to my office, I was sadly tempted to spend the rest of the afternoon idling in Central Park. What a meal! What a dizzy group! What a Princess!

At the time Madame Rubinstein, the Princess Gourielli, was reputed to be nearly eighty; yet her firm chin, pale olive complexion brightened by carmine lips, rouged cheekbones, and the skillfully drawn contours delineating her eyes—those eyes which were seldom at rest and must even have glowed in the dark—suggested a woman a third her age. Then there was her vitality, her powers of concentration, and her curious speech. It could be soft, modulated, singsong or blunt—a whiplash!

She was frightening and yet lovable; but what had really bowled me over, besides her opulence and the magic of her surroundings, were her parting words: "Remember, I'm your friend."

# *"How Much? Too Much!"*

---

❦ ❦

"What's the use of looking back?"
    I later found out that this was the standard answer Princess Gourielli gave when playing the part of Helena Rubinstein, the cosmetics tycoon and Empress of Beauty, if quizzed by the press about her past.

Not so myself. I'm a hopeless sentimentalist and, like all the Irish, love to wallow in retrospection. Looking back is my thing. It gets me through difficult days; lulls me to sleep at night; and, when I have to make a decision, encourages me to do so with a clearer eye.

Memories!

I first arrived in New York on a troopship filled with cackling Cockney war brides. Most of them were pregnant and amorously inclined. It was an incredible overture, in the fall of 1948, to what was to be my new life in America. I was still hobbling on a stick, due to damage sustained on my legs while attempting to cross the Rhine, at Nijmegen, in 1944. But in those distant days, when I was in my early twenties, nothing could stop me. I was entranced with all I saw. I longed to investigate and to discover what was to be my home for the next twenty-odd years. I was also joyful to be alive and, finally, out of uniform.

After a few weeks of pleasurable inactivity, of soaking in my new freedom, I began to feel restless. My parents, who had preceded me and with whom I was then living, gently urged me to find a job, and, much to my surprise, I landed one as a junior editor on *Town and Country* magazine. The salary was fifty dollars a week—or, as the current editor, Nicky De Gunzburg, explained in a low monotone, "Just enough for your laundry bills and minor vices." My duties were far from arduous, but they helped me rapidly to enlarge a small circle of friends and acquaintances on every imaginable level—from subbasements in Greenwich Village to walk-ups in Harlem, via Park and Fifth Avenues.

Greenwich Village, before the architectural onslaughts currently known as New York University, was compact and crummy. A three-course dinner at the Jumble Shop on Eighth Street cost less than a dollar. It was even cheaper on the other side of Washington Square where, in the garlic-scented atmosphere of Little Italy, I first stumbled on Marlon Brando. He was perched on an icebox, wearing a T-shirt, spouting Shakespeare to an unreceptive audience drinking gin out of Dixie Cups. The setting was a loft furnished with packing crates; its owners were unknown to most of their guests. Brando's declamations were not completely unheeded. A small man with a neat mustache, sharp eyes and a benign smile kept egging him on in a Southern drawl: "Now, honey, try Henry V's Agincourt speech!" Brando took up the challenge, still seated on the icebox, posturing with an imaginary sword. The small man beamed with delight. Was it then, on that evening, in that dingy loft, that Tennessee Williams first met his future star? I don't know. But *A Streetcar Named Desire* is somehow linked in my memory with this cameo scene.

Next I met Pavel Tchelitchew, the Russian painter, whose speech sounded as if a tornado had formed in his larynx and couldn't quite get out. Ruth Ford, the actress, and her poet brother Charles-Henri were in the vortex of his eclectic group which included the bearded editor Leo Lerman. He had been christened by his friends "The Marshmallow Lenin" because of his shiny bald pate, pointed beard, and an aura of mysticism which always accompanied his lesser pronouncements. In his house, on the borders of Spanish Harlem, I was introduced to Glenway Wescott, Carson McCullers, and Brooklyn's poet laureate, the frail but indomitable Marianne Moore. George

Davis was also there. It was because of him, when he became managing editor, that I was hired on *Flair*—my first big break, since my salary was doubled and I was now making one hundred dollars a week!

As for Harlem, I was sometimes lucky enough to be invited to Blanche Dunn's fried chicken Sunday suppers on 124th Street, where the cast was no less varied. Carl Van Vechten, the writer, presided; Jimmy Daniels, the intimate singer, cooked; and sometimes, even Nancy Cunard—wearing monkey fur and Ubangi bracelets—trailblazed integration with the fervor of a Methodist preacher.

Park and Fifth Avenues? Well, before leaving London a maiden aunt, who had savored American triumphs before me (and had since turned to raising pug dogs), wished me Godspeed with a letter. I looked upon it with suspicion. It was merely addressed: "Mrs. Cornelius Vanderbilt, New York."

Months elapsed before I used this introduction—by then I was working for *Flair*. Mrs. Vanderbilt, whom I now discovered had ruled over New York society for more than half a century, was over eighty, blind, and sufficiently vague for my youthful and odd presence not to ruffle the elaborate ceremonial surrounding her.

She no longer lived in her huge palace on Fifth Avenue but had moved to smaller quarters situated on the southeast corner of Eighty-sixth Street and Fifth Avenue, facing Central Park. Her brick mansion occupied half a city block, had a mere forty-six rooms, and a permanent staff of eighteen. (Small wonder I had been hesitant, intimidated.) I was told that Mrs. Vanderbilt never ventured out of her home without a footman hurling a red carpet on the sidewalk, linking the front door with an old brown Packard, so that she might not soil her shoes. This thrilled me. So, when an English friend, Michael Duff, forced the issue and finally brought me into "Her Grace's" glittering orbit (Mrs. Vanderbilt's first name was Grace), I acquiesced with pleasurable anticipation. He was staying with her. They were related through her sister who had married into the Pembroke family. "Come to dinner on Monday next," Michael suggested. "That's opera night. The food's bloody good and we'll hear *Salome* at the Met."

I duly clocked in.

To my unsophisticated eyes the Vanderbilt mansion seemed to combine all of the visual affluence of the Paris Ritz with the glitter of Versailles' Trianon. There was marble everywhere. It covered the hallway, as if in a plush bank; lined the stair well; exploded in multicolored patterns on the walls of a series of galleries leading to the reception rooms on the first floor. These were furnished with an Edwardian's love for clutter. Boulle, gilded Louis XVI chairs, six-foot Chinese vases filled every nook and cranny—as did love seats curling gently beneath jagged palms and vitrines crowded with jade ornaments.

Michael Duff, to my relief and alarm, was on hand to receive me. He was immaculately dressed in tails. These threw me into a panic. I was wearing a "utility" dinner jacket. Fortunately, other guests arrived, many of whose clothes seemed to be just as scruffy as mine. We were a motley group that included Serge Obolensky, several very social ladies escorted by their decorators, and . . . the Duchess of Windsor.

Punctually at eight, the drawing-room doors were flung open by two footmen as Mrs. Vanderbilt was wheeled in by a third. She was small, pink, and glittering. Her features could have been those of a very old Marilyn Monroe—vapid and innocent. A diamond-embroidered bandeau encircled her forehead; diamond shoulder straps held her dress; miscellaneous diamond clips and brooches sparkled from her neckline down to her pointed shoes; while serried bracelets barely permitted her, such was their weight, to raise her arms.

Everyone gathered around her.

Although she couldn't walk, could barely see, her greetings were those of a diva. She trilled in a high, piping voice, extending two fingers (and never more than three) to each of her guests, who in turn murmured their names.

"Ooh . . . Wallis! And where's my favorite king?" Mrs. Vanderbilt said to the Duchess of Windsor. There were never too many kings for Mrs. Vanderbilt and although she had difficulty overlooking the abdication, she had, finally, accepted the Duchess. The Duchess tactfully explained that her husband had a head cold. In point of fact, he loathed opera, she told us later, and was enjoying an evening's solitude in the Waldorf Towers writing his memoirs.

Some days after my first Vanderbilt dinner and my first night at the Metropolitan Opera, I arrived at work, on a Monday morning, to find a pink slip on my desk.

In four curt mimeographed lines it informed me that *Flair* had suspended publication. I was fired—as was everyone else on the staff —with six weeks' severance pay.

At lunch, several of my colleagues concentrated on discussing their future plans while drowning the past in martinis. For my own part, I sat stunned. Later that evening I again studied my pink slip. It reminded me of Madame Rubinstein, of Princess Gourielli. Not only did it match her table setting, it was proof of her psychic powers: "*Flair* won't last!"

I sat down and wrote her a short letter offering my services. Weeks went by without an answer and I was forced to seek work elsewhere.

Being unemployed and hard-up in New York is a rough but edifying experience. But with unemployment benefits, a few savings, and liberal free-loading whenever the opportunity arose, I survived. Mrs. Vanderbilt's Monday dinners became the cornerstone of my diet. I had passed the initial test and was firmly established on her guest list, thanks to her genial secretary, Mrs. Payne, who seemed to enjoy our chats on the telephone—particularly after I had informed her of my plight.

"You can always depend on us for a couple of good, nourishing meals a week," she told me. "And it might help you to get a job if I asked Mrs. Vanderbilt to have you listed in the *Social Register*."

When I discovered that this honor would require a small fee, I turned it down. Twenty dollars, in those days, saw me through a whole week. In the meantime, there were countless interviews, none of which produced tangible results. I was later told by a friendly would-be employer that my appearance, which he described as "pleasing," did not inspire confidence. I was too "off-hand." I also lacked "direction," "compulsion," "ambition." These words alarmed me. I knew my potential, but evidently failed to get it across. Then, one day, I was summoned by Carmel Snow, the editor of *Harper's Bazaar* —the queen of the fashion press, of the fashion world. We had a rapport. Often, at cocktail parties, she had grabbed me by the arm. "Get me a little drink . . . let's have a good gossip!" We shared Celtic memories and, although much awed by her—possibly because I could never quite understand what she was saying—our relationship was relaxed. She enjoyed my chatter. I admired her mumbled yet acid pronouncements.

When I called on her, Mrs. Snow received me punctually. She sat, primly upright, behind a small white desk, wearing a pink linen suit and a matching straw bonnet. She was neat as a nun; a very chic nun, whose puckish features, half-closed eyes, turned-up nose, turned-down mouth reminded me of a stubborn but ageless sprite.

She was explaining, in her usual muffled voice, some of the finer fashion points just observed on Seventh Avenue. An equally *soignée*, angular, dark-haired lady stood attentively by her side. This was Diana Vreeland, her principal fashion editor, who was later to become *Vogue*'s editor-in-chief.

Mrs. Vreeland's hands were like antennae. They seemed to snatch Mrs. Snow's pronouncements from the air. Her mouth kept revolving as if savoring them. She undulated, from pelvis to fingertips, like an Egyptian belly dancer: "I getcha! This season navy blue's the pink of India!" Her voice sounded like a saxophone imitating a buzz saw.

Mrs. Snow sat stock-still while Mrs. Vreeland bounced out of the room (a fawn who had been given birth by a kangaroo?). Mrs. Snow then turned to me and said, "We don't pay much!"

I now gathered I was a candidate to write a free-lance monthly travel piece for her magazine. The fee was a hundred and fifty dollars. More woolly words sealed our agreement. Mrs. Snow rose, teetered on ankles no larger than the stems of champagne glasses and, with a trailing motion of her hand, dismissed me: "Your first article will be about Chile." I had never been to Chile.

Contributing to *Harper's Bazaar* was a jolly diversion, if not a meal ticket; but I somehow managed to keep my head peeking over the high water mark of solvency. To do so, I had to use every means with which youth and the optimistic nature of a born hooker had endowed me. Besides, I still had my "utility" dinner jacket first worn at Mrs.

Vanderbilt's. In those days, a dinner jacket was a life raft on which insolvency, a speck of breeding and good manners might just survive.

Toward the beginning of 1951, many months after I had written to Princess Gourielli, I received an answer. It was typewritten on elaborately crested paper and bore a Paris address. Her style was terse, matter-of-fact. "When in need of work, take anything you can get," she had dictated. "Then, you can improve yourself. I expect to be back in a month. Call me at my Fifth Avenue office after the New Year. I'm sure something good will come out of it."

I did. The breathless voice of her secretary again greeted mine. With many a pause (due to the fact, I learned later, that the Princess monitored such conversations on an extension), she suggested that I meet "Madame Rubinstein" on the following Saturday, for lunch at The Colony restaurant. Licking my lips, I accepted.

When I arrived on the dot of the appointed hour, my hostess, whose face now reminded me of an impassive carving on a totem pole, was already seated in a secluded corner of the bar—which was then considered to be the fashionable part of the restaurant, reserved for the most desirable guests.

She was dressed in inky black. Her shiny, form-fitting *tailleur* matched the inevitable bowler hat. It was decorated with a star the size of an order of chivalry, set in rubies and emeralds. Around her short neck were eight massive strings of knobbly, milk-white pearls secured by yet another monumental brooch. This also looked like an order. "Surely the Garter," I thought as I sat down.

"Want a drink?" Princess Gourielli's voice was barely audible. "I've ordered a Bloody . . . you know? Mary!" She sipped it, when it arrived, holding the glass with two fingers cocked vertically. One of them was enriched with a pearl the size of a gallstone.

"Hungry?" she asked, pronouncing it "hongry."

Pallavicini, who often lunched with her, had previously warned me, "Eat what she eat; otherwise she eat you!" Before I could admit that I was hungry, or even examine the menu, the Princess called out to a hovering maître d'hôtel: "Two 'paillardes' of beef, spinach, beer. . . ." And, eyeing me, asked, "Like beer? I do!" Her voice was now strong. Her look and her query called for complete agreement.

While waiting for our food, we exchanged generalities. When these were exhausted, she munched energetically on a roll and then announced: "I have tickets for a film. It's called *Ben Hur*. 'My Little Girl' tells me it's educational . . . *religious*. Want to go after lunch?"

"It will be a pleasure."

She nodded, gave a series of small shrugs, and concentrated on her steak—the "paillarde" of beef. It vanished in a matter of seconds, as did the spinach, the beer, and two more rolls.

Who, I wondered, was "My Little Girl"?

(Months later, I learned that Princess Gourielli referred to all her secretaries, collectively and sometimes even affectionately, as "my little girl." Some were doddering with age. No matter. It was easier than trying to remember their names. But should "my little girl" come into disfavor, she was promptly written off as "My zero! You know, the nebbishy one who tries to type.")

Our meal was not prolonged with chat. I had to wolf down my food in order to catch up with Princess Gourielli, who seemed in a rush to reach Broadway. Even before coffee appeared, she called for the bill, studied it carefully, and paid with cash plucked out of the large crocodile handbag permanently looped around her arm. I glanced quickly inside during the lightning moment it was open. My head reeled. It looked like the contents of a salad bowl—filled with greenbacks of every possible denomination.

She now took an extra handful, and, carefully wrapping herself in a sable stole, rose to her feet, tipped every waiter in sight with a single dollar, and tottered out.

"Taxi!" She now gave the doorman yet another dollar bill, then turned to me: "Hop in first! It's easier that way."

We drove to Broadway in silence. As the cab approached the cinema's neon-lit marquee, I felt impelled to produce my own dollar bill.

"No! Don't. . . . I have lots of small change," Princess Gourielli snapped. She had evidently thought I was going to give a forty-cent tip for a sixty-cent fare.

"Are you *that* extravagant?" she queried, rolling the "r."

"No. I was going to ask for change."

"Good. You can pay!"

*Ben Hur*, a revival of several revivals, was now splashed upon the widest of wide screens. This production, created by Cinerama, was an innovation. The huge screen almost engulfed the audience.

"I always like to sit close," Princess Gourielli confided as we settled down in the third row.

When the lights went out, I experienced a feeling close to panic, but my companion, perched on the very edge of her seat, alternately clutched my arm and her throat. She produced an arpeggio of gull-like sounds, thrust her elbow in my ribs, and—especially during love scenes—kept demanding in a loud whisper: "What are they doing? . . . Are they kissing? . . . Will they get married?" Our neighbors began to hush her, but she was not one to be intimidated and continued with her cries, sighs, and nudges until the climax of the famous chariot race—when Ben Hur's horses are caught in a life-and-death struggle with Messala's black equipage. Then her excited groans, prods, and queries almost knocked me out of my seat until, in a resounding voice, she demanded: "Has the Jewish boy finally won?"

Three hours later, deaf in one ear, bruised and dazed, I led her out of the cinema. She was smiling to herself.

"Most interesting! I'm glad the Jewish boy won."

"Why?"

"He was the more *gentlemanly* of the two."

When we reached her apartment the front door was wide open. There were no servants around.

"Sit there!" The Princess pointed to two chairs in a corner of the marble hallway. "I'll get something to drink and then we'll have a chat."

Her footsteps echoed as she raced away and, after a brief absence, returned with two glasses in one hand, an ice bucket in the other, and a bottle of Scotch tucked under her arm.

"Now we can relax!" The Princess seated herself, raised her legs onto a footstool and indicated, with a quick gesture of her right hand, that I should do the honors.

"Mixing drinks," she said, "is a man's work."

For a while we both sat in silence. She studied me as I pretended to look vaguely at the sensational view beyond the windows. A sharp kick in my shin brought me back with a start: "Now, now tell me . . . tell me what you really want, what you really want to do with your life?"

My hands rose and fell.

I was at a loss to answer her question.

"Well. *Let Me tell you!*"

In her singsong voice, with surprising intensity, she first enumerated my failings. "You give the impression of being a playboy. You need stability, direction. You must be ambitious!" I was reminded of the man who had recently turned me down for a job. He, too, had said— but without her warmth or interest—practically the same thing.

Next, she listed what few characteristics I benefited from: "You are nice, honest, clean-cut . . . *gentlemanly*." "Like Ben Hur?" I queried. She nudged me. "Yes, almost."

And finally she described her business, herself, her own problems: "I have too much on my shoulders. I'm surrounded with people, but I can't get to them. . . . There's the family, aai! They all want to prove their worth, but they all want to enjoy their own lives. People . . . people . . . and I'm alone! With burdens . . . such burdens! In New York things are easier for me. In Europe! You can have it! Nothing but intrigue, disagreements. I swear, I swear, it's killing me."

She pounded her breasts so that the pearls jangled. She raised her eyes to the ceiling, hit my knee, shook a fist at imaginary enemies. It was difficult for me not to laugh. This funny little lady seemed to epitomize all of the distress, anger, of a classical Jewish mother.

Then, picking her words she said: "I'll tell you something. You could be most useful to us . . . to me! You could have what I call a real job, a career, a future. With us . . . with me!" Again, I was jabbed in the ribs as she pointed to herself. Again, I was stunned. That this powerful, strangely maternal woman had to unburden her heart to a stranger such as myself confused me. The impact of her personality seemed almost smothering. I longed for another drink, for air, for escape.

She must have felt this. Her voice lost its urgency. It became soft, almost conspiring: "We've talked enough. You've had a long day. So have I. Come and see me on Monday. Yes. Come to the office in the morning. Then we can really talk shop!"

With another wave of her arm, she dismissed me. I kissed her hand gently, thanking her for lunch and the movie.

"Don't forget," she called out after me. "Monday. I expect you at ten sharp, in the shop!"

"Shop . . . to talk shop!" These words echoed in my mind as did the curious inflection the Princess gave them. Her accent was captivating. It could be satin-smooth, rich as treacle; or rough and imperious.

Yes, as at our previous meeting, I was hooked.

As I wandered home, to my one-room apartment, I somehow realized she was my future. She gave me strength and I needed it. While I, I somehow also stimulated her.

I couldn't sleep. My thoughts were filled with the forthcoming interview on Monday morning. I kept wondering: "But what will I do for her? Where will I fit in? What does she want from me?"

The telephone jangled. My friend Pallavicini's excited voice brought me back to my senses. "The Princess," he said, "she call me this evening. She talk about you, in German. Very good sign! She want you. She don't pay much. Ask lots," he added, "she cut everything in half!"

On Monday morning, as I walked the short distance from my apartment to the Helena Rubinstein offices, I was still queasy, uncertain. I stopped before a drugstore window, passed daily but ignored, and briefly studied the towering pyramids of jars, bottles, compacts, lipsticks. "Golly! Who ever buys all this crap?" I marveled. Elizabeth Arden, Germaine Monteil, Dorothy Gray, and, always, prominently displayed, Helena Rubinstein's white and gold-topped jars.

"Women's names! Woman's work?" I wondered.

But also, in the same window, there was an equal profusion of products with Max Factor, Revlon, Charles Antell labels. This comforted me. "Men's names! Men's work?"

Then, for the first time, I realized, as I pushed my way in and out of the crowds rushing to work up and down Fifth Avenue—"The beauty business is an enormous industry!"

Ten A.M., the hour of my appointment, chimed from the belfry of Saint Patrick's Cathedral as I reached a beige, eight-story building on the corner of Fifth Avenue and Fifty-second Street. At second-floor

:[ 29 ]:

level, large gold letters spelled out the words *Helena Rubinstein*. I must have seen them a thousand times. But now, and only now, was I conscious of them, was I conscious that there *was* a Helena Rubinstein, and, evidently, Helena Rubinstein was conscious of me—even wanted to employ me.

The entrance to the business offices was on Fifty-second Street. I dashed into an elevator. It took me to the fifth floor, where a reception room, decorated in muted shades of pink, smelled of spring flowers.

A curvaceous receptionist—murmuring reassuring words—now led me down a long corridor to a suite of offices where several secretaries hammered away on cerise-colored typewriters. Their smiles were enigmatic. I sat down on a tufted sofa. From behind one of several doors I could hear the Princess's voice. It seemed raised in anger. But since the secretaries flashed warmth and amiability, I focused my attention on a copy of *Glamour* magazine. I had selected it at random from a pile resting on a small table carved in the shape of a black-amoor. The Princess—Madame—was consistent. She liked, even in her offices, exotic objects.

Several paper clips, placed at regular intervals in the front of the magazine, revealed sundry Rubinstein advertisements. Some piece of foresight made me concentrate on these.

Princess Gourielli's voice, accompanied by a series of loud thumps, rang out emphatically. The word "rotten" kept echoing from behind the door. Was she on the telephone? Could she be having a solitary tantrum? No other voices seemed to interrupt hers.

The secretaries worked on with undisturbed concentration.

The door nearest to me burst open. Three harried women, looking neither to left nor right, hurried out. They fled down the corridor.

The Princess was now in my line of vision. Regal, diminutive, one hand balanced on a hip, she stood behind a carved Renaissance desk of monumental proportions. Her other hand was raised to heaven. The desk seemed to fill half the room. I recognized her bearded son, Horace Titus, towering above her. He was tugging at his Vandyke, gazing vacantly into space. Two women, one fat and heaving, the other thin and defiant, filled the foreground.

Their attitudes suggested a court-martial. A third woman, trimly energetic, revolved about them emptying ash trays, realigning chairs, straightening papers. She did so with total unconcern.

I now realized, peeping from above my magazine, that I had never seen the Princess without a bowler hat. Her blue-black hair, raked back in a tight chignon, dramatized a smooth forehead that rose above carefully arched eyebrows, while her mouth, curved in anger, could have been a shark's.

"I call it rotten . . . rubbish . . . zero!" She banged her desk with both her hands and, while spitting out these words, caught sight of me. Her features were immediately transformed. A welcoming smile replaced the gargoyle frown. I was beckoned into her office.

"Come . . . come quick and look at this dreck!"

Without bothering to introduce me to those present, the Princess held up a full-page advertising layout, similar to one of those I had just been studying in *Glamour*.

"Let us see what he thinks?"

I looked carefully at the layout. It was fortunate I had not wasted my time while waiting examining Rubinstein advertisements in *Glamour*. I remembered that the headlines, printed in a bolder type, proclaimed the words: "I, Helena Rubinstein. . ."

The Princess gave me an encouraging wink. "Don't be shy!" she said. "Speak up. . . ."

In a hesitant monotone I voiced the opinion that the copy was hard to read.

The Princess's head bobbed agreement.

Feeling bolder, I added, "It seems, also, somehow impersonal."

Down came the ad.

Bang! Her hands again pummeled the desk.

The fat lady, standing behind me, sighed. The thin one murmured, "But, Madame . . ."

"That's enough!" The Princess pointed to the door. "We talk later."

Dismissed, they both scurried out. Horace, still tugging at his beard, followed them.

"What's got into him?" His mother turned and asked the energetic young woman who was now opening every window in the office. She silently pantomimed several of her employer's gestures as Princess

Gourielli indicated I was to sit down on one of the upright Louis XIII chairs facing her desk. It was very uncomfortable.

"Now, let us talk . . . let us talk shop! I hope something will come out of it. My day has already started badly." She sighed and sat down, almost vanishing behind the desk. I was able to study her office during one of those brief silences she seemed to enjoy. It was entirely furnished with cumbersome, masculine antiques, although a Venetian glass chandelier, hanging in the center of the room, gave a fleeting note of femininity to the austere surroundings.

A loud burp shattered. my brief reverie. Princess Gourielli didn't trouble to disguise it.

"Too much black coffee," she said. "Now, now tell us what you can do?" Her secretary, who seemed to be in perpetual motion, continued to prance around the room. Before I could formulate an answer the Princess enumerated my few talents, notching them off her fingers with a pencil.

"He writes. He speaks English, French, Italian. He knows about art. He . . ."

She scratched her head, shrugged and turned to her secretary: "Pfft . . . what he doesn't know, he'll soon learn from . . . from me!"

Both ladies nodded in unison.

"How much?" The Princess next whispered.

"How much . . . what?"

"Money! How much do you think you're worth?"

She now eyed me speculatively and folded her arms as might a landlady claiming back rent. I remembered Pallavicini's warning: "Whatever you ask, she cut in half!" With what I thought to be a genial and disinterested smile I half-murmured: "Fourteen thousand?"

Princess Gourielli sprang to her feet. She clasped her hands as if in prayer, pointed to me in disbelief, then to herself, shook her head and slumped back on her chair.

"He . . . he wants to ruin us!"

In a slightly higher key I now suggested: "Twelve thousand?"

Again she was on her feet, flaying the air with a fist and next slapping a hand to her brow: "Oy! He's mad. Such chutzpa, I swear."

"Ten?" My voice was choked.

"How much?" She roared back at me and before I could answer asserted, ". . . *too much!*"

I was still unaware as to what we were bargaining for. I knew it was a job, but what was the job? The Princess, also, seemed totally oblivious. We had not discussed my future functions. We were bargaining in a marvelous vacuum and she was thoroughly enjoying herself. Her eyes glittered. She whacked her secretary who, fascinated, had finally stopped in her tracks.

"Take some notes!" the Princess ordered before thrusting five fingers under my nose. An emerald dazzled me. I weakly countered with five fingers of *both* my hands. She now produced six. I retaliated with eight and, finally, like an auctioneer sensing victory she held up five fingers of one hand and two of the other.

By then I was thoroughly muddled, tired, dispirited—but I somehow managed to counter the proposal again with eight fingers. My tormentor, glaring furiously at me, snatched an envelope from her desk and with slow deliberation wrote a brief message which she handed me.

"My last offer," it read, "is seven thousand dollars a year." The word "seven" was underlined once, the words "a year" twice.

I nodded weakly and murmured, "Beggars can't be choosers!"

At that the Princess finally spoke for the first time during this, our uneven contest, affirming, "You're damn right!"

She now led me to the door and, with a conspirator's dig in my ribs, shook my hand.

"Wait and see. I'll bring you luck!"

I reeled out of the building and directed my dazed footsteps to the nearest bar, laughing, laughing out loud. For months I had been looking for a job; and now, now that I had one, I didn't even know what it was!

# *"Are You Learning?*
# *Are You Getting Strong?"*

֎ ֎

I t was a strange feeling, being more-or-less unemployed one day, dependent on a minute, uncertain income, and then waking up the next with what seemed to be a princely salary—*seven thousand dollars*. I could hardly believe my good fortune.

Elated I bought myself three new ties, some books, and sent flowers to my mother who duly congratulated me, but advised caution. "I hear your Beauty Queen doesn't keep people. She grabs them, milks them, and fires them."

My mother was a confirmed Elizabeth Arden fan. She had obviously been chatting about my future with some of her friends—many of whom were anti-Semitic. But on questioning her more closely I discovered that it was her Jewish friends who looked down upon Helena Rubinstein, Princess Gourielli.

"She's a Tartar," they told her, "a witch!" One of them even added: "And then, there's her dreadful family." But it would have taken much more than these warnings to dampen my enthusiasm. I felt rich and already successful. In my eyes the Princess was a lamb, a jeweled lamb, whose clothes could hardly be likened to those of the proverbial wolf. As for her family . . . I had yet to meet them and, when I did, they seemed hardly worse than anyone else's caught in a difficult situation, ruled over by a matriarch who was also their employer.

On the morning after my interview, although still confused by it, I called up the Princess's office for further instructions. Her secretary (the breathless lady who had gyrated with such energy while my salary was being discussed) informed me that my new employer had gone to her factory in Long Island City.

"Madame left her home at eight. But before doing so she called me at my home, at my home! to tell me that you were to start working for her as soon as possible."

"What does that mean?" I asked.

"Today, now, *tout-de-suite!*" Ruth Hopkins answered. It was then I discovered her name. "I'm Ruth Hopkins at work and Ruth Weill in the kitchen." I immediately took to her, particularly after she told me, some days later, "Not only did Madame want you under her thumb *immediately* but, guess what? She pointed to me and said: 'There's a young Irishman coming to work and *you'll* find him something to do!'"

I hurried over. The Princess's wishes were obviously not to be trifled with.

Miss Hopkins led me into her cubbyhole. It was a utility room, painted a metallic gray, cluttered with filing cabinets on which a vast assortment of discarded bottles and jars gathered dust in old Delman shoe boxes. The furnishings included a steel desk, two upright chairs and a large framed photograph of Princess Gourielli dressed in wild Asiatic trappings suggesting the starring role in *Turandot*.

Over coffee, Miss Hopkins discussed my future. "I honestly don't know what Madame Rubinstein—I mean, Princess Gourielli—has in mind for you. It's no use worrying. I'm sure when she returns she'll have figured something out . . . even if it's just emptying wastepaper baskets."

Not relishing the idea of the wastepaper baskets, I changed the subject. "Do I call her Princess Gourielli, Madame, Madame Rubinstein, or what?"

"In the office," she answered, "it's Madame to her face; Madame Rubinstein behind her back. Socially," her voice rose an octave, "it's Princess . . . Princess Gourielli. You see, Prince Gourielli, her husband, insists on it. He's Russian—or, rather, Georgian. Titles are very important to the European aristocracy."

I nodded, having already experienced this lust for glamorous identification among some of New York's noble expatriates.

"But why Madame?"

"That's another story." Miss Hopkins, although seated, was still a victim of the fidgets. "You see there's 'Miss' Arden up the street; 'Mademoiselle' Chanel in Paris; Señora Perón wherever she is. . . . But 'Madame' has been a part of Madame Rubinstein's name, of her legend, for years." She paused. "Different stories are told as to how she became 'Madame.' The nicest concerns Chanel. Madame, the Princess, was being fitted by her and she asked Chanel, 'Why haven't you ever married? Why didn't you marry that rich Duke?' You see, Chanel's name was then being linked, romantically, with the Duke of Westminster. 'What?' Chanel stormed. 'And be the third Duchess of Westminster? I am *"Mademoiselle"* Chanel just as you are *"Madame"* Rubinstein! These are our rightful titles. What's more we've earned them!' " Miss Hopkins heaved from the effort of telling me this story which, even if apocryphal, was charming. I bowed, impressed.

"Madame . . . so be it, during office hours. Princess . . . from there-on-in."

"You're catching on." Miss Hopkins gave me an encouraging smile. "Now let me tell you about Madame's family—*the family*."

"Aah!" I thought. "Here comes the real dirt." I wasn't to get it, however; only a genealogical appetizer.

"First comes Prince Gourielli, Madame's husband. He's the titular head of Gourielli, a Rubinstein subsidiary specializing in perfume. Their offices are next door to the St. Regis Hotel, in a lovely brownstone. 'The Prince,' as we all call him, is a sweetie-pie."

She paused to let this sink in.

"Next, in order of importance to Madame Rubinstein, there's her younger son Horace, Horace Titus. You know him. Madame's first husband, his father, was called Edward Titus. Then there's Mala, her niece. Her married name is Mrs. Victor Silson. There's also Roy Titus. He's Madame's elder son and president of our board. You probably won't see much of him—no one does. Lastly, in the immediate family, here in New York, comes Oscar Kolin—Madame's nephew, Mala's brother. He's our executive vice-president, Lord Pooh Bah and chief executioner."

While I attempted to memorize, digest, and unravel these names, Miss Hopkins continued: "And besides the 'family' who work here, there are four living sisters out of a total of seven, several nieces, cousins—some employed, others not—plus six brokers, three lawyers, one important accountant and . . . two grandchildren."

At that moment, a dark, plumpish woman dashed in. She had humorous eyes and a preoccupied manner. Miss Hopkins, using her formal telephone voice, introduced us.

"This is Miss Fox, our director of advertising and promotion. Her office is next door. Madame Rubinstein never does a *thing* without her."

Miss Fox asked me my connection with the business. "I don't have the slightest idea," I said. "Princess Gourielli engaged me yesterday. Miss Hopkins and I are trying to figure out what she wants me to do."

"I've been with Madame for twenty years," Miss Fox shot back. "She hired me because I wore my hair like hers. There are still times when I'm not too sure what she requires from *me*."

Wishing me luck, she bustled out.

Miss Hopkins resumed her briefing. "Your first duty will be to work closely with Madame Rubinstein. She likes to teach people her business system, particularly those in her immediate entourage. It's really quite simple. All she wants is to be constantly informed about anything and everything!"

"Next, I would suggest that you get to know Miss Fox. She's Madame's trusty. They work hand-in-glove. What's more, they think alike. Madame even took Miss Fox on her honeymoon with the Prince in 1938. The three of them went round the world!"

Miss Hopkins produced a large scrapbook to substantiate this startling statement. It was filled with press clippings and photographs of the newly wedded princely couple. The most sensational ones had been taken in Hollywood, where the diminutive Princess and her distinguished, gray-haired Prince were wedged between phalanxes of glittering stars—Gary Cooper, Clark Gable, Joan Crawford, Myrna Loy, and even Mae West—while, in the background, there was the inevitable Miss Fox!

Noticing my fascination, Miss Hopkins snapped the book shut: "We must be serious."

She now outlined various ways in which I could be useful. I had to learn how to file. My typing had to be improved. It would be wise if I knew shorthand.

My eyes were rapidly glazing over. Miss Hopkins opted for an hour's break. "Come back at one. Madame Rubinstein will have returned from the factory by then. While she has her lunch at her desk I know she'll probably want to talk to you."

I left and walked over to the nearby offices of *Harper's Bazaar* to inform Mrs. Snow about my new job. After a brief wait I was shown in.

Magazine layouts carpeted the floor. Alexis Brodovitch, her art director, and the photographer Richard Avedon were busily reshuffling, discarding, exchanging this photographic layout for that, in what looked like a game of pictorial hopscotch.

Mrs. Snow, now resplendent in shades of lemon, directed the operation with her white-gloved hands. She paused and peered at me over her glasses. "We are closing the March issue."

I hovered against a wall watching. Like chess players, they worked in silence, occasionally nodding to one another. There were sudden sweeping motions as the layouts were shifted around the floor. Then, with the quixotic impulsiveness of all great editors, Mrs. Snow flicked her fingers. "That will do, Brodovitch," she murmured. Collecting their layouts, the two men left.

Mrs. Snow now turned to me. Before I could open my mouth, she mumbled what sounded like, "Hosanna."

"Helena," she repeated more clearly, "called me. I know she engaged you. I'm delighted. She's an extraordinary woman . . . you'll learn a lot from her!"

Her voice trailed away, regained momentum. "Of course, the family may be a problem. If they are, you can always come back and starve with us. Good luck!" I was dismissed.

Punctually at one o'clock, I returned to the Rubinstein building and was quickly propelled to what was now, in my mind, "the Madame's presence." Seated at her desk, dressed in a purple silk suit with some ten strands of carved emeralds dangling from her neck, Madame Rubinstein nibbled on a chicken leg. Her chignon was unraveled. A beautician was rhythmically brushing her jet-black hair. It reached to the small of her back.

"No time to pretty myself. . . ." She shrugged. "Had lunch?" In the crook of her arm nestled the inevitable paper bag. She shook its contents. Bits of chicken, a few salad leaves, two apples, and a quantity of dollar bills landed on the desk. Now I knew what she carried in her paper bags—her lunch and spare cash.

"Eat!" she ordered, handing me an apple. The dollar bills vanished into a drawer. While I munched on the apple, she bit on her chicken leg until it was picked clean. Wiping her lips with the back of her hand, she fired brief questions at me.

"Where d'you lunch?"

"Hamburger Heaven, Halper's Drug Store, the Automat."

"Good food, the Automat . . . big turnover . . . fresh!" She spat out a piece of chicken skin, which landed on my shoe. Then, turning to the beautician who had just finished knotting her chignon: "Here, dear!" She plucked a dollar bill from the desk drawer.

The door to her office was wide open. During my brief culinary third degree, the Princess kept eyeing the empty desks. She did so in a series of sharp, quick glances, like a store detective who had just spotted a shoplifter. Finally, unable to bottle up her mounting fury, she snatched the telephone at her elbow, flattened all five buttons with the palm of her hand, and bellowed through the receiver: "Where the hell *is* everybody?"

Seconds later, five breathless women answered her summons. Loaded down with papers, they hovered in the doorway. Outside, the sudden clatter of typewriters reminded me of an infantry battalion marching on a city street.

Madame Rubinstein's momentary flash of anger was now replaced with a benign smile. Beckoning with her hands and head, she summoned everyone in at once. I stood to one side of her desk, ignored and again unintroduced, while the staff members lined up in single file—petitioners before an empress?—and handed her papers to read, sign, and comment on. She disposed of everything quickly. One woman was given a slap on the back; another was told that her skin was sallow, but that her letters were neatly typed; a third, "You say too much and not enough!"

Soon a second wave crowded in the doorway. Madame sat precariously on the edge of her chair, cradling her chin in one hand, sometimes sucking on the end of her pencil like a small child working over sums. She barely moved. Her eyes were creased with concentration behind a pair of heavy-rimmed tortoise-shell spectacles. These had slid down, past the prominent curve of her nose to its tip. Her expression was that of a somnolent turtle.

She worked her way through the second wave and had barely finished stroking the hand of the last smiling minion when Miss Fox sprinted through the door, closely followed by two men carrying large trays piled high with an assortment of colored boxes.

Madame Rubinstein looked up and slowly, but with theatrical deliberation, studied a circular clock hanging on the wall.

"Had a nice lunch, dear?"

"I didn't have lunch. I-was-at-the-Agency-working . . . Madame!"

"Better! You won't get fat." She pronounced it "fet."

Meanwhile, the trays were unloaded. Brightly hued boxes, of all shapes and sizes, covered the desk.

"Pretty?" Madame's eyes sparkled. But her expression had changed from that of a studious child to a greedy one—surreptitiously sneaking a look at her gifts on Christmas morning. And, indeed, these were Christmas packages, designed some eleven months ahead of the next holiday season.

"No!" Miss Fox protested. "They are not pretty and they're exactly the same as last year."

"Don't get angry, dear," Madame soothed. She then asked:

"Did last year sell?"

"The returns were staggering!"

Madame Rubinstein jumped to her feet and shouted to the secretaries in the outer room: "Call him in! Get him . . . get him here! I want the packaging man . . . Mister, Mister What's-his-Name." She fell back on her chair, heaving, shaking a fist at no one in particular, "Wait and see! He'll get some hell."

With a speed I now recognized as company policy, the culprit appeared. He oozed Middle-European charm from a tightly fitting, pin-striped suit and was attended by a bevy of youths burdened with more trays filled with yet another selection of festive boxes. These were lined up on the desk. It was almost impossible to differentiate the first batch from the second. When the operation was completed, Madame Rubinstein, eyes blazing, arms flaying, knocked over most of the boxes, and then berated everyone, repeating over and over: "Expensive nothings, trash, *billig!*"

Finally striking her breasts so that her emeralds danced, she said: "I swear, on my solemn word of honor, I swear, you're all ruining the business!"

Undismayed, the packaging director turned to Miss Fox. His speech matched his looks. Both were oily.

"We win all the awards. We have beautiful Christmas merchandise . . . elegant, stylish, luxurious. What do you know about taste?"

"More than you do. I know what sells!"

It was then I learned, during their heated exchange, that Christmas merchandise, especially gift-wrapped items from the regular line of perfumes and cosmetics, was sent out on consignment during the late summer. If unsold, these "returns" had to be broken up, repackaged, or disposed of in special, cut-rate promotions.

Deaf to the verbal swordplay raging about her, Madame Rubinstein peered down at the packages still standing on her desk. She turned to me and inquiringly held up a garish gold cardboard sleigh in which nestled two beribboned bottles.

"What woman wouldn't be pleased?"

I longed to tell her that only an Eskimo might find it attractive.

Madame asked Miss Fox. "How much does this precious object sell for?"

"Two dollars and fifty cents."

"Ridiculous!"

The sled was thrown to the floor.

"What d'you think we are? Woolworth's?"

The packaging director—a circus trainer introducing a musical seal —now pointed to one of his assistants and clicked his fingers,

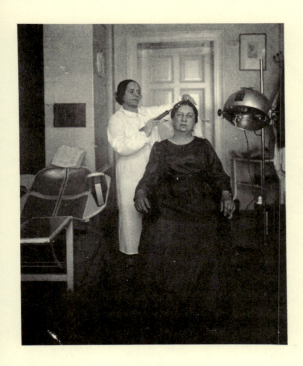

"Don't be nervous!"
Madame at work on one of
her "guinea pigs," Paris,
1923.

"I'm happiest working in
my 'kitchen.'"
Madame in her Paris
laboratory, 1932.

"Poiret made the dress. . . ."
Madame in a pre-Raphaelite pose.

"Charts!" Mathematically tabulated documents were unrolled like the Torah before Madame's nose. These listed the cost of raw materials, bottles, boxes, advertising, promotion. There were plus and minus columns. The minus columns were very small.

"I don't understand all this dreck!"

"But our profit is still four to one."

"Five, it should be five!" Madame Rubinstein pummeled the desk with both her hands and barked: "Think of the cost of your silly charts! Think of the time we're wasting! Think of the rent, the electricity!" Lastly, pointing an accusing finger at the packaging director: "Think of the huge salary we're paying you!"

She slumped back in her chair. Only her fierce eyes, frowning brow, smooth black hair were visible between the stack of packages covering her desk.

A dark-haired man glided in. He walked rapidly on the balls of his feet, while toying with his silk tie. Gold links, the size of fifty-cent pieces, enriched the crisp cuffs of a fine poplin shirt. A gold watch sparkled on his wrist.

Madame cried out: "Oscar! Christmas is killing us."

She might have been Phaedra or even Medea, such was the woe coloring her voice.

"So this is Oscar Kolin, Madame's nephew and 'our vice-president,'" I thought. After bowing to her and then carefully looking around the room to check those present, he leaned intimately on her desk. He had the elegant look and the carefully trimmed mustache of an Adolphe Menjou—and even purred like him, as if in a love scene, with an indefinable accent. Was it French?

"Christmas is killing us?" he queried. "Excuse me, Madame, with Rexall and Thrifty Drug doing over a million?"

"Dollars or units?"

"Dollars, of course."

"I don't give a damn! What about Lord and Taylor, Saks, Bonwit's? What about that smart store on the coast and the other one in Dallas?"

"We sell Magnin and Neiman-Marcus. We do very well with them. We sell everybody!" Oscar soothed. He picked up the sled from the floor and, caressing it, sinuously repeated: "Excuse me! But with prestige items such as this we are leaders in our field."

The packaging director beamed. Miss Fox's mouth curled with derision.

Madame said: "I hate 'prestige.' That's an Arden word. If only we could have beautiful packaging like hers . . . I should live so long!"

She clutched her heart, and sank even lower behind her desk.

Next, popping back on her feet like a piece of bread from a toaster, she spun around, fiddled with some bottles lining the window ledge and triumphantly held one of them at arm's length.

"What really interests me is bread-and-butter . . . like this! The new cleanser. . . ."

"Bread-and-butter! The new cleanser," everyone chorused. It was a scene from Gilbert and Sullivan.

"The new cleanser should sell ten million!" Madame said, squeezing the bottle. A few drops of white fluid landed in the palm of her hand. She applied them to her face, massaged, patted, smoothed away for a few seconds. Her make-up streaked as if caught in a cloudburst. She looked like a Sioux Punchinello as she handed the bottle around:

"Try some, everybody. Don't use much! It's very economical. . . ."

Oscar tapped Madame's desk with a pencil: "Excuse me!"

He smoothed his hair, ran a finger over his mustache, shot his cuffs.

"For five years Madame has worked on the cleanser. Even if I do say so myself, it's a miraculous product. Its scientifically formulated. It contains new ingredients, has new advertising claims, new promises of beauty!"

Before the murmurs of appreciation could reach a crescendo, he curtly dismissed everyone with another tap of his pencil. "Excuse me . . . I must talk to Madame privately!"

In single file we all trooped out and dispersed. Oscar closed the door, grandly, to closet himself with Madame Rubinstein.

I was left standing in the anteroom. The secretaries had covered their typewriters. It was already closing time. They were all busily touching up their make-up before leaving for the day. Miss Hopkins darted out of her cubicle, pulled me in after her.

:[ 44 ]:

"What happened?"

I recounted the scene while attempting to rid my hands of the cleanser. It clung to them like glue.

Miss Hopkins puffed with excitement. "Fox hates the packaging man. The packaging man hates Fox. Oscar hates them both. Madame is fully aware of the situation. She enjoys it . . . plays one against the other. The cleanser is a diversion but, mark my words, it *will* sell ten million!"

As I left Miss Hopkins to go home, the door to Madame's office was still shut. Through it, closely followed by several resounding thumps, I could hear her voice: "To hell with Christmas! To hell with prestige! The cleanser's our only hope!"

During the next few days, this scene was often repeated. The cast varied, as did the subjects discussed. Madame treated all her staff with matriarchal firmness, discussed all her products with proselytizing fervor, made every decision, ruled imperially, dictatorially.

In the New York Fifth Avenue offices, and in the salons which were part of them, she employed several hundred people. The factory, which was then in Long Island City, had an equally large staff. At the time, there were salons in Boston, Chicago, San Francisco, and, of course, the House of Gourielli on Fifty-fifth Street.

The American business, in the early fifties, grossed around twenty-two million dollars a year. Theoretically, it was publicly owned, although Madame Rubinstein personally held fifty-two per cent of the outstanding shares (reportedly worth some thirty million dollars). Besides this nest egg, Madame owned, *in toto,* all of the foreign subsidiaries, with the exception of the English business and its subsidiaries in South Africa and the Far East—these were the property of a foundation already set up to avoid the murderous inheritance taxes. Then, there was the Australian business. Australia, where Madame had emigrated from Poland at the turn of the century and where she had first originated her business, had been "partitioned." This was a constant source of irritation to her. She didn't hesitate to inform me: "I gave a third of the Australian business to Roy, a third to Horace, a third to my sister in England, Mrs. Cooper. That was before the second war. It was peanuts. They each received ten thousand dollars a year . . . but now, ha! Little thanks do I get for the forty or fifty thousand dollars they each pocket!"

Madame Rubinstein frequently felt, I was to discover, that she was surrounded by ingratitude. Her laments were actually part of a "power game"—she liked to play such games with various members of her family, with her staff—to let them all know who held the purse strings. She did, in a vise of steel.

As the weeks went by, I settled down to the Rubinstein office routine. It centered around Madame, whose working days varied. Sometimes she clattered in at nine A.M. trumpeting, "Where's everyone?" but there were also days when she stayed home, lying in bed, surrounded by lawyers, brokers, secretaries—plotting, buying and selling stocks, dictating, and telephoning.

In the office, Madame treated the telephone with the suspicion of an aborigine. She had never learned to dial a number; but simply held the receiver at arm's length and bellowed into it. If it was an "important," and, therefore, a business conversation, Miss Hopkins, and later myself (or anyone, for that matter, who happened to be around) was ordered to listen in on an extension. Madame believed in witnesses.

My duties, so vague in the beginning, began to clarify. I was to be in constant attendance as an extra secretary.

"Listen. Say less than more. If you want to be smart, play stupid!" My new boss gave me these instructions. Then, there were times when I was told: "Hop it! Take a walk around the building. Find things out. Come back and tell me. That's how you'll learn."

At first I was treated with suspicion by new co-workers. Many were openly hostile. As for "the family," they politely ignored me; although Horace, occasionally, would lure me into a corner and pump me. He constantly wanted to be reassured, to know how he stood in his mother's favor (which changed daily, as did Madame's opinions of everyone surrounding her, especially her family).

I was soon known as "Madame's new protégé," and, sometimes even told by well-wishers: "You won't last."

Madame had had many office "protégés" before me. Some had survived a few days, others a few months. One of them, introduced enthusiastically by Madame Rubinstein to her staff as a "lovely woman, so well-spoken" was even given an office (as yet, I didn't have a desk). When she failed to live up to Madame's expectations, she had to be dismissed. This was done by the personnel manager. Madame never fired anyone herself. She thought it was bad luck—for her. The following morning, consternation: "The Lovely Woman" was still in her office and, although reminded repeatedly she was no longer employed, refused to budge.

That evening, well after the official five-thirty closing time, Madame Rubinstein trotted around several of the five office floors on a tour of inspection. She liked to do this about twice a month, and would switch out lights ("Electricity is so expensive!"), assess the contents of wastepaper baskets ("Why don't they write on both sides?"), acquaint herself with "the real workers"—those who stayed late on the job.

She froze. There was "The Lovely Woman," comfortably seated at her desk, reading the evening papers—reading them in a fully lit office! Rushing back upstairs, Madame Rubinstein hammered her telephone buttons while yelling, "The beast's still here!"

When finally informed of the problem, she nodded. "Stubborn? I'll show her," and then instructed that the furniture in her office be immediately removed. "The Lovely Woman" was never heard of again.

My status in the company gradually changed. It was evident, after three months, that I was there to stay. My duties continued to be ephemeral and secretarial, but always centered around Madame Rubinstein, who still didn't remember my name.

She referred to me vaguely as "Mister?" to my face, "The Young Irish" behind my back. If I was out of favor, particularly when I came to work late after an evening on the town, she singled me out as "The Butterfly."

Her memory for names was zero. During one of her brief rages directed against Oscar Kolin she even said to Miss Hopkins: "Go tell my nephew, What's-his-Name, that he's a rotten vice-president!"

In order to overcome this problem, Madame endowed her associates, her staff, her friends, even her own family, with graphic sobriquets. There was, of course, "My Little Girl" and "My Little Girl's Little Girls" (secondary secretaries were kept in reserve, on ice, so to speak, should "My Little Girl" quit).

Harold Weill, who directed Madame's complex private affairs from his own law firm, was known as "The Young Lawyer." His duties included advice on all legal matters (shared with several other lawyers); the forming of the Helena Rubinstein Foundation; and the preparation of a huge document known as "My Testament"—her will.

Mr. Weill accredited his success with Madame to the fact that he visited her at home three times a week at eight A.M. and was always punctual.

"The Bookkeeper," Jerome Levande, was the company's comptroller and Madame's favorite "fall guy." She picked on him unmercifully. She had an infallible eye for a victim: "Our expenses are killing us! It's all your fault. . . ."

Besides these two or three key figures and members of her immediate family, there were many others: George Carroll, director of sales, was known by Madame as "The Salesman"; Amy Blaisdell, whose fief was publicity, went by the obvious appellation of "The Publicity Woman" (when not called "The Fat One"); the export director, Richard Augenblick, a great favorite of Madame's, was alternately designated as "The Polish Lawyer" or "*Le Grand Seigneur.*" He was absent-minded, romantically inclined, and extravagant. For years, he had accompanied Madame on her foreign travels. She had forced him to master bridge, and curbed his love for fine food and expensive cigars. He was one of the few "outsiders" in her empire whose devotion she valued: "He knows much more than he seems to. Besides, he's very honest."

With her family and friends, the name game was more complicated. Their designations were even vaguer. What was startling was that while her acquaintances could have filled Madison Square Garden, her friends were easily notched off on the fingers of her two bejeweled hands. "I have no time for them, so why should they have time for me?"

New York, where I first knew her, was her favorite city. Here she had a number of close friends whose company was sought in spurts —usually after a row with the Prince, Horace, or another member of her immediate family.

"Sara, Sara! I want to talk to Sara!" she might say, pointing to the telephone.

"Sara Fox?" I queried.

"Pfft, no. The other one. The one who writes beauty articles for *Harper's Bazaar*. Her husband decorates Bergdorf's windows. They have a house in Greenwich. Sara Lee . . . ," she finally remembered.

Madame could enumerate intimate details about a person's life for half an hour at a time. She would get angrier and angrier while his or her name continued to elude her. Finally, with a return of memory, she smiled benignly: "See, I can remember when I want to!"

In order to curtail these guessing games during which Madame Rubinstein's mounting exasperation made her turn puce with rage, and bruise my ribs with repeated nudges, I finally drew up a list with, among fifty others: "The Broker with the Car" (Milton Traubner, one of her brokers), "The Man Who Makes Good Hats" (Mr. John), "The Little One Who Was Once Married" (a purchasing agent who had worked for Madame for thirty years and, even after retirement, was still known by this descriptive phrase).

Having resolved the problem, my stock momentarily rose. "He's clever, maybe. . . ." Miss Fox, years before, had rendered a similar service by cataloguing Madame's enormous collection of jewelry.

Sara Fox described her triumph as being "mere common sense." She went on to relate: "Madame wanted to wear what she called 'her good diamonds' one evening when she was going out. I was with her, helping her dress. She didn't have a private maid. You know what? She got down on her knees, tugged away, and produced a battered Hattie Carnegie box from under her bed! It must have been five feet long. 'Don't tell a living soul,' she cautioned throwing open the lid. On top were several old girdles. These camouflaged piles of jewels —necklaces, bracelets, rings—thrown in without regard to value, settings. I was horrified. I immediately went out and bought her an office filing cabinet, an ordinary steel one. We spent the whole of a Saturday afternoon putting her diamonds under 'D,' rubies under 'R,' emeralds under 'E,' and so forth. There was even a drawer for 'M,' miscellaneous. Madame was delighted."

One of my early office duties was sorting out Madame Rubinstein's mail. This operation preceded her arrival or, had she come in at nine in the morning, it was conducted under her supervision.

:[ 49 ]:

Next to a well-worded contract, or a dividend slip, few things gave Madame more pleasure than a lucid business letter. In the days before Xerox (whose stock she immediately invested in, clearly sensing the usefulness of this photo-copying device), Madame Rubinstein ordered every "good" or important letter to be copied several times and, in her own hand, underscored vital paragraphs. These copies were forwarded to various associates, peppered with enigmatic marginal notes. "Oscar, I'm sure you'll learn from this." "Horace, I hope you'll see that a little patience goes a long way." "Fox, 'The Nail Man' is going to eat us up unless you do something to stop him!"

"The Nail Man" was Charles Revson, the success of whose rival cosmetics company "Revlon" alternately stunned and angered Madame.

In 1932, so the story went, he established, with his brothers, a small nail varnish company. His total capital was three hundred dollars. First, he assiduously copied his peers, next, he produced—invented—"Coordinated Lip-and-Finger-Tip Make-up." These twin items were brilliantly named ("Fire and Ice" is a good example), advertised, and merchandised. In less than a decade, Charles Revson parlayed a fly-by-night operation into a cosmetics empire. Madame had "slaved" for more than fifty years, really pioneered, to attain the same results. Small wonder her nose was out of joint.

"No sooner do we bring out something new," she groaned, looking as if she wanted to feed him arsenic, "than 'The Nail Man's' copies it . . . *only better!*"

Charles Revson had succeeded Elizabeth Arden as Madame's pet bugaboo. For years, she had feuded with "The Other One"—as she called Miss Arden, not wishing to give her the benefit of a name—who once hired the whole of the Rubinstein sales staff away from her. Madame immediately retaliated. She captured Miss Arden's ex-husband, T. J. Lewis, and made him *her* sales manager. "Imagine the secrets he must know!" She was disappointed. Mr. Lewis did not last long. But now Revson-Revlon kept her awake nights, particularly after his "$64,000 Question" TV spectacular had clicked and catapulted his business into a company which grossed more than Madame's. What irked her chiefly was that the "$64,000 Question" had first been offered to the Rubinstein Company. Not even owning a television set at the time, Madame had turned it down. "Only poor people watch those awful machines!"

The Revlon headquarters were in a brand-new building across the street from Madame's Fifth Avenue offices. She was fond of pointing to it, as if to the inner circle of Dante's Inferno: " 'The Nail Man's' busy in there, copying us . . . I swear!"

When she was finally introduced to Mr. Revson at a party, Madame Rubinstein failed to register, until she was safely home.

"His skin looks dry," she said. "He should use our products!"

As for her old enemy, Miss Arden—although they frequently attended the same parties and sat on nearby restaurant banquettes—they were never actually to meet. But Madame always showed a keen interest in "The Other One," or "Mrs. Graham" (Miss Arden's full name was Elizabeth Nightingale Graham. It was rumored that she had picked "Arden" as her commercial sobriquet because of her admiration for the novel, *Enoch Arden*.)

Madame studied her from afar, whispering: "Looks well! Nice skin, good chin, but too much color in the hair for her age!" Madame's own hair was rinsed blue-black every six weeks.

Thus, the average working day at the office began with disposing of Madame's mail in a series of colored folders (red for the U.S.A., pink for England, blue for France). This took me about an hour.

Then began a stream of her appointments with company executives. They reported the activities in their departments. Some of these appointments became full-scale meetings at which twenty people might be present; others were held "in camera." Madame liked a secret, particularly if the information she gleaned could then be of use to needle others.

Madame's arrival at the office in the morning was heralded by her hurried footsteps echoing in the hallway. She would hustle in, breathless, and would let her coat fall into my arms, give her hat to Miss Hopkins, throw her lunch bag on a chair. She slumped briefly behind her desk, and heaved a sigh.

"What's new?" The question was automatic and, like a middle-aged husband's greeting to his wife when returning home, it didn't require an answer.

After the mail was sorted Madame assiduously worked her way through each of the colored folders.

"Aah! A lovely letter from my other nephew. The one who runs Canada—Oscar's brother. Read it carefully. He describes a new promotion for 'White Magnolia' . . . it's a cheap perfume. Here, in the States, they tell me it only sells in Harlem. Why not? Make three copies: one for my sister, Mrs. Cooper, in London—she controls South Africa. Another for my niece in Rio—they have lots of black customers. And a third for the woman in Switzerland—Maeder. She can sell anything to anyone . . . even to the Swiss!"

This simple method of keeping the left hand informed of the successes, or failures, of the right was foolproof. Madame's remarks, annotated with a few boldly pertinent words in the margin, jogged even the laziest executive to action. Sometimes her spelling failed to keep abreast of the richness of her invective. "I am shuttered [shattered] . . . to hear of your impotence [incompetence] . . . ," she scribbled in a moment of anger to one of her agents.

In major countries—France and England—Helena Rubinstein subsidiaries were run by members of the family. But having exhausted (in more ways than one) her initial supply of sisters, nieces, nephews, and cousins, she was forced to find agents who sold her products on a commission basis.

If congratulated about the family's achievements, Madame would snap: "Better they work!" And indeed they did—not only in England and France—but throughout South America, in Australia, and in the Middle East, where a distant cousin or two kept the pot boiling in Persia, Lebanon, Israel with occasional shipments of whatever could be spared from more important markets.

Having disposed of her folders, Madame now turned to me and dictated a cheerleader's letter to the agents, adding, "They can also learn from 'White Magnolia.' I always say, 'What's good for one country is good for another.' "

There were agents all over the world. The principal ones, hand-picked by Madame, flourished in Germany, Italy, Mexico, Spain . . . countries she liked to visit and, by so doing, stimulate. Naturally, they thrived.

Madame's mind now turned to "the cleanser." Like a hummingbird she required more than one flower to feed on. And the more honey it produced, the better.

"We must also write the agents a lot of blah-blah about the cleanser. It will save postage. But first we need a name for it."

Every beauty product, in every cosmetics line on the market, was carefully baptized with a hopefully beguiling name—catchy, feminine, evocative. Some were wildly fanciful; others direct and down to earth.

Madame favored the latter. Her knowledge of English, after more than half a century spent working in various Anglo-Saxon countries, remained sketchy; but her ear for the right words never failed her. She could pick a name for a product with the same infallible certainty of success, of timeliness, as Cole Porter when he baptized one of his songs.

Miss Arden, due to a demoniacal interest in horses, had a tendency to relate many of her products to the turf. (Her "Maine Chance" stables siphoned a large part of her company's profits; but since it was her company, no one dared complain.) Thus, she named the fragrance "Blue Grass" as a loving tribute to Kentucky's misty hills; and she not only recommended "Eight-Hour" cream to choice customers but also to her trainer, ordering him to massage the sensitive fetlocks of two-year-olds with it.

Mr. Revson was more direct and scientific. Having first observed the triumphs (or the mistakes) of his competitors, he next spent liberally on market research, thoroughly testing a derivative name, then backing it with millions of promotional dollars. This threw Madame Rubinstein into a tizzy. "He's nothing but a copycat! I call it downright dishonest." She hollered when Revlon's "Youth Dew" emulated her "Skin Dew" and his "Ultima" cream closely followed the golden hormone claims of "Ultra Feminine."

Such was Revson's success with "Ultima" that he named his ocean-going yacht after it. Madame Rubinstein never owned a yacht, but, hearing "The Nail Man" did, she secretly bought stock in his company. "Wait and see . . . I'll complain at their next stockholders' meeting about his extravagance. . . ." Dissuaded, she finally admitted that her investment was paying off—"Why bother?"

Naming products, in the Rubinstein company, was a free-for-all, over which Madame presided. Practically anyone was invited by her

:[ 53 ]:

to join in the fun as she worried all concerned, for weeks on end, as a terrier might a bone. Now that the cleanser was uppermost in her mind she regularly smacked her forehead with the palms of both hands, groaned, whimpered: "Aai! Besides the cleanser . . . so much more! So much more to do. . . ." Meetings were held with a frequency suggesting a governmental crisis. Miss Fox now took over. Her genius bridged that gap between Madame's vagueness, effervescence, and the public's appreciation for a good product, evocatively named. Madame recognized and appreciated this skill. But first, emulating Mr. Revson, she studied competitive products—unless, as was often the case, she was launching something entirely new and had to start from scratch.

The cleanser wasn't a novelty, although it had an unusual formula.

"First, we must describe the ingredients . . . sensibly, wisely. Then, then we must find a good name."

When shown lists of the names of existing products, Madame was equally lucid: "Ha! 'Milky Cleanser.' Sounds like a dairy. . . . 'Flowing Velvet.' Can velvet flow? 'Penetrating Cleanser.' Good, direct, to the point. . . ."

While checking Miss Fox's suggested names, the two words kept cropping up: "deep" and "cleanser."

" 'Deep!' That's good," Madame cried out. " 'Cleanser' . . . that's even better! But, best of all, the two together, 'Deep Cleanser!' "

The problem was resolved. She looked like Radames—triumphant. Now, everyone in the company, from her favorite elevator operator to the youngest salesman, was questioned by her: "How do you like 'Deep Cleanser'?"

Affirmative answers were overwhelming—decisive.

The product was finally named.

Even so, details, endless details, continued to concern Madame Rubinstein. She kept asking me: "How does 'Deep Cleanser' sound in German, Italian, French, Japanese? No matter—if the Japs can say 'Coca-Cola,' they'll soon learn how to say 'Deep Cleanser.' "

For the next month, I was kept busy coordinating her wishes.

"We must have good literature!"

"We must have a plastic bottle!"

"We must have lovely instructions!"

I worked wherever I could—on every menial job she gave me—seated at the corner of her desk, in the outer room with the secretaries, or on one of Miss Hopkins' dusty filing cabinets.

Madame liked the feeling of activity around her. She enjoyed the confusion, and, even if fully occupied, she kept her office door open so as to monitor traffic outside, through the corner of one eye.

"Come in, come in!" she beckoned. "Sit down. Tell me . . . What's new?" At such times, I endeavored to slip away for a breather. My escape hatch was the men's room.

Sensing I was an "artful dodger," Madame Rubinstein finally intercepted me as I emerged from this hideaway with the *Herald Tribune* tucked under my arm.

"Read in there?"

I was speechless.

"I do. But seldom during office hours."

She walked back with me, down the pink corridor, to her office. Her features were those of a schoolmistress who had caught a favorite pupil smoking. When we reached her office a benevolent smile softened the contours of her steely jaw. She turned to me:

"Need a desk? I'll give you one!" With that Madame pointed to a small, empty space in the corner of the room. "There . . ."

I was now a prisoner but, sitting virtually under her nose, listening in on meetings, observing the tactics she used to encourage, placate, or stymie the people revolving about her taught me much. When alone, together, Madame kept inquiring: "Are you learning? Are you getting strong?" On receiving an affirmative answer she patted my arm or nudged me.

Now, finally, I was courted by my co-workers. It was somehow imagined by them that Madame held no secrets from me, but indeed she did. Often, when members of her family, or lawyers, called, she turned and nodded at the door. "Hop it!"

I soon thought I knew when to disappear on cue and did so. But this had the opposite effect. Madame would call as I sidled out: "Stay! Learn! Listen!" It was difficult to know what to do. Meantime, everyone in the company kept muttering, "It's time for Madame to go to Europe!" She made two or three such voyages a year in order

:[ 55 ]:

to keep up with her equally vast interests abroad. This produced a general *détente* among members of her New York staff—and even a collapse or two.

"Let her agitate in France," they said, heaving sighs of relief. But who was to accompany her? She needed a general factotum attuned to her demands. It was Horace who first broached the subject to me, somewhat deviously, as was his habit: 'Mr. Augenblick isn't well. He has always traveled with my mother in the past. And now that she wants to go, there seems to be no one available."

"Why don't you?" I suggested.

"We've had a slight falling-out. Besides, my mother doesn't really trust me."

"She doesn't trust you?" I was incredulous. This was the first inkling I had that disagreements existed between Mother and son.

"Yes. My mother says I'm impulsive and unreliable."

His handsome bearded features took on a look of even greater suffering than usual. He might have been one of Christ's disciples, painted in the *quattrocento*, about to be martyred. It was strange to hear him confess to me, a comparative stranger, that his mother thought him "unreliable."

I bided my time.

Finally Madame raised the subject herself. In her blunt way—shy, imperious, but somehow also on the defensive—she inquired, "Want to come to Europe with me?"

"Yes, indeed!" I answered, trying hard to hide my glee.

"You'll have to work hard, even week ends."

"It's still yes!"

Now that she knew I was anxious to accompany her, caution replaced the original note of uncertainty in her voice.

"You'll have to work terribly hard!" she repeated.

"Of course." I tried again to reassure her.

"Good. We'll first go to Paris. Then maybe Austria, Switzerland, Italy. Aii! We'll have so much to do. . . . Come to the house tomorrow morning, early. We'll discuss everything then. We'll make our plans."

# "Madame Must
# Always Come First!"

***

O n the following day, I walked up Park Avenue to Madame
Rubinstein's apartment—early, as she had instructed me—to
discuss our forthcoming European travels.

All of Madame's homes—whether in London, Paris, or New York
—were used by her as annexes of the office she maintained in each of
these cities. "I always lived over the shops," she was to explain to me,
"until we expanded and I was forced to move into apartments. So I
bought the apartments. Next, I bought the buildings. Then I built the
buildings. Why not? *Real estate's a good thing to have.*"

Besides her apartments, she owned country homes in Greenwich,
Connecticut; near Grasse, in the South of France; and at Combes-la-
Ville, outside Paris. These were week-end retreats where, between
marathon games of bridge sprinkled with business discussions, Madame infrequently took a quick spin in the garden to view the agrarian
output. "Each lettuce costs more than five dollars to grow. What can
you do? It takes gardeners, caretakers, accountants . . ."

Madame Rubinstein always maintained her many homes with several objectives in mind. First, she needed a roof over her head, and it
couldn't be any old roof. Next, entertaining was an important consideration: "It's good for publicity." Lastly, owning land and
property gave her a cozy feeling of security.

Madame had acquired her New York apartment, where I now directed my footsteps, for a song, just after war was declared in 1941. "I always looked for apartments on the top floor," she explained, "so I found this place. It was a white elephant. Imagine, thirty-odd rooms, three floors. But it suited me. I was about to take it when my agent—a nice, honest woman—rang me up. 'You can't have it,' she said. 'Why?' She didn't answer. 'Don't be stupid. Tell me!'"

Madame Rubinstein, recounting the story, smiled sadly. "Jewish people were not allowed in the house. So . . . so I bought the building!"

"It suited me!" Her own triplex matched the complexities of her character. It was oddly laid out. The picture gallery was on the top floor, the reception rooms on the next, while the bedrooms were situated on the lower floor. The heart and hub of this thirty-six-room maze was Madame Rubinstein's bedroom. Here, as the years progressed and her strength declined, she liked to hold court, to receive intimates while comfortably ensconced in bed, sometimes somnolent, always wary. "I seem to think better lying down. . . ."

When I arrived at Madame's apartment, my eyeballs were still glazed with sleep. Rising early is my private brand of hell. Fortunately, the cold winter air on Park Avenue had snapped my brain to a certain degree of awareness. I could feel a pleasant, if vacant, smile stretching my features. Having rung the doorbell once, I waited, rang it twice, waited further. After interminable minutes, Albert, Madame's Filipino butler, eyed me suspiciously as he opened the door. His manner was grudging, sullen; and without acknowledging my greeting, he pointed a grubby thumb to a nearby doorway, saying, "She's in there!"

Albert had then been in Madame's service for fifteen years. He was, she admitted, "one of the crosses I have to bear," but, "Albert's honest," and "Albert's soups are good!" Albert, in point of fact, understood his mistress's idiosyncracies, catered to them, and often stimulated them with cruel intent. Theirs was a curious relationship in which one and then the other took the upper hand.

"*Entrez!*" Madame Rubinstein's voice resounded in French as I fiddled with the knob.

I stepped into her bedroom. It was huge, at least thirty feet long, and freezing.

Pale winter sunlight filtered through lace curtains hung from three tall windows on the rough surface of a gray homespun carpet. The sunlight was reflected in quantities of mirrors, on masses of furniture, on walls painted in the same washed-out shade of violet as the door.

"Phew!" I thought. "What a dust trap!"

I now focused on Madame Rubinstein. She was reclining in state, at the far end of the room, on what appeared to be a crystal sleigh.

"Come in! Come in!" she summoned me impatiently with both her hands. She had the look of a Chinese doll—tightly encased in a red quilted bed jacket, black hair streaming over her shoulders, while masses of pillows propped her up.

"You're late! Sit down. . . ." She pointed to one of several high-backed chairs made of the same transparent material as her bed. The sun's reflections seemed to illuminate Madame and her bed with subtle, incandescent light. Then I realized, with a start, that the curved head and foot boards were actually lit by fluorescent bulbs.

I must have nervously examined the chair Madame pointed to, wondering if it would hold my weight, because, as if reading my thoughts, she said: "Perfectly safe! Lucite! Same stuff as our powder boxes."

Most of the furnishings surrounding us were molded in this hardy plastic. The effect was both airy and eerie. In addition to the bed and matching chairs, there were numerous tables covered with papers, books, jars of cosmetics; there were sideboards on which pyramids of boxes rose uncertainly in the air; there were vitrines stuffed with pink, blue, and white opalines. And, in odd corners, a chaise longue, a Georgian highboy, a modern make-up table equipped with a huge, circular gold-plated mirror. These elements added functional touches to the outrageous décor.

"Have some coffee?" Madame suggested when I was safely seated. She snatched a cup from the discarded breakfast tray and thrust it in my hand: "First, go wash it. . . ." She pointed to a nearby doorway. My eyes fairly popped, as I walked toward it, snared by the contents of a glass vitrine I had not yet noticed.

On serried shelves, huge amethyst brooches nestled with jade necklaces, with carnelian and rock crystal ornaments, with Mickey Mouse watches. There were belts of hammered gold, emerald-encrusted boxes, combs decorated with pearls, old paper flowers. I paused, mesmerized.

"Hurry, hurry!" Madame screeched behind me. "We have work to do. You can look at the dreck later."

Her bathroom maintained and even supplemented the atmosphere of confusion in the bedroom. It was also violet, and disorderly. There were dirty towels and undergarments strewn about the floor, draped over chairs, thrown over the side of a marble tub the size of a Roman emperor's sarcophagus.

While rinsing my cup in the sink, I glanced at the fixtures encircling it. They seemed to be of solid gold.

"Where are you?"

I trotted back to her bedside. "Read! Read aloud!" she ordered, handing me a sheaf of papers.

When I first arrived, Madame had been sitting in bed cross-legged, like a buddha. Now, folding her hands over the roundness of her belly, extending her legs, she settled completely back in her pillows and closed her eyes. Her face, at rest, was amazingly unlined. It was covered with a thin coating of cream. The taut skin on her forehead was smooth as a duck's egg and of about the same subtle hue. She wore no lipstick, but the streaked remnants of yesterday's mascara accentuated the curve of her prominent cheekbones.

"Read!" Madame repeated through the corner of her mouth. It was pursed with concentration. I quickly examined the papers. These were a detailed itinerary concerning her forthcoming European travels, submitted by the Paris office. I cleared my throat and read: "Princess Gourielli and party will leave Idlewild Airport for Orly via Pan American flight 100, February 4, at 0900 hours. . . ."

Madame's left eye flicked open. She pointed a red lacquered finger at me: "So, so you're the party?"

I nodded, and droned on. "Paris from February 5 to 15. Appointments have been made with . . ." There followed a long list of names. After each of them, eyes closed, Madame interjected: "He's a chemist." "He's a nebbish lawyer." "He's the good-looking young perfumer. . . ."

I read on, quoting further dates of arrivals and departures, appointments, names of people to be seen all over the map of Europe.

By the time I had finished my mind was reeling. In the five weeks allotted this trip we would cover thousands of miles, meet dozens of strange people, hold press conferences, attend luncheons and dinners for store executives and buyers. I was to be her sole companion, although associates, managers, and agents connected with the business had been alerted to reserve hotel rooms, to attend to all of the arrangements in their territories. But was I up to the job? Would I stand the grueling pace?

As these thoughts buzzed in my head, I again looked at Madame Rubinstein. She seemed blissfully asleep. I was about to tiptoe out of her room when she sat up and flipped the covers from her bed.

"Buzz off! I've got to go to the toilet!"

I wandered out, dazed and puzzled. Was I to stay, or return to the office? The hallway decorations kept me busy while I mulled the problem. These were abominably lit. Two bare bulbs screwed in the ceiling cast uncertain shadows on African masks clustered in groups, on Renaissance sideboards strewn with pewter plates and mugs, on Chinese mandarin chairs.

I had just decided that Madame's taste was a blend of Byzantium and the Flea Market, when the elevator door flew open and Miss Hopkins, her secretary, whirled in. "Phew!" she greeted me. "And how's the First Lady of Beauty this morning? I've been shopping for her. Bloomingdale's—for stockings. There's a sale on seconds in the basement. Madame can't resist them. Ninety cents a pair!"

She threw her coat on a chair and when I quickly told her my dilemma advised, "Stick around! Madame probably wants you to do so," before darting to the violet door and calling out: "Yoohoo! It's me."

While waiting for Madame's summons, I wandered into a nearby sitting room. Here, lace curtains flapped in an open window. They were trimmed with a bright floral chintz whose cheerful design, repeated on incidental chairs and a Sheraton sofa, almost captured the atmosphere of an English country house. I say "almost," because never had I been in an English country house where seven Renoirs spiraled over a fireplace crammed with old newspapers.

These paintings, the seven Renoirs, were a motley group. Two were of fish, two of bright anemones—flanking a portrait of a tough-looking lady—and one was of an exquisitely painted young boy. His identity, I discovered, was Jean Renoir, the painter's son. Madame had had each of these treasures carefully labeled and numbered; and, as in every room, particularly those thrown open to the public for charitable occasions, a purple catalogue entitled "The Collection of Prince and Princess Archil Gourielli" was at hand. Using this catalogue to guide me, I discovered that in addition to the Renoirs there were a Toulouse-Lautrec, two Modiglianis, several lesser works by painters unknown to me. And, rounding off the appointments, propped against the wall facing the fireplace, was a pair of tall vitrines crammed with silver. Their contents, described as "English, French, German, Brazilian silver" included bangles, statuettes, goblets, medallions, miniature forks and spoons. Obviously, when Madame collected, she did so with abandon. She bought in "lots," in "bulk."

Facing the window, a monumental desk proclaimed the *raison d'être* of this crowded room: it was Madame's home office. The desk, I thought, must have been carved by a demented Bavarian for King Ludwig II. Never had I seen such convolutions, so many nymphs and satyrs cavorting on a single piece of furniture. I casually opened a drawer. It overflowed with papers, pencils, cosmetics samples, and sweets. While working, Madame was prone to suck on sugar balls, toffee, or crystal mints.

Before I could close the drawer, Miss Hopkins reappeared at her usual hurried pace, followed by Madame Rubinstein, wearing a trailing housecoat of Episcopal purple.

"Ha! Pinching my sweets!"

She swept up to the desk, grabbed three candies, handed one to Miss Hopkins, another to me, while she popped the third in her mouth. Then, Madame sat down on the couch with her hands tucked in her sleeves.

"Who are we waiting for?"

Miss Hopkins examined a scrap of paper.

"The bookkeeper, Mr. Levande."

"He's late! Wait and see. I'll give him some hell."

Mr. Levande soon arrived, puffing slightly. He was a small, affable man inclined to stoutness, whose well-manicured nails were one with the gloss of his suits, his matching shirts and ties. Because of these accessories, he was known by his colleagues as "White on White."

"You're late!" Madame hailed him in the same manner in which she had greeted me earlier on. Before he could excuse himself, sit down, or say "Good morning," she spat, "Our expenses are killing us!" Attack was one of her basic principles.

Mr. Levande obviously knew her methods. He sat down with great care and, taking his time, opened an attaché case. Madame eyed him like a cat might a caged bird. She began to rock uncertainly. From his case, Mr. Levande slowly unfurled a bundle of papers, placing them on the surface of the desk. Madame looked down at them absent-mindedly.

"These are the expenses you claim are killing us, Madame." He paused. "Expenses incurred by you, by members of your family, *and* by the sales staff."

Madame nodded agreement—then, freezing Mr. Levande with a look, she said, "So tell me more. And whose company is this? And whose money is this? And whose family is this?"

Mr. Levande was a one-shot man. He seemed to shrink in his chair as Madame now embarked on what was, for her, an eloquent speech.

"My life! I give my life to the business and you begrudge me a meal or two. . . ."

Her voice, like the tide on a beach, rose, fell, and throbbed as she enumerated her services and sacrifices. Mr. Levande attempted to extricate himself by changing the subject. Madame would have none of it: "As for my family . . . let me see their expenses."

She studied the columns of figures without making a single comment. She was storing the information in her brain for future retribution. When it came to the sales staff, she dismissed them, saying: "To sell, you have to travel; to travel, you sometimes need a drink!"

For the next hour, Mr. Levande dealt with generalities—the company's insurance policies, the need for new machinery in the Long Island City factory, the need for a new factory.

Madame listened. She jotted down short notes on the backs of old envelopes, and, finally, without rancor, closed the interview: "You keep an eye on your business and I'll keep an eye on mine."

After Mr. Levande had left, Madame turned to Miss Hopkins:

:[ 63 ]:

"He thinks he's a *macher*, when actually he's a *nudnik*!" I was later to learn that in Yiddish a "macher" is a big shot, while a "nudnik" is a nuisance.

"Doing anything for lunch?" Madame asked me. "I have three newspaperwomen coming. You can learn lots from them. They're all beauty editors." She turned to Miss Hopkins. "What in the devil are their names?"

"Ruth Mugglebee of the Boston *Globe*, Eleanor Nangle of the Chicago *News*, and Lydia Lane of the Los Angeles *Times*."

"Good! Nice, important group." Madame turned to me. "Go upstairs and wait for them. I have to dress. I'll be there in a jiffy!"

A circular marble staircase linked the lower bedroom floor with the hallway and the reception rooms above. Up I went, examining every detail. This was the first time while in Madame Rubinstein's employment I had been left alone in her apartment—free . . . free to idle a few moments in exploration.

The relationship of decoration and owner always fascinated me— particularly with someone of Madame Rubinstein's mettle. Her life was intimately linked with her possessions. These were rich, avant-garde, schmaltzy; but they meshed perfectly with her personality as did the clothes she wore and the jewels she studded herself with.

Born on Christmas Day, Madame was a Capricorn, and I knew from my occasional studies of horoscopes that, as such, she was stubborn, withdrawn, but resourceful. I also realized that some of her complex shadings were those of a Sagittarius. She favored quick action, was spirited, independent, ruthless.

The décor in Madame's New York penthouse, faithful to the stars guiding her destiny, was a wild mélange. Viewing it, like shooting the rapids, produced a surprise at every turning.

Having climbed the staircase, I stepped into the upper hallway, which might have been designed by Philip Johnson for a modern bank, such was its opulence compared with its dingy counterpart below. Sunlight beaming down on the checkerboard marble floor gave it the luster of ice, and the massed potted plants added their jungle flavor to a room whose generous proportions—those of a skating rink— were dramatized by a few pieces of Indonesian furniture and a dozen white marble heads mounted on tall pedestals.

I recalled my first visit, for the Sitwell luncheon months before, when these statues had made me think of second-rate *art-nouveau* confections. Now that I was an employee, my satirical eye had mellowed. They were stylish. The name Nadelman, carved on the base of one of them, failed to ring a bell. Later, I heard Madame say, "Nadelman was a Pole. I made him come over from Paris to New York in the early thirties. Arranged a show for him. Nothing sold. So I felt responsible. Bought the lot. That's how Nadelman became known, and I got to own thirty-six pieces of his stuff."

In the living room, which I had only seen vaguely, purple and magenta velvets covered some twenty Victorian carved chairs placed helter-skelter on the acid green surface of a carpet designed by Miró. Chinese coffee tables, aglow with mother-of-pearl inlay, blended with the muted golds of Turkish floor lamps, the grays of life-sized Easter Island sculptures, and the vivid blues of opaline vases, six feet tall.

A huge fireplace, decorated with mirrored panels and a phalanx of grinning African masks, held the center of this busy stage—while on every wall, hung frame to frame, row upon row, was the incredible assortment of paintings.

"What a mixed bag of bagatelles," one art critic had said on first viewing the collection. Another wrote that the collection represented: "unimportant paintings by every important painter of the nineteenth and twentieth centuries."

Madame, who never failed to read anything concerning herself, couldn't have cared less. "I may not have quality, but I have quantity. Quality's nice, but quantity makes a show!" The "show" included works by Matisse, Braque, Chagall, Derain, Gris, Rouault, and Picasso, interspersed with a few Dalis, Tchelitchews, Marie Laurencins.

But the *pièce de résistance* of the collection—Madame's words for the "cornerstone"—was a large Fauve-period Matisse of swirling trees, hung directly facing the fireplace.

"Gosh!" I thought. "Two things that don't trouble Madame Rubinstein are chronology and frames." Some of her frames looked as if they had been gnawed by hungry rats. My attention, now, was riveted on a golden icon. It was twice the size of the entrance doorway and hung at the far end of the room between a pair of Rouault tapestries.

While trying to decipher it, I felt a nudge in my back. Madame had crept up behind me without a sound. She was dressed to kill in a pepper-and-salt suit. Wrapped about her neck were some ten strands of black and white pearls; matching rings, earrings, and bracelets glowed on her fingers, earlobes, and wrists; while her feet . . . her feet were shod in felt carpet slippers of the type that French *concierges* wear.

"Like it?" she said, using a shoulder to designate the icon, as she held a silver tray covered by a tattered scarf. I rolled my eyes in an effort to express admiration. "Bought it in Moscow, 1938, before I married the Prince."

Putting the tray down, she pointed to the collection of African sculptures lining the fireplace.

"What's his name . . . Jacob Epstein . . . started me off when I first lived in London. He had an eye for the African stuff. I used to often hop over to Paris. That's where all the important sales took place. Epstein, you know, was a sculptor. He kept up with what was going on, received catalogues, announcements of sales. So, so he told me what to buy for him, adding, 'I'll spend up to three pounds for each object.' That was fifteen dollars, then! If the price went higher, I bought it for myself." She paused and scratched her nose with her sleeve. "My big collection came later, in the thirties, when Hitler started being difficult. There was this German Jew who managed to get out of Berlin with a wagonload of African stuff. He was broke. I helped him out. Pfft! That's how to collect . . . by the wagonload."

Madame finished her monologue about her African collections, saying, "The best pieces are in Paris. The French appreciate such things more than they do here in America. Wait and see! You'll be surprised. I hope you'll take an interest in them. We need a catalogue. . . ."

She pointed to me—this was evidently going to be one of my jobs, cataloguing her works of art—before reaching for the silver tray. It contained an assortment of jewelry. "For the newspaperwomen coming to lunch . . . little gifts. Nice?" Madame queried.

She picked out a silver filigree bangle and slipped it onto her wrist with a conspiratorial wink: "I always say jewelry makes a better gift if it's personal, so I wear it, then I give it." She added, to her own considerable armature of pearls, a coral clip and slipped a tourmaline ring on one of her fingers.

"Three pieces. Three newspaperwomen. Where the devil are they?"

Her query was answered by the sound of the elevator door opening, of feminine voices twittering in the hallway. Three ladies now advanced into the room, and, seeing Madame at the far end, accelerated their pace and their movements, like a flock of rare birds about to be fed.

Madame all but vanished in their collective embrace. On emerging, she pointed to me: "That's Mister. . . ."

They were an oddly matched but enthusiastic triumvirate, whose clothes and faces belied their calling of "fashion and beauty editors." Ruth Mugglebee, the first to shake my hand, was dark, plump, and exotic. Boston seemed an unlikely city for her native habitat. Eleanor Nangle, whose center of activity was Chicago, where her newspaper, the *News*, printed several million copies a day, almost conformed to my idea of a Middle-Western matron, gray-haired and capable. I felt that an angel food cake, baked by her, would never dare collapse. Lydia Lane, who represented the Los Angeles *Times*, was slick and businesslike. Her tan suggested long hours spent by a Hollywood swimming pool interviewing Esther Williams. She was effusive, and kept hugging and kissing Madame, whose features froze: ice on granite.

It was then that I realized something I had instinctively felt from the very first day we met: Madame Rubinstein didn't like to be touched, particularly by strangers.

Miss Lane kept up her act until Albert announced lunch.

As Madame followed the procession, she urgently whispered in my ear, flipping a thumb in Miss Lane's direction: "Get that woman away from me. See that she sits at the other end of the table. She's driving me crazy!"

"I don't think your boss likes me," Miss Lane quietly said to me during lunch. We were sitting at the far end of the table—out of Madame's hearing.

"She's a creature of moods," I answered.

"She's hell on wheels," Miss Lane countered.

:[ 67 ]:

With that, we established a rapport. It was silently understood that Miss Lane couldn't complain to me about Madame's attitude, so we discussed Hollywood, her home, film stars. She was a vivid raconteur.

"Twice a year," she then told me, "I come East to case the scene, to view the new fashions. I'm interested in beauty. What woman isn't? That's why I'm here. Madame Rubinstein may be hell, but she's still news!"

I was surprised. It had never occurred to me that Madame was "news." Until then, I had thought of her as a superbusinesswoman—a personality, but hardly "news."

"Why is she such news?" I asked.

"Look at her! Look at what she's done! Why she's changed the face of every woman in America, in the world, for all I know. She's a pioneer, she's an instigator, she's a doer! And, for all her rudeness to me, she still has magic! There isn't a woman alive who isn't fascinated by her."

I looked down the length of the table to where Madame sat. She was listening to her neighbors, Ruth Mugglebee and Eleanor Nangle, like a sphinx, immobile, but her eyes occasionally flickered imperceptibly toward me. Suddenly she sprang to her feet, removed the tourmaline ring from her finger, and gave it to Ruth Mugglebee: "For luck!" She next pried the coral clip from her dress, pinned it on Eleanor Nangle's: "For luck!" she repeated. Lastly, she tugged at the silver filigree bangle on her arm and summoned me. "Patrick!" This was the first time I had ever heard her using my name. "Give this to your new friend."

I rose, fetched the bracelet, placed it carefully on Miss Lane's arm. She patted my hand, before thanking her hostess, and whispered: "She needs you!"

Before I could digest this remark, Madame inquired, "Anyone want to see my clothes?" and led us in single file down the circular staircase to her bedroom, thence to the bathroom beyond, where she busied herself throwing open closets.

"Keep your friend away from me!" Madame urged me again in a whisper. I retired to a corner, dragging Miss Lane after me. For the next half-hour, Madame displayed her collection of clothing. For the next fifteen years, I was to see this performance repeated. I never tired of it. There were always new clothes, new patter, new anecdotes delivered by Madame with her splendid bluntness: "Ha! Chanel first made this coat in 1922. It's inspired by a Breton fisherman's blouse. Chanel doesn't change. She only improves existing models . . . clever?"

Madame must have had a hundred dresses, coats, and evening gowns stored in the bathroom and hanging behind the sliding glass panels in a narrow L-shaped corridor adjoining it. There were more stored away in her Paris and London homes, her country houses; but the bulk of her wardrobe was kept on Park Avenue because: "The closets are lined in . . . in . . . what's it called? Good for colds. Better for moths. Camphor!"

Her clothes, like her jewelry, were carefully classified. Thus, in one closet, hung all her pre-1914 gowns; in another, what she called "little street costumes" (pronouncing it "cosh-tumes"); in a third, evening gowns; a fourth, furs. Madame adored furs, kept them under separate lock and key, revealed their existence only to the discriminating. "Why make people jealous?" But, when she did, the accompanying dialogue was soft, like a fugue: "Somali leopard! Dior made it. There are only six coats like this in the world!" "Russian sable! Molyneux's creation. I've had it for over twenty years. When it starts getting red and fuzzy, all you do is send it back. They repaint it. Hair by hair!" "Mink! I can't remember the exact brand. Tour-ma-line? Yes, that's it. Comes from Maximilian. They're clever with furs. Russian Jews know more about working skins than anyone else. . . ." The fact that she was Jewish seldom prevented her from uttering such slight but derisive designations.

On this particular day, Madame first led her audience to the pre-1914 dress closet from which she plucked an elaborate beaded gown. It was of orange and yellow crushed velvet, cut on the bias in uneven panels, fringed with silver tassels. "Poiret!" she announced grandly; "Poiret made it. He was mad for women. Went broke because of them. Gave away too many free dresses."

She strutted around, draping the brilliant gown on her short body. It was still amazingly contemporary. Then, seizing a cloak of purple satin studded with crimson velvet appliqué flowers, she spun it on her shoulders, snuggled in the immense collar, and struck a pose reminiscent of the twenties—one hand resting on her left hip, the other poised on her shoulder blade: "Lanvin! Madame Lanvin, not the current mish-mash. She started out making children's clothes. Then she dressed demimondaines; next her daughter married a count; then all of Paris came to her. What more can I tell you?"

By now, the ladies of the press had all produced pencils, notebooks, and were joyously scribbling away in the bathroom: Ruth Mugglebee perched on the tub, Eleanor Nangle sat on the toilet, while Lydia Lane propped herself on the golden sink. In quick succession, Madame produced gowns designed by Doucet, Rochas, Schiaparelli, Fath, and Dior. She ended the show with one of her latest French acquisitions—what looked like a vast golden lampshade. "That's by Balenciaga! He's the king! Look at the lining, see the embroidery, examine the seams!" She held out the evening dress, first pressing it to her stomach. Her eyes glittered: "Imagine! It cost three thousand dollars!"

Madame now selected, at random, one of her favorite bowler hats. "Mr. John. Nice man! He invented it for me!" She next chose a close-fitting toque decorated with a cabbage rose dangling, at eye level, on a long green stem: "Callot Soeurs. They've gone out of business. Dead or something. But, in their day, no one made better hats." Hardly had these details spun from her lips than she lunged for what looked like a black felt shoe, snatched it, set it on Lydia Lane's head. It was, indeed, a black felt shoe, skillfully cut to fit the head: "Schiaparelli!" Madame trilled. "She was some jokester. Suits you. Your period. 1938. You may have it!" Miss Lane barely blinked: "Thank you so much. I hope you'll excuse me now, but I have to call on Miss Arden. Miss Elizabeth Arden."

Madame's jaw went slack. Relentless, Miss Lane continued: "Yes. Miss Arden has had an accident. One of her horses bit her finger off."

"I'm so sorry," Madame answered. And, savoring every word: "Is the horse all right?"

I was forced to take refuge beyond the closets, in what appeared to be an ironing room, where I stood a while and rocked with laughter.

"Where did you vanish to?" Madame Rubinstein greeted me on my return. She didn't wait for an answer. "Please see the ladies out. I have work to do at home." On this uncertain note we all left.

Strolling down Park Avenue, on my way back to the office, Lydia Lane shed further light on Madame's behavior. The other two ladies had left us. We could and did talk.

"Poor thing. I think what really bothered her was that you were paying too much attention to me . . . to me! She was just a little jealous . . . of you!"

"What else was I to do?"

"Nothing . . . except to remember that in her eyes Madame must always come first!"

# "Paris Is Some Hell"

Madame never again mentioned Lydia Lane. But she seemed to watch me, almost speculatively, during the next few days. These went by in a flash of feverish preparations for our forthcoming trip to Europe. Her appointments, at the office, stretched until well after seven in the evening when, calling out, "I'm late, I'm late!" she reeled home to further meetings which lasted long into the night.

Madame seemed possessed by demons. She had to see everyone, from each department. She had to hear them justify their employment. She urged them to increase their efforts and issued instructions which she countermanded later; next she switched her attentions from one subject to another—ordering boxes of her favorite matzoh crackers, lipsticks by the gross, traveler's checks, laxatives. Her staff was green about the gills. Her family, more than ever, kept out of sight. Her secretaries exchanged formulas for the newest tranquilizers.

Finally, at dawn (seven A.M.) the day of departure, observing Madame's instructions, I was on her doorstep.

Dressed in what she called "my traveling cosh-tume"—an ancient, belted cossack coat trimmed with faded Persian lamb, matching shako hat, plastic rain boots—she stood tapping one foot, surrounded with an extravagant collection of luggage, mostly held together with string.

"You're late! Ha. Lots of rubbish . . . overweight!"

We drove off in a hired limousine looking, I thought, like two immigrants who had struck oil. Madame sat up front, next to the chauffeur; I was wedged in the back between several large suitcases, hatboxes, dress cartons emblazoned with the Dior and Balenciaga labels; and, half a dozen pieces of unzipped hand luggage crammed with woollies, books, and papers.

In 1952, the International Terminal at Idlewild was housed in a small, temporary building. Jets didn't yet exist. Transatlantic travel took some fourteen hours on lumbering DC-4's.

Madame insisted that I carry most of the hand luggage. I was weighed down like a Sicilian mule. So was she. We both struggled to the Pan American counter, followed by two porters wheeling the rest of Madame's heavy bags. These now rose on the scales, almost brushing the ceiling.

"Wait and see!" Madame hissed in my ear. "It's going to cost a fortune."

Before the official could tot up the bill, Madame ordered a suitcase removed from the scales, opened it, grabbed two mink coats, and flung them at me. Then, with an assured smile, sweetly announced: "I'm sure there's no overweight." She next gave him a crumpled bill— I knew it was only a dollar, but, judging from his reaction, he thought it must have been at least twenty—and grandly inquired: "Where's the VIP place?" Looking bewildered, for he hadn't had a chance to tot up Madame's overweight, he led us to the VIP lounge, overwhelmed by her forcefulness and what he thought to be her generosity.

Madame sat down, thanked him profusely and, when he was safely out of sight, nudged me: "See how easy? With one dollar, I've saved at least a hundred." She fiddled with the lock of the rawhide beauty case she had been carrying. The lid sprang open and two apples rolled to the floor. I scurried to retrieve them. "Ah!" Madame beamed. "All the way out I was wondering where they were. Have one? Stops the ears from buzzing when the *avion* goes up."

If on our drive out to Idlewild we had looked like immigrants, walking to the plane we must have reminded the crew of two of the Marx Brothers—if not all four. I tottered forward in little bursts of speed, fur coats trailing from my shoulders, clutching paper bags and hatboxes, while Madame called out: "Another fifty yards. Don't give up!" swinging her make-up case at my rump to prod me on.

When we were finally settled in our seats, Madame instructed me to place the beauty case under her feet, fix the catch on her safety belt, and, without another word, fell asleep, arms folded on her purse.

For the next few hours, occasionally glancing at her, I went over our itinerary in my head, and recalled snippets of advice proffered me by various members of her staff. Mr. Augenblick, Madame Rubinstein's export manager, with whom she had always traveled in the past, could only suggest: "You'll be living with her. Make sure you turn off your bedroom lights." Miss Hopkins, between hoots of laughter, cautioned me to keep carbons of every letter I might be called upon to type, adding: "Always check the zippers on her dresses. If they're open, there's a storm brewing." I also recalled Lydia Lane's hint: "Remember, Madame must always come first!" But it was Horace, Madame's younger son, whose farewell was most confusing. He had dropped in to say good-by to his mother on the eve of our departure—none of her family was ever allowed to take her to the airport—and after a few peremptory words signaled to me to follow him into the corridor. "I don't envy you," he said when we were well out of hearing. "I've traveled with my mother in the past. She'll get you up at seven; you'll start typing letters; she'll keep after you all day and all night if you give her a chance. In Paris, there's bound to be trouble with Mr. Ameisen, the general manager. He's a good man . . . and a nice one—which is more than I can say for a lot of people surrounding Madame Rubinstein. But she enjoys torturing him. She thinks he's lazy because he never appears at the office before ten in the morning. Then there's Stella, my aunt. Stella Oscestowitcz. She's the president of the French corporation. All she does is make trouble for Ameisen. She's frightened of my mother. Recently, to make herself interesting in Mother's eyes, when all her schemes had misfired, she threatened suicide. D'you know how Madame Rubinstein reacted? 'Stella won't kill herself; she just ordered four new dresses.'"

With that, Horace shook my hand and gave me a mock blessing. I wasn't sure how to interpret his farewell. Was it a warning of the traumas facing me? Or was it a confession of his own inadequacy as a son, of his failure to make any contact with a boss who was also his mother?

Of all the people close to Madame Rubinstein, Horace was the most ambiguous. She adored him, and yet her love was like a seesaw. With him she blew hot and cold: "Horace is brilliant!" "Horace is gaga!" This did little to settle his lack of direction or his instability. On certain days, he liked to think of himself as an aesthete; on others, a business tycoon; and then, in quick succession, he would be an art director, merchandising expert, copy writer, man-about-town. "Poor Horace!" Madame was fond of repeating. "He's just like his father . . . all over the shop."

Until then, I had only known him as a fleeting figure. His appearances, at the office, made Madame alternately beam and rage. At the time his mother paid him a retainer as an "artistic" consultant. She seemed reluctant to give him definite duties—would do so for a few weeks and then take them away from him—and yet he had first call on her attentions; could "wheedle" her (as she was the first to admit); then "bamboozle" her (another of her expressions).

"Poor Horace!" indeed. Within the next few weeks, I was to participate in a fearful confrontation of this devoted, demanding, and possessive mother and her adored son—neither of whom would give in an inch—for each, without fully realizing it, was set upon destroying the other.

Madame now stirred in her seat by my side. She knocked her hat back, gave a huge yawn, stretched, and sniffed the air.

"I'm starved!"

Soon menus were produced, hors d'oeuvres came wafting by, bar carts clattered down the aisle. In those days meals, on planes, were copious and leisurely.

"Order me vodka. It kills the poisons . . . in case the food's not fresh," Madame said to me in an undertone. She then picked two of every hors d'oeuvre and piled a small reserve of them on a plate under her chair. Since we were flying east, by the time the seven-course meal had ended, night was falling.

"Where's the toilet?" Madame asked, wiping her mouth with the back of her hand. She had just gobbled down a cream puff.

I indicated the door.

"Come with me. Stand guard. I don't want to get locked in. I'm clumsy with the hands."

Having accomplished this mission we returned to our seats. She again propped her legs on the beauty case, wrapped her coat around them, and gave another huge yawn. Then, turning imtimately toward me, said, "Let's chat."

While I groped for a suitable subject Madame had already found hers. "I'm not looking forward to Paris," she said, "nothing but irritation, headaches, problems!

"First there's Stella, my sister. She's a pain in the neck. She doesn't even speak to Ameisen, the manager, and he's a lazy bum, but clever, shrewd. What I call a real Jesuit."

In her own way Madame elaborated on the muddled French business scene that Horace had briefly described to me. She did so with relish, obviously reveling at the thought of charging into a mare's nest, of routing her adversaries.

"Then there's Eugénie and Gaston at Quai de Bethune—both are hell!"

She now explained to me that these last two characters were her servants, and had been since 1934—from the moment she first moved into her Paris apartment on the Île Saint-Louis.

"Eugénie's a terror. Worse than Albert in New York. As for Gaston—that's her husband, although they're not really married—he's like . . . he's like a little Hitler!"

It was obvious to me that Madame's way of life in Paris was consistent with what it had been in New York: difficult relatives, ornery servants, self-inflicted problems and . . . lots of hysteria.

"Things in France have changed since the war," Madame went on to say. "Since both wars. I first knew Paris in 1906. Imagine! I opened my salon there in 1908! I can even remember seeing that fat old Edward VII driving down the Faubourg Saint-Honoré. . . ."

She paused, savoring her memories.

"What was Paris like in those days?" I egged her on.

"Paris is Paris . . . smart, difficult for business! I much prefer London. London is really cos-mo-po-litan. The English are easier to get along with than the French. You see, I don't speak much French." She then, closing her eyes, hearkened back to the distant past. "When

:[ 77 ]:

I first went to London from Australia it was a triumph! I opened my salon there. I was married there. Both Roy and Horace were born there. But Paris, for our business, was—how do you say it—more avant-garde. Lots of Romanians and Hungarians—clever with skin—taught me masses. Then, the couture was getting to be important. With big houses like Worth starting to show collections instead of just making clothes for rich people came the make-up. I understood all this. Took advantage of it."

Madame chatted on, rocking slightly, arms cradled around her bosom, eyes half-closed. She was evoking events that had taken place more than half a century ago. I recalled old articles concerning her beginnings. "Little Polish girl makes good in Australia with family beauty formula!" They told how, as the eldest of eight daughters, Helena Rubinstein had left her native Cracow to visit relatives near Melbourne with little more than twelve jars of a beauty cream; and those jars had been the foundation of an empire. But it was the very lack of details, of dates and figures, that was always to tantalize me. Later I managed to piece some of them together; but on the plane, that night, all I knew were the barest facts. Madame only liked to look back in the form of vignettes, thumbnail sketches, snippets of information; she refused to fill the gaps. How did she travel all the way from Poland to Australia? I asked. "By boat. . . ." Where did the money come from? (For she had readily admitted that her family was poor.) "Mother sold a trinket!" What were her first impressions after seven weeks spent at sea, of a country called "Down Under" by the average Englishman and still looked upon as a penitentiary colonized by riffraff? "Pfft! I had three proposals of marriage on the boat. I hated Australia, my relatives, the whole shebang! Still, I worked . . . worked. Even if every day only had twenty-four hours, I worked fifty!"

But, beyond these scanty details, she said little. She did this with everyone, especially the press, who soon adorned her statements and enhanced (as she well knew they would) her legend.

That night, as we flew to Paris, Madame was only concerned with her business there.

"D'you know what's killing us?" (She always used the word "us," like royalty, instead of "me.") "Holidays! That's what's killing us!

The French take too many holidays. A month in the summer, a week at Christmas . . . religious holidays, political holidays. I swear, they have more holidays than anyone on earth. All paid for, what's more." She pointed to herself as the prime victim of French sloth. She then thumbed her nose at no one in particular. "That's what I say to the French! What they need is another Napoleon. A strong hand. A dictator!"

De Gaulle had not yet returned to power, but, when he did, Madame sent him a congratulatory telegram. "Wait and see," she said. "Now there'll be less holidays!"

The plane's lights dimmed. A sign in front of us proclaimed, "No smoking. Fasten your seat belts." We were about to land at Shannon, in Ireland, to refuel. "Good!" Madame said. "I need some air."

It was a cold starlit night and, as we walked to the terminal, Madame inhaled and exhaled with a great show of appreciation. "Your country," she said, "has nice air. Fresh. We must come back some day for a visit!"

In the early fifties every plane crossing the Atlantic on its way to and from Europe refueled at Shannon. It was a free port and, as such, prospered until the advent of jets. Liquor cost about a dollar a bottle; French perfumes were sold for a fraction of their American price; Irish handcrafts—tweeds, knitted goods, linens—were all purchased by a captive audience of travelers in quantities which made members of the Dael (Eire's governing body) dance jigs of joy.

"Everything's so cheap!" Madame exulted as we wandered around.

A group of nuns, en route to Rome from their convent in Boston, recognized my traveling companion. "We once saw a picture of you in the *Globe!*" They formed a cooing, fluttering circle around her, requesting autographs.

"God love you! My niece back home will be so pleased to hear of this. She dotes on your 'Apple Blossom.'"

"Get her name and address!" Madame ordered me, as she scribbled hers, over and over, on any scrap of paper available, including the backs of one or two holy pictures. "I'll send her a sample when we return to America."

This was no empty promise.

Foreign travel stimulated Madame to sudden flights of generosity and, during the next decade, I was to fill several notebooks with the names, the addresses, the requests—for a special shade of lipstick, a jar of cream, a bottle of toilet water—from strangers met, as it were, on the wing.

"Customers . . ." Madame said, carefully weighing her words, "particularly future customers, are not to be sneezed at. Besides, a little sample won't ruin us."

An hour later, just before landing at Orly, the Paris airport, Madame slipped her bank roll in my pocket. "Don't forget to give it back!" Little did I know that American money was then not allowed in France. If caught with it, I could have gone to jail.

We were met by a bald-headed man whose pale blue eyes seemed to float in the middle of a round, plum-colored face. He greeted Madame with Old World courtliness. They spoke in Polish. Their conversation, as we reached the customs shed, grew quite heated. Madame was giving him hell, and, from the odd word in English she used, I gathered it was all due to the number of porters he had summoned to help us with our hand luggage. This was now aligned for inspection.

"*Rien à déclarer!*" Madame said firmly. "Nothing to declare."

The inspector thought otherwise. He ordered everything opened. While Madame tried to untangle her keys, repeating to herself, under her breath, "Curse him. Curse them all!" the bald-headed man helped me untie the knots on those pieces of luggage held together with string. "My name is Emanuel Ameisen," he said, as we both tugged away.

So, this was the put-upon manager whom Madame considered lazy. His manners were both gentle and distant; his speech, in English and French, velvety. I had heard that he was vaguely related to the Rubinstein family, through Madame's first husband, Edward Titus, and he later recounted to me, with considerable humor, his Polish youth, his French upbringing, his life with Madame during her brief but hectic visits to Paris twice a year.

"She's a hydra . . . and of her nine heads eight are constructive, one is destructive."

We stood to one side as Madame faced the customs inspector. His

"The Prince is very distinguished." Prince Gourielli, circa 1949, on a holiday in Saint Moritz.

Edward Titus: "He was very dapper . . ." Madame always said of her first husband.

A rare photograph of Roy Titus and his mother,
taken in 1950.

detachment boded ill. Vaguely, he examined every piece of luggage until he caught sight of Madame's unopened beauty case. He now pointed to it.

"What's that?"

"My beauty case."

"Kindly open it."

Attempting a delaying action, Madame Rubinstein emptied her pockets of handkerchiefs, keys, Life Savers.

"Take your time, Madame. I have the whole night before me."

Her eyes narrowed. She knew she had met her match. Seizing the case, she examined the lock, spun several numerals until it snapped open, and, with a disdainful gesture, said *"Voilà! Regardez. . . ."*

He threw back the lid, scratched his head, whistled.

It was filled, indeed, overflowed, with what at first sight might have been an exotic stew whose principal ingredients were jewels. There were rubies, emeralds, diamonds mounted in brooches, necklaces, rings, and bracelets—all coated with face powder—nestling in scraps of Kleenex. Madame's familiar strands of pearls (her "best pearls"), like a mess of cold spaghetti, were glued to her polished rubies, knotted with her emeralds.

I now realized why she liked to travel with her feet safely anchored on this make-up box; why she never allowed it out of her sight. It must have contained hundreds of thousands of dollars of what she called "my rubbish."

The inspector scooped a handful, held it up to the light.

"Costume jewelry!" Madame spat. *"Bijoux de fantaisie."*

*"Ça se voit,"* he answered as he dropped them back in the case and flicked his fingers to signify that the inspection was over.

Madame thanked him with a great show of feminine graciousness but, spinning around, whispered: "Idiot!" She then glared at Mr. Ameisen and myself: "You're also a pair of idiots . . . no help!"

In a silent procession, led by Madame, we wended our way to a waiting limousine. It was an enormous black Chrysler, equipped with a roof rail for extra luggage and tended by an unshaven chauffeur wearing a green baize apron over his uniform. He bowed low, if unsteadily.

:[ 81 ]:

"Drunk, as usual . . ." Madame shrugged as she heaved herself into the front seat of the car. "He's a mess. But what can you do? He serves a purpose."

Mr. Ameisen and I settled in the back. It was then he explained that the tipsy chauffeur, Vladimir, was also the concierge at Quai de Bethune, Madame's Paris home.

"He is a Pole," he cupped his hand so that Madame wouldn't hear, "and since he acts as concierge, chauffeur, and occasional butler in the household, he's given to a nip. Overwork . . . no doubt!"

Mr. Ameisen shrugged as we drove at a breakneck speed through the somnolent streets linking Orly with Paris. Judging from Madame's head, bobbing up and down next to her driver, she had again fallen asleep. It was only when we reached the Pont de la Tournelle, facing Notre Dame and linking Paris's Left Bank with the Île Saint-Louis, that she sat up and shot an inquiring glance at the Tour d'Argent. This famous restaurant faced the bridge, looked down upon the Seine River, and encompassed a view which included Madame's home.

"The duck . . ." Madame inquired over her shoulder, "Is the duck still as good? Expensive? Up there." Without pausing, she then asked: "Mr. Ameisen . . . has the house been painted?"

"Only the hallways, Madame."

"Can we raise the rents?"

"I'm afraid not."

"More waste! I hate Paris. *Paris is some hell!*"

The old Chrysler shuddered to a halt. I peered out. A massive doorway of carved wood—what the French call a porte-cochere—opened, allowing a thin shaft of light to dance on the damp pavements. We had reached Quai de Bethune, Madame's Paris home.

"The Île Saint-Louis . . . ," she liked to remind me, "is very smart. Only the best people live on Quai de Bethune."

In the dead of night, it looked dismal, dank, and deserted. I could vaguely see the gray shapes of eighteenth-century buildings, backed by a church's steeple, lining this narrow, one-way street which is on the south side of the island. Behind us, as I glanced through the car's rear window, Notre Dame was barely visible, shrouded in river mists.

Madame led the way through the porte-cochere. She was greeted by an angular woman whose pale, strained features were swaddled in a black knitted shawl. This was Madame Vladimir, the chauffeur's wife, who, with the help of her erratic husband, guarded the building from a one-room cubbyhole—the concierge's *loge*. It faced an equally diminutive elevator. Urged on by Madame: "There's plenty of room . . . just breathe in. Then you'll fit!" we all piled in, and, packed like sardines, reached our destination on the top floor. I had to sidle out backward, inhaling deeply to do so.

Spinning round, I barely refrained from whistling. It was as if I had stepped onto the movie set of *Grand Hotel*. The entrance hallway epitomized the glittering thirties as once interpreted by Hollywood. Had Greta Garbo and Joan Crawford been standing in the open doorway—an incredible construction of Lalique glass and plated chrome—I wouldn't have been at all surprised. Instead, two tired-looking maids, both dressed alike in shabby white dusters, counterpointed the visual grandeur surrounding them. There were Greek statuary, African masks, Louis XVI sideboards, opaline vases, Samarkand rugs, and mirrors—mirrors everywhere—reflecting and counterreflecting the shimmering scene.

"Eugénie!" Madame barked at the plumper maid whose vapid pudding face, taut gray hair, made me think of what the French call "Madame Pi-pi"—the traditional guardians of public lavatories: "*J'ai très faim*—I'm starved! Get me some soup, a few slices of Polish sausage, bread. . . ."

I sensed animosity as Eugénie bustled off. Not a word of greeting had been exchanged between employer and employee. Madame next turned to the other maid, an ageless wisp of a woman whose thick woolen stockings, felt carpet slippers, were at odds with her modishly bobbed hair.

"*Bon soir*, Marguerite. . . ." Madame's voice was warmer, as she first shook, then patted Marguerite's hand. Now that these brief formalities were accomplished, she turned to Mr. Ameisen, and said, "Follow me!" They both vanished through a curtained doorway. I was left standing, staring at Marguerite. She returned my gaze with that mixture of deference and disdain French servants project when uncertain if faced by a superior or an equal.

"Monsieur? Monsieur is a guest? No, Monsieur must be Madame's new secretary. . . . I'll take Monsieur to the Prince's room. That's where all the other secretaries used to sleep," she added dramatically, leading me down a corridor filled with a practicing witch doctor's collection of African art.

We passed through a small dining room furnished with tactful Biedermeier pieces to what appeared to be an exotic greenhouse. It was, I decided, definitely a greenhouse. Masses of exotic plants spiraled upward to a domed, glass ceiling; poured down from mirrored shelves; grew in such rich abandon that if Eve had emerged from there I wouldn't have batted an eye.

Noting my look of amazement, Marguerite explained that *la serre* (the greenhouse) was built on a bridge linking the main apartment with a smaller one where, when in residence, the Prince lived and, when he was not, anyone did who accompanied Madame Rubinstein on her visits to Paris.

"There are two wings, Monsieur." Marguerite no longer addressed me hesitantly. "In the wing facing us, Madame has her bedroom. It is linked with this side of the apartment by *les salles de receptions* (the reception rooms), a salon, a library, a card room, a music room, the main dining room. There's lots for me to dust! *Pensez*, just think, *six cent vingt-deux nègres* . . . six hundred and twenty-two blacks for a start."

I assumed she meant the collection of African sculptures we had passed in the corridor, but, like a stock-keeper in a small country store, she continued to enumerate: "Sixty-two paintings, forty-six drawings, ninety-four opaline vases, eighteen different sets of table-ware—besides the Louis XVI furniture, the Boulle, the mother-of-pearl in Madame's bedroom. . . ."

Madame Rubinstein's collecting impulses obviously flourished in Paris with the same lack of restraint they had in New York.

We now entered a small room furnished with oddments, including a large desk. "This is where Monsieur will work," Marguerite told me as I glanced around, focusing, finally, on a glass vitrine filled with tins of food. I examined them at closer quarters. Carefully stacked, under lock and key, were delicacies such as *pâté de foie gras*, asparagus tips, mushrooms, smoked hams.

"Those are Madame's little reserves." Marguerite gave me a sly wink. "She doesn't trust Eugénie with them in the kitchen. Keeps the key herself!"

So this was to be my office—the auxiliary larder! I now looked at the pictures on the walls. These were all of Madame Rubinstein who, like Big Brother in George Orwell's *1984*, would be constantly watching over me as I toiled on her behalf.

"Aggravation, irritation, problems! . . ."

Madame's repeated description of life in Paris echoed in my ears as I studied her portraits. One was by Raoul Dufy, circa 1935; a breezy water color in his familiar slapdash style. The likeness, in a series of quick brush strokes, was uncanny. Madame seemed to be saying, "Off with his head!" like the Red Queen in *Alice in Wonderland*. Another by Vertès, done in the early 1940s, was a fashionable pastiche that revealed her social side: enigmatic, distant, bejeweled, shy. It was the third that made me pause. There, in an ancient copper mezzotint, an egret stuck in her towering pompadour, one hand balanced on her hip, Madame as a young woman eyed that world as if it already belonged to her. The signature meant nothing to me—Helleu. I was later to meet Helleu's granddaughter, Eliane Orosdi, who told me, "That print was made from a drawing done in 1908. My grandfather, in those days, painted everyone of note able to pay his fees—Consuelo Vanderbilt when she was Duchess of Marlborough, the Duke of Alba, all of those Hungarian Palffys; and members of the various governments in Europe, including quite a few crowned heads. The fact that he did a drawing of Madame Rubinstein shows how well, even in 1908, she must have been established in Paris society."

This surprised me. I was often skeptical about the stories of her success—it seemed to have been so rapid—and, yet, here was proof positive. As a very young woman she was not only a beauty, but "established in Paris society." For all of Madame's vagueness about the past, for all of her cries of "work and more work," she still seemed to have had time to go out into the world, to meet people, to marry, to bear two sons, besides setting up a business which, by 1908, included salons in Melbourne, London, and Paris. Here again, little by little, Madame was to fill the gaps in her seemingly ephemeral past. I never

:[ 85 ]:

ceased to marvel at what she had managed to accomplish from around 1900, when she first set out for Australia, to the present. And, for the next decade, there was to be no letup in the grueling pace of her daily life. In fact, to the very end, she continued driving herself, and all those around her, unmercifully. Often, when our relationship was sorely tested by her incessant desire to dominate me, to run my life, to keep me by her side—"Think of me as a mother!"—I still had the strength to hold on, to be patient, until there was a change in the wind, and, from a raging virago, she subsided back into her true self: *an old lady bypassed by the love she craved because she was unable to show her true feelings.*

Marguerite stood beside me. She was pensive. "*Voyez, elle était belle!* You see, she was beautiful. I've been her maid for more than thirty years. I've seen her change as her business expanded, as she dumped Titus—the first husband. He was a card! Couldn't keep his hands off the ladies. She stood it for years, but it made her grow harder. She loved the man. When they separated, her life was only the business. Even the Prince couldn't change that, although he tried!"

Marguerite sighed: "She's impossible, but she knows what she wants. She knows how to hold people as long as she needs them. And then . . . then, she has a magic! Now, let me show you your bedroom—Prince Gourielli's bedroom." Marguerite led me down a short corridor to what, at first glance, looked like a padded cell (padded entirely with slivers of wood, cunningly joined together) whose sparse furnishings—a small bed, two upright chairs, and a chest of drawers—were monastic rather than princely.

Noting my look of disappointment, Marguerite tried to cheer me by first pointing to an aging chinchilla bed-throw: "At least you'll be warm. It used to be Madame's best fur coat." And then she led me back into the corridor, and threw open a door: "Look! You have your own private entrance. There's the elevator, there's the back staircase. Monsieur can come and go as he pleases. No one . . . ," she nodded her head in the direction of Madame Rubinstein's bedroom, which must have been at least a five-minute walk from where we stood, "will be any the wiser. You can escape! It's not as bad as you think."

As I climbed into the Prince's narrow bed my thoughts were again a jumble: "Why was the Prince's bedroom so far from Madame's? So austere? Why did Marguerite think I would want to escape? What would tomorrow be like?" Still, I had made friends with Marguerite, who was to turn out to be, as Madame reluctantly admitted, "a jewel." I wondered about Eugénie, the glum-looking cook. Why did her employer treat her with such callousness? Where was Gaston? Her husband-who-wasn't-a-husband, whom Madame had called "a little Hitler"? What a household, what a hornet's nest I seemed to have fallen into!

There was a loud buzz by my bedside. I groped in the dark until my hand found a telephone, pressed one button after another: "Hallo!" Madame's throaty voice echoed in the room. "Are you sleeping?"

"Yes, I'm sleeping."

"Good! Go on sleeping. Tomorrow we have a terrible amount of work to do. . . ."

# "Watch Her Zipper!"

Psychologists say dreams are usually related to the previous day's experiences. Freud insisted they extended these experiences, giving them a new dimension.

I was dreaming that Madame Rubinstein and I were still on the plane, and that *all* our fellow passengers were nuns—the nuns we had met at Shannon Airport. Instead of their customary black habits, they were swaddled in loose-fitting nylon smocks usually worn in beauty salons.

I knew they were nuns because their heads were still incongruously encased in the wimples of their order; great flapping wings of highly starched linen.

Madame also wore a smock. It was entirely embroidered with pearls. She strutted up and down the aisle. I followed her, dressed like an intern, wheeling a refreshment tray. It was piled high with jars, bottles, tubes of Helena Rubinstein cosmetics.

With the precision of a circus ringmaster introducing a musical seal, Madame matched her words to her gestures. She was giving her famous beauty lesson: "Three Steps to Beauty." "First, my dears, you cleanse the skin with my wonderful, new 'Deep Cleanser.'"

She snatched a bottle from my tray, emptied a few drops of white fluid on her fingertips, applied them to her face in a series of quick, upward strokes: "Up, up, up . . . always UP! *Never down*. That's how you loosen the muscles and make the face sag." The nuns all sat forward in their seats, as Madame beat a rapid tattoo under each of her eyes and cooed with pleasure, "Next step . . . refresh!"

The plane's lights went out as a wild buzzing noise woke me up with a start. It was the phone ringing again, but this time morning sunlight flooded my room.

"Hallo! Still asleep? It's time you got up! I've been awake since six. Come, come quick. I need you. We have heaps to do!" Madame's voice rasped at me.

I shot out of bed, shaved, dressed at the double—thankful for my early military training. As a young soldier, I had often made it from my bunk to the parade ground in three minutes flat.

As I reached what must have been the kitchen door, Eugénie materialized with a cup of steaming coffee.

"Monsieur will need this to give him strength," she said. "Madame's been wanting to ring him since six. Not even daylight, yet! I told her to wait until eight. I told her that young men need their sleep!"

There was a touch of warmth in her taut smile. She led me at a trot down the witch doctor's corridor into a recessed room furnished with a clutter of Victorian chairs tufted in bright yellow silk, past the Lalique front door to the curtained doorway Madame had vanished through on the previous night.

"Par ici, Monsieur!" Eugénie raised the corner of the curtain, revealing a magical sight. I assumed it to be the drawing room—the main drawing room—since it was so formal. Ionic columns supported a domed ceiling; green love seats nestled in mirrored alcoves; tall windows jutted out over the river: the Seine River, sluggish and flooded, winding into space, to some distant *pointilliste* horizon.

"Vite, Monsieur!" Eugénie urged me on. She tugged at my sleeve and guided me to a quilted yellow satin door beyond another small hallway filled with Egyptian, pre-Columbian, and Khmer sculptures. Here, she rattled a bronze handle—knocking on satin would have been a waste of time. "Entrez! For God's sake, come in, hurry. . . ." Madame's voice was a tocsin.

If her Park Avenue bedroom with its cold, formal furnishings reminded me of an icebox—overstocked with glass, mirror, and lucite—

this one made me think of the padded warmth Colette had once written about with such sensuality. Precious fabrics, wood, bronze and mother-of-pearl were wedded with an orgy of graceful furnishings. I blinked before my eyes settled on Madame. She was lying on her side in a huge golden bed, like a sea lion sunning itself on a rock, wrapped in satin sheets and covered with enough paper to confuse a garbage collector.

"Ha! Slept late." Her eyes were a challenge. "I've been hard at work with all this dreck." She impatiently brushed aside some papers, which fluttered around her.

Dreck. There we go again on a multilingual binge, I thought. "What's next?" In an effort to collect my wits, I praised her bedroom, complimented her on what I had seen of the apartment.

She snorted, but rose to the bait: "We have better furniture here than in New York, better objects, pictures. I learned, years ago, that the French judge people by such things—by *le tout ensemble*." Her French, even in a brief sentence, was almost musical.

Madame rattled on: "I bought this bedroom furniture from Misia Sert. It had belonged to a relative of Napoleon's . . . not the first Napoleon, the other, the one with the beard, the one who looked like Horace."

As with people's names, Madame's historical associations were apt to swan off on unpredictable tangents—but by comparing the dead with the living, particularly the living in her own family, she invariably managed to produce the needed clue.

"Napoleon the Third," I said.

"Yes. That's him. The relative was his aunt. Very grand, intellectual. She had a literary salon. Now, what the devil was her name? Same as my maid in New York . . . Mathilda."

"Napoleon the Third's aunt was the Princesse Mathilde," I suggested.

"Yes. That's her. Anyway, this was her bedroom once; before Misia bought it. Now, do you know who was Misia—Misia Sert?"

Madame now cozily settled down to "a little gossip"; work was forgotten. She enjoyed such disjointed and aimless chatter. So did I. We were like a pair of fishwives. I acted as her foil, occasionally urging her, while she reminisced in fits and starts, flashbacks; and thus it was that she sought a moment's respite from her "irritations," "problems," and imaginary "pressures." She repeated the word "Misia," rolling it on her tongue, savoring it. "Misia Sert was some meshuggenah, an eccentric. She's dead now. Died of drugs. But when I first came to Paris—pfft! more than forty years ago—she was a Queen. Rich. Social, artistic . . . Polish! That's why she took to me. We spoke the same language, shared similar memories. Besides, I wanted to learn. You see, London and Paris were new experiences for me after Australia and Poland. I was green. I didn't know about society. I had to make my own way. Someone had to show me, to guide me. That's where Misia came in. Like Princess What's-her-Name—Mathilde—she had a salon, and every Thursday entertained the best writers, painters, titled people."

Titles intrigued Madame. It wasn't just a question of snobbery. She was too impatient to be really snobbish. But, as a secret romantic, she appreciated them, and was impressed by the sound of a grand name suitably prefixed. In the company of titled people she always insisted on using her own, hissing at me, "Call me Princess, then they'll know." I often disregarded her and, later, she gave me hell: "Stupid! Don't you know it's easier for one princess to talk to another, or for a princess *not* to talk to a countess?" To which I answered: "But people in Europe are more impressed with Madame Helena Rubinstein than they are with Princess Gourielli." "Smart aleck!" she snapped. "That's not the point. First, you must do what I tell you. Second, I like being called Princess Gourielli. It makes me think I'm someone else. It makes me forget the business!"

"Titled people," Madame continued, "were more important in those days than they are now. Misia was very cosmopolitan. She was one of the first to mix artists with dukes, princes, even kings. She really knew everybody—even that Jewish writer who slept in a room lined with cork and wrote the famous book I could never read. You know, Marcel something."

"Marcel Proust?"

"Yes, that's the one. Nebbishy looking. I met him once at Misia's. He smelt of moth balls, wore a fur-lined coat to the ground, asked heaps of questions about make-up. Would a duchess use rouge? Did demimondaines put kohl on their eyes? How should I know? But, then, how could I have known that he was going to be so famous? If so, I might have told him a thing or two. But I was shy. . . ."

Madame stared at the ceiling in an effort to conjure Misia Sert and her glittering circle back to life. She was no longer lying in bed on her side but had assumed a lotus pose.

"Misia was a meshuggenah, but always busy. I like that sort of people. I only knew her well after she divorced Nathanson. It was before the 1914 war. He was rich, very rich. A publisher. By then, Misia's only interest was for antiques, for writers, and for artists. She collected them all. Many of the good artists painted her portrait—Renoir, Bonnard, Vuillard. It was through her Helleu and Dufy did things of me. . . ."

So now I knew the true origins of the two portraits. Madame continued nonstop. She occasionally wiped her face on her satin sheets and, then, carefully selecting a corner, blew her nose in them.

"Misia was very knowledgeable. It was she who gave me the idea of being painted, of all the portraits. Good for publicity, good investment, good for all the empty walls! She also helped me collect things. She had an eye . . . she had an eye for the unusual."

Madame now hearkened back to the early thirties when, just after the Wall Street Crash, she had returned to Paris after selling her American business to Lehman Brothers, the investment bankers. I had read about this financial coup. For eight million dollars in cash, Madame disposed of her American firm and retired to Europe. This was part of her deal with those she called "the bankers."

Morning sunlight—that strange, pale, French winter sunlight—shone on her satin walls. She still sat in her favorite lotus position and slowly unwound the story.

"I knew that they would make a mess of things. What do bankers know about the beauty business? Except that it can make money for them. After they bought me out, they tried to go mass; to sell my products in every grocery store. Pfft! The idea wasn't bad. But the timing was all wrong. So, so they wanted me out of the way? So I could now afford to be out of their way! I came here, to Paris, with all of my money—with eight million dollars. I built up my business in Europe. I built a few houses. I got separated and then divorced from Titus!"

:[ 93 ]:

Madame skirted around this last event, although I was later to hear her say it was one of the tragedies of her life. For Edward Titus, her first husband, remained to the end of his days, and hers, the only passion she was to experience as a woman.

When in Paris, in her younger days, Madame Rubinstein had always lived "over the shop." In 1930, armed with her American millions, she moved to Boulevard Montparnasse where Edward Titus worked as an art dealer and a printer; but after her divorce, she was faced with the problem of finding new quarters. Misia Sert's second husband, the Spanish painter José Mariá Sert, owned a tumble-down eighteenth-century house on the then unfashionable Île Saint-Louis. Prodded by his wife, as always, short of funds, he sold this property to Madame, who, with her eye for real estate, recognized a bargain: "I bought it for a song, but it cost me a fortune to get all the tenants out. One old woman insisted that I get her a small house in the country. The others settled for cash. That was just the beginning. I then had to tear down Sert's old building. Misia found me an architect, contractors, helped me to get the permits. Truly, she was well-connected. Knew important men in the government. Still, it took three years and lots of the Lehman money to finish the place. By 1934, I was finally able to move in . . . but I was alone!"

On that winter morning lolling back in her huge yellow bed, Madame only divulged the scantiest details concerning her second "coup" in her dealings with Lehman Brothers. She wasn't one to crow about financial success, and when discussing money, particularly hers, always played it cool: "Why blabber? It only makes others envious. Brings beggars to the door!"

Still, little more than a year after Lehman Brothers had bought her out in America, she forced them to sell the business back to her.

To do so, she wrote hundreds of personal letters to small stockholders—mostly women—pointing out, "as one woman to another," that men, particularly bankers, didn't understand the beauty needs of the average woman. With the Crash, the Helena Rubinstein stock plummeted. Meantime, she bought whatever shares came on the market, while collecting proxies from her new adherents. Her own holdings, by now, were considerable. She was then able to force "the bankers" into selling the company back to her—at her price! For well under two million dollars, Madame was able to resume her position as "president" of the American Helena Rubinstein Company. She had made a net profit of six million.

"All it took was a little chutzpa," Madame concluded before screeching: "Nine o'clock! Aii . . . too much gossip! Too little work! Here, take these papers." She scooped up a handful. "Study them. I'll be ready in a jiffy. We must go to the Faubourg, to the office."

I left and for the next quarter of an hour amused myself by wandering around her apartment—built with Misia Sert's help, financed by Lehman Brothers, fostered by Madame's heartbreak.

The light in the drawing room gave the illusion of a spring day. It bounced off the green damask curtains, the Louis XVI chairs covered with flowering tapestries, the malachite tables, and was reflected in the mirrors and the crystal objects scattered around the room. There were treasures everywhere. Fayum mortuary portraits with glazed eyes smiled down from the leaf-green walls onto enigmatic Egyptian sculptures; silver and gold ash trays seemed to throw sparks at the massive Empire crystal and bronze candelabra hanging from the ceiling; while the Aubusson carpet, covering the floor, was a field of verdant hues.

The next room produced a radical change of mood. It contained the bulk of Madame's collection of African sculptures. Here the color theme was red on pale sand. There were red curtains, upholstered chairs, cushioned settees; while on recessed shelves and in vitrines, some two hundred pieces of African sculpture were decoratively displayed—dramatically aligned against stripped oak paneling. I wandered on whistling quietly to myself. This wasn't just a home, but a mausoleum in the guise of a museum. Everything looked slightly dead and definitely dusty. In her New York apartment, there was quantity; in her Paris apartment, there were both quantity and quality. And yet, for all the dramatic extremes of presentation, of visual drama, there was an unlived sadness about the place, and although Madame liked strong colors—reds, purples, yellows, greens; mixed modern furnishings with antiques, valuable objects with kitsch, allowed one period to merge or clash with the next—the final result was cold, even depressing, in its formal opulence.

Beyond the "African room" came a small antechamber and the

"main" dining room—as opposed to the "small dining room" that led to the suspended greenhouse and my new quarters. In the main dining room, the stone walls—great slabs of dramatic concrete—again gave me a chill, even if it was a luxurious *"frisson."* A long black and white marble table, which must have weighed at least a ton, was surrounded by twelve upright gilded Louis XIV chairs. Several large paintings—most of them by Miró—softened the monastic austerity, as did the rich surfaces of Boulle chests, sideboards, and serving tables; but it was a sepulchral room—designed for a wake rather than a roistering banquet. A door in the wall swung open and Eugénie sidled in.

"Monsieur! Madame says she'll be ready to leave for the office in five minutes. Here's her lunch."

She handed me the inevitable paper bag, and, seeing that I was still hypnotized by the dining room, said: "Sue, Monsieur Sue, decorated this room for Madame when he built Quai de Bethune. He was her architect. It's not her taste, but his. Madame always wanted more than less. She's like that . . . take, take, take! I just gave her my household accounts. Do you know what she did? She cut them in half!

"I've been with Madame since this building went up. Before that, I worked for Monsieur Titus. He was a real gentleman. Their marriage broke up only because of money. Madame will tell you otherwise. She'll say he had mistresses. That's true. What else would he do? She never gave him a moment. God only knows how she found the time to have two sons!"

So this was the other side of the story but Eugénie, who was obviously smarting at the fate of her household accounts, begged me once more to hurry. Although I would have gladly heard more, I ran back to my room, stuffed the papers Madame had given me in an attaché case, collected my overcoat. When I returned to the entrance hallway, Madame was standing there. She wore only gray—from her fur bowler hat to her patent leather shoes—and even the pearls looped around her neck were gray.

"You waste time!" she said, grabbing the paper bag with her lunch in it: "Come, the car's waiting. We have a hundred and one things to do!"

From the Île Saint-Louis to the Faubourg Saint-Honoré, where the Helena Rubinstein salon and offices are situated, is a good half-hour's drive through unending, hysterical traffic snarls. I still turn pale at the thought of them.

Vladimir, the chauffeur-concierge, made it in twenty minutes maneuvering the old Chrysler like a souped-up sports car. Madame seemed totally oblivious of the perils she was running while she bounced up and down on the faded gray upholstery by my side. Other thoughts preoccupied her. First, there was the morning's mail. She produced it in stages—emptying her purse, a large envelope, and finally her pockets. "Look at all the letters we have to answer! Open them." I did so. "Now read them. One at a time." I refrained from pointing out (sucking in my breath since Vladimir had almost knocked down a policeman) that "one at a time" was the only way they could be read careening through the streets of Paris at sixty miles an hour.

Before I managed to get through the contents of the first letter, Madame cried: "Stop! I want to talk about Horace." She seemed unusually perturbed. Her breasts heaved like a trapped pigeon's. "Horace is a fool, a dreamer. Ameisen told me last night that he had just left New York for the South of France. Imagine? Why didn't he come with us? But he's in trouble. He's run away. And now he wants to stay in my house near Grasse. Know about it?"

I knew that Madame owned a lavish *mas*, as houses are called in the rural districts of Provence, in the flower-growing countryside around Grasse. It was called "Maison Blanche."

"The Prince made me build it after the war. It's not far from Cannes. He was mad for Cannes because of all the white Russians living there. Imagine! He's only been down once. Pfft! I should have named it '*Éléphant Blanc.*' Cost a fortune. Useless. And now Horace wants to move in. He'll fill the place with his rubbishy friends. He's already bamboozled me into spending millions on a perfume research place nearby—just to keep someone he likes employed. I tell you, I'm being used, bled! Where will it all end?"

"Let me tell you where it will end! It will end in a showdown. Better have it now than later. Got a pencil? Let us write to Horace. Here, write on the back of this envelope. Ready? 'Dear Horace.' No.

:[ 97 ]:

Make it just 'Horace. I'm your mother. You're my son. I wish you well. I wish you more than well. But . . . but?' Oh, to hell with Horace! To hell with the letter! Why write? He's just like Titus— the father. Another . . . another waster!

"In a few weeks we'll go down to Grasse. Just you and I. We'll surprise him. Meantime, I won't say 'yes' or 'no.' I'll act dumb. I'll sit back and wait. Know something?" Madame leaned into my ear. "Horace has been having an affair with a Negress. She's been trying to blackmail him. Found out about me. That's why he's run away. Stupid! One should always face responsibilities . . . then there's no blackmail."

Madame, feeling she might have said too much, suddenly changed the subject to her sister Stella, Stella Oscestowitcz, the current titular head of the French corporation.

"Another agitator!" she spat. "Another troublemaker! Another fool! Give . . . give . . . give. That's all I'm called for. And now, know what? Now she wants a dowry!"

Stella was the fifth sister, born after Regine and before Manka. She headed the second wave of females in the Rubinstein family and was considerably younger than Madame. It was soon evident she had always been a problem. While a teen-ager, she had followed Madame to Australia, then flitted around Europe, America, without ever properly settling down. During her travels she had married twice— "unsatisfactorily," to use the word Madame spat out like a pip.

"And now, now she's found herself another man! A count . . . a French count . . . a French-count-of-no-account. Well, he won't get a penny from me. A dowry? Stella doesn't need a dowry! Stella's sixty-six!"

Madame's right hand crashed down on her lunch bag. I heard an egg crack.

"Besides, Stella gets a huge salary for doing nothing. I gave her an apartment. She made me buy her another one in Cannes. I invest her money for her. I buy her dresses. It's still not enough. She wants a dowry! As God is my witness, I swear . . ."

While Madame recovered, I waited for the next installment. But her mood had again changed. Now she was benevolent and said, "Poor thing! Just like Horace. She has a chip on her shoulder. Let us write her a nice note. . . ."

I was given another envelope, locked my knees around the jump seat to steady myself, and waited. Madame's message was conciliatory. She praised her sister, asked for details concerning the future bridegroom's background, overlooked the dowry. As with all of her dictated correspondence, she ended with the words, "Full stop!"

"Type it up the minute we get to the office. I'll be seeing her shortly. It may help me to say the right thing. Even so, she'll cry. And I'll . . . I'll give in."

Madame had a passion for dictating such memos and she used them in various ways. But their primary purpose was to clarify her thinking and her approach when face to face with the recipient. Sometimes these memos were delivered before a meeting; or else, if a stalemate occurred, she handed out the memo during the meeting: "Here. Study this and let me have your answer later!" But, more often than not, the memos were never delivered. She used them as a reference, sneaking quick glances at the piece of paper as a military strategist might at a map.

We had reached the Faubourg. Madame peered out of the window, recognized the British Embassy, and hollered: "Stop! *Arrêtez la voiture.*" Vladimir's impulsive use of brakes matched the impulsiveness of her command. We both pitched forward. Madame collected her bits and pieces and got out of the car. "Come," she said. "We'll walk a block so that they don't see the car. It will give them a jolt when we arrive." Surprise, as with Von Clausewitz, was one of her favorite strategems. She led me briskly, some two hundred yards, to an eighteenth-century building.

While the New York salon and offices were lavishly housed, their Paris counterpart appeared to be small and dingy. At street level the retail shop, enhanced with the legend HELENA RUBINSTEIN, SALON DE BEAUTÉ, SALON DE COIFFURE, was wedged between an oculist and an upholsterer.

Madame briefly studied the jars and bottles in one of the two shop-windows. "Not enough merchandise!" she cracked and marched in. The narrow room, lavishly mirrored but sparsely furnished with twin counters on which more Rubinstein products were displayed, ended in an alcove where, behind a pair of columns, several salesgirls sprawled around a cash register—gossiping.

"Look at them!" Madame hissed over her shoulder, "Lazy bums! Little do they care, what with their social security. Wait and see! I'll give them some social security."

Before the salesgirls could even get up, Madame was on them. "Having a nice rest? Litka! Go and stand by the doorway! And you, whatever's your name, dust the counters, rearrange the products, look busy!" She snapped a few more orders, snorted, and pushed me into an elevator.

"What did I tell you? Nothing but irritation!" We ascended gently to the third floor where Mr. Ameisen stood waiting for us. Apparently forewarned of the approaching holocaust, he looked infinitely sad.

"The shop's a cemetery!" Madame greeted him. "Those girls down there would do better walking the streets. Except who would want them?"

She led the way into a nearby office, tossed her bags on the desk, sank in an upright chair behind it, and toppled over the wastepaper basket with her feet. It was then, as she stretched out her legs, that I noticed the zipper on the side of her skirt was wide open.

"Watch her zipper!" Miss Hopkins had warned me in New York. For the next quarter of an hour, without a moment's pause, Madame lambasted Mr. Ameisen in a mixture of English, French, and Polish. Standing at attention in a corner of the room, unable to understand what was going on, I quietly surveyed our surroundings, plotting my escape. There were four doors. The walls were paneled in modern oak. Two of the doors were pendants to a vitrine filled with what looked like pre-Columbian and Greco-Roman statuary. Hanging on the wall over Madame's head was a portrait of her painted in tones of raw umber. It must have been done right after one of her tantrums. She looked like a squaw about to burn a few white settlers. No escape, I thought. Stiff upper lip, I decided.

Suddenly the bombardment of poor, silent Mr. Ameisen ended, the fire in Madame's eyes abated, and her jaw line slackened. She now emptied her lunch bag on the desk, selected a salad leaf, shelled an egg, and, comfortably folding her arms about her waist, said in English: "Now that you know what I think of you, what do you think of Stella?"

As she mentioned her sister's name, one of the four doors opened. An exact duplicate of Madame Rubinstein edged uncertainly in. She had the same blue-black hair, forehead, eyes. The only difference between the two ladies was that this new apparition was a mess. Her unknotted chignon flapped around the back of her neck, her eyebrows were drawn on crookedly, a rivulet of lipstick ran down her chin.

"Ha, Stella!" Madame beamed. "Speak of the devil. I was just asking about you. Your lipstick's on crooked!" By now, Stella had reached the desk, still walking sideways, still silent. "Where did you get your dress?" Madame winked at me. "I hope you've brought your marriage contract? We must study it. Have an egg. . . ."

Mr. Ameisen gave me the eye—a very pale blue eye—indicating that the time was right for us to leave the two sisters alone, and we excused ourselves. Madame shouted after me: "Type out the letter I dictated. You know . . . the one for 'The Pill.' I may need it later. Meantime, Mr. Ameisen, show him around, tell him all you know. I want him to report to me exactly what goes on in this place."

Mr. Ameisen's pained expression quickly changed into a puckish smile.

"Who's 'The Pill'? Stella? Madame's right—arsenic and old hate. But Madame tortures her. She's always liked a willing victim. Still, Stella knows how to handle her. Wait and see. She'll get her 'dowry' *and* marry." He paused. "It's really rather marvelous for a woman of her age to even want to get married. But then, like all the sisters, she has a sort of magic. You wouldn't think so, seeing her now, but twenty years ago she was a *femme fatale!*"

As we walked around the third-floor offices, Mr. Ameisen introduced me to various members of his staff as "Madame's new confidential secretary." Most of them had the shabby, preoccupied look of sedentary French workers whose days are spent in unaired, ill-lit offices and whose pay checks (for all of Madame's cries of social security) barely kept them solvent.

Compared with the glossy New York setup Helena Rubinstein S.A.,

Paris was a run-down operation blending French frugality with Middle-European sloth. The building crumbled with age. It had none of the glamour I associated with beauty products.

Mr. Ameisen now guided me to a series of cubbyholes where various departments, each dealing with a specialized aspect of the business, were housed. In quick succession, I visited sales, merchandising, advertising, publicity, personal services, and "accounts payable." The latter, he told me, was Madame's pet. She had even managed, on one of her recent trips, to cart over from America a huge IBM machine. It was carefully covered with old newspapers and stood unused in the corner of a room that smelled of cabbage, boiled beef, and human sweat. The gray-haired drudges surrounding it preferred to scratch away at their ledgers.

Our next stop was in the hair salon, on the second floor. Here pandemonium reigned. Women wearing pink Rubinstein shifts wandered around, sat under the lunar machinery, telephoned, played with their dogs, and gossiped. A fog, an emanation of damp cooked hair, hung over the suffocating room. It reminded me of a North African sook, a demented auction sale, and a Turkish bath operated for the benefit of psychopathic females—all rolled into one.

"You see what we have to contend with. . . ." Mr. Ameisen led me on to the face and body department, one floor down, where the atmosphere was both sinister and serene. A vague but elegant lady sat at a desk, her myopic eyes fringed by a sky-blue hairdo. She was busy examining the liver spots on the backs of her hands. *"Ah, cher Monsieur!"* Looking up, she greeted Mr. Ameisen. *"Comme vous êtes élégant!"* Her intonation was Slav—possibly Polish. Her manner was superior, almost deprecating.

"Madame Giza," Mr. Ameisen introduced us, "is a cousin of Madame Rubinstein's and one of the cornerstones of the house! This is Madame's new secretary. Her *'bras droit!'* Her 'right arm!' "

Madame Giza's elegant head bobbed at me. It was evident that she had seen a procession of "right arms" and wasn't a bit impressed. "What can I do for you?"

"Madame Rubinstein wants Monsieur to know 'every aspect' of the business. I thought that this important department, that you, *chère Madame*, were of such importance to our house that I immediately brought him here."

Her handsome features softened. She was no longer suspicious. Rising, she led us on a tour of her fief. Not unlike the minotaur's maze, it was all winding corridors. These were punctuated by mysterious doors over which a red or white light glowed. If the light was red, Madame Giza pressed a finger to her lips: "A customer!" If white, she opened the door and showed us the appointments. They were clinical. Each room had been painted in a subtle shade of pink: "It makes people look younger, feel better," Madame Giza informed us grandly. In some of the rooms, there was only a massage table; in others, a chaise longue, a stool, and a table full of products. "This is for the body; this is for the face; and this is for special services," she pointed to what looked like a dental drill, *"dépilation!"*

I was beginning to realize that beauty—or its maintenance— required more than a couple of jars of cream and a bottle of astringent, when Madame Giza threw open a door whose overhead light failed to proclaim it was occupied. In the room, an ancient hulk of a woman swaddled in sheets and connected by wires to several pieces of machinery was stretched out reading *La Vie Parisienne.*

*"Excusez moi, Madame la Marquise!"* Madame Giza trilled. *"Madame la Marquise,"* being French, aged, and happy to see two men, summoned us in. *"Rentrez, rentrez!"* she cackled.

Madame Giza tried to prevent us, but I marched past her, fascinated. "I'm the house guinea pig," the marquise informed us. "The doctoress is testing some new machinery on me for *cellulite.*" With that, she flipped a sheet, and revealed her legs. They looked like two overpoached turbots, tattooed with a riot of varicose veins, wired to several of the sinister machines.

"For twenty years Madame Rubinstein has employed my services to benefit humanity, to contribute to beauty, to help her discover new ways of satisfying every woman's wish for eternal seduction!" The marquise declaimed: "Like Helen of Troy I once had a beautiful face, body . . . but now my poor body, no longer desirable, is dedicated to research so that others may triumph over men's passions!"

In a husky tremolo she then advised us that, due to her dedicated services, sagging breasts could be pumped up, hips reduced to velvety curves, legs firmed to dimensions that would be the envy of "*ces dames du Casino de Paris et du Lido.*"

Before more secrets could escape from the marquise's lips, Madame Giza pushed us out. "A crackpot. Nothing but a crackpot! The doctoress only uses her because of her long friendship with Madame Rubinstein." Mr. Ameisen tactfully added, "Madame Rubinstein loves her 'research.' She even employs a special woman doctor whose only job it is is to supervise the removal of warts." Judging from his tone, he was obviously also tortured by all these people.

"But where did Madame ever find 'the Marquise'?" I asked him when we were out of Madame Giza's hearing. "Oh, she picked her up at the Flea Market," he said airily. "The marquise had a booth there. Madame liked to buy opalines from her. One thing led to another. The marquise wouldn't come down in price for one of Madame's purchases, so Madame told her to come and work off the difference. Madame saved on her purchase . . . had a willing guinea pig. Both were happy!"

We completed our tour in Mr. Ameisen's office. Here he introduced me to his affable secretary, Sylvia Bedhjet. After I had typed up my notes for Madame to give Stella, he explained that the Paris salon lost money. "Still, it keeps Stella busy, Madame Giza, too. It also helps the marquise to survive. You might call it 'a charitable institution.'

"Women these days have learned how to treat their skins, shave their own legs, exercise. They do it all at home. We can only survive on wholesale. But when Madame first opened a salon in Paris, she was a pioneer. Why, she even introduced such simple practices as Swedish massage. No one had ever heard of it then. You see, Madame always traveled a lot, even in those days. And wherever she went she picked up a local formula, beauty idea, *objet d'art* . . ."

Before he could tell me more Madame trotted in. She nursed several voluminous files and quickly dumped them in my lap. "For you to study when you've finished gossiping!"

"We were not gossiping, Madame. Mr. Ameisen was telling me how you introduced Swedish massage to Paris."

"Ha! How would he know? I'll tell you. I'll tell you both."

For the next half-hour we were all silent as Madame tacked from one subject to the next. She described the origins of massage, depilation, electrolysis (pronounced "electricks"), Scotch douches, and even high colonics ("very good for the skin, those colonials!"). Finally, she returned to the subject of massage: "I wrote letters to a few of the smartest women in Paris. That was around 1912. Poiret was all the rage. He had started designing loose clothes. Women had to give up their corsets. They had to do something about all the flesh." Madame's expression, her mouth curled with distaste, gave me a fleeting vision of fat pouring down on the sidewalks of Paris from every "smart" woman. "In my letters I offered them a complimentary massage. A free consultation. Few women, particularly French-women, can resist something for nothing. Colette, the writer, was among the first to show up. She was scandalous, very scandalous in those days. So, so I warned a newspaperwoman I knew. 'Come,' I said, 'Come to the shop' and I gave her a scoop. After Colette's massage—you know, it wasn't just an ordinary massage, they did little extra things. After it was over Colette felt good, so good that she told the newspaperwoman, 'Massage is a woman's sacred duty. The women of France owe it to themselves. Without it, how can *they hope* to keep a lover!' That did the trick. Headlines! You should have seen the crowds," Madame chuckled briefly. "Now, back to business! Those days are all over. What we need are some good new products, clever advertising, better merchandising. Call up the lawyer, Mr. Ameisen. I want him to check Stella's marriage contract. Can you beat it? She's going to be a bride!"

Madame beamed; she had given in to her sister. "Imagine? The count plays bridge, owns a car, has his own income. Stella's made good at last! Mr. Ameisen, give me some money, I want to go shopping. I must buy Stella a gift."

He asked how much she required.

"Half a million francs." This amounted to about a thousand dollars.

"Whom shall I charge it to?"

"Stella, of course."

During the lunch hour I was led on a tour of some of her favorite Parisian shops. Our first stop was Dior, on the Avenue Montaigne.

"I must buy some shoes. They have the best in Paris. Expensive, but comfortable. Besides, the man who makes them always gives me something off. I never have to bargain."

As we were walking into the Roger Vivier shoe shop, then still a part of the House of Dior, cries of "Helena!" from a large black Cadillac stopped us. "See who it is," Madame said. "Why it's Caramel! Caramel and Marie-Louise. . . . Come." We walked over to two pairs of beckoning arms and as we reached the car out popped their excited, diminutive owners who fell upon Madame, enveloping her in a series of embraces.

She stood her ground, preventing herself from being swept into the gutter by grasping their waists. Thus linked, all talking at once, they lurched into the Dior shoe shop.

"Caramel," as Madame pronounced Carmel Snow's first name, was my old boss from *Harper's Bazaar*. During a lull in the verbal free-for-all Madame introduced me to her companion, Marie-Louise, who sounded like a macaw impersonating a factory whistle. Her full name was Marie-Louise Bousquet and I remembered that not only did she represent *Harper's Bazaar* in Paris; she was looked upon by her many friends as a "character," a "personality," one whose imprint was felt at every level of fashion and international society.

*"Quel beau garçon!"* she croaked, looking at me through hooded eyes and throwing her arms around Madame. "What taste you have, *mon Helena*. The Prince will be jealous." Madame giggled, patted her, pushed her away. The half-dozen bangles Marie-Louise wore on each wrist jangled as she minced around us in a happy gavotte. She was even smaller than Madame—almost as thin as the gold-headed cane she propelled herself with, and kept banging on the floor to give her words greater emphasis. A Breton sailor's hat, glued to wisps of frizzled hair, accentuated features that reminded me of Jimmy Durante.

The three ladies—Madame in gray, Mrs. Snow in pink, Marie-Louise in yellow—fluttered around the shoe racks grabbing a pump here, a mule there, calling endearments to one another, until, finally, they all slumped down in a row of chairs.

*"Helena, ma chérie . . . ,"* Marie-Louise growled lovingly at Madame, "try the crocodile!"

"And the purple lizard, dear," Mrs. Snow took up the refrain in her teakettle's hiss.

Madame slipped on one of each, tottered forward and . . . fell. We all sprang forward to help her up. "No! Let me catch my breath!"

This was the first time I was to see Madame fall and lie, for five or ten minutes on the ground, "catching her breath." Her ankles were weak. Her equilibrium was poor. She was always in a tearing rush and seldom looked where she was going. But in the many falls she sustained in my presence, she never broke a single bone or suffered greater damage than "a shock." She always lay still, like a felled animal, muttering, "God is good to me"; "stupid"; "I'll have some awful bruises." After a while, she would get up alone, refusing all help, breathe in and out two or three times, straighten her clothes, check her jewels ("Sometimes a stone flies out"). And then, if the fall had been particularly severe, order whoever was standing by: "Get me a drink!"

While Madame was still stretched out on the floor in the Dior shoe boutique a further commotion among the attending salesgirls heralded the arrival of Monsieur, Christian Dior himself.

The great couturier had heard that Mrs. Snow, Madame Bousquet, and Princess Gourielli were in his establishment. He had come down to present his respects. Quite unfazed by the scene that greeted him, he balanced himself on his haunches, kissed Madame's hand, and joined in the conversation centered about her reclining figure. When she finally got up to her feet, another wild melee ensued as all three ladies, stimulated by the "Master," sought his advice as to what shoes would be best for them. Roger Vivier joined them. Accessories were produced, models appeared wearing the latest evening dresses and fur coats. An impromptu fashion show developed under Monsieur Dior's benign and subtle supervision. His manners, like those of a French parish priest supervising a garden *fête*, were gentle. "*Ma petite*, the sable must drape over the left shoulder!" "Princess, this pearl-encrusted dress is made for you!" "Madame Snow, observe the hemline!" The ladies goggled. So did I. It was as if he were conducting a string quartet and in full control of both the performers and the audience. I had always imagined that hysteria and temperament were part and parcel of the French "*Haute Couture*" as was an extravagance of dress and flamboyance of manners. Not so with Mr. Dior. He seldom raised his voice. His features were those of an elderly cherub. He walked with the dignity of a banker and when he sat down, to admire his handiwork or chat, he did so straddling a chair back to front, like a good French peasant watching a game of cards in a *bistro*.

When the show was over, Madame had ordered six dresses and Mrs. Snow a coat. They now concentrated on their feet as Mr. Dior vanished, promising to ask them to lunch so that they might see his newly refurbished home. Before turning to fashion, right after the war, Christian Dior had sold pictures and antiques. Knowing this, Madame was obsessed with a desire to see his house, to find out what he owned, where he had picked up "little bargains." She had an immense curiosity concerning self-made people. Rich, established, and inherited homes, however well-appointed, seldom interested her: "They didn't have to work for it. Someone else did it for them." An appointment had to be made "soon" with "Monsieur." She left the details to Marie-Louise who, writhing like a puppy, assured her that Christian's house was *"un chef d'oeuvre . . . un miracle . . .* beautiful, *mon Helena!"*

It was then that the three ladies discovered that each was wearing the other's shoes. A brief scrimmage followed and soon we left to the sound of Marie-Louise's raucous farewell: *"A bientôt, ma chèrie!"* Tell your lovair to call me! I adore you!"

"Pfft! Marie-Louise is very exhausting. Still, she's a wonderful person. No money, crippled, old . . . and yet she keeps going. Remind me to give her something when we next see her. The magazine doesn't pay her much. She needs help."

On our way back to the office we stopped off at Madame's *corsetière*, visited two antique shops, and ended our tour at Hermès, the saddler, where she bought five bags: "Four for me, one for Stella . . . after all, think of all the money I spent at Dior." I did. It amounted to some ten thousand dollars. This, in due time, would be paid by the Paris office for, as Madame carefully explained: "I have to look good for the business." She invariably also asked for duplicate bills and presented them to Mr. Levande, "The Bookkeeper" in New York, using the same valid excuse and ordering me to keep mum:

"Think of all the money I spent *on you*" she would snarl, "without ever being reimbursed!"

(Years later, after one of our regular financial tiffs, I was to discover that when I first lived in her Paris apartment, Madame received a daily subsistence allowance for me, and pocketed it although she occasionally gave me a "tip," particularly if she felt I was getting cranky from overwork: "Here, go to a movie!" But since she invariably decided to join me, I was stuck with both tickets—and a loss!)

We were finally back at the Faubourg: "See, they are all still at lunch! Devil take them. . . ." Madame settled down behind her desk, feet again propped up on the wastepaper basket. The afternoon followed a pattern I was soon to get used to, based on extemporization and whim.

As in New York, her office door was kept open and anyone walking by—even a cleaning woman—was apt to be summoned in. *"Entrez!* Who is she? What does she do? Find out. . . ." Whereupon, using me as an interpreter, Madame would question her new victim.

By six on that first day in Paris, my head reeled. But Madame, sitting well back in her chair, still sparkled. An Italian newspaperwoman, whose thirst for news matched my boss's energy, wandered in, propelled by Mr. Ameisen. Fully aware of Madame's penchant for interviews, he used this ploy to get out and go home.

"This is Madame Melik from Milan. She's the beauty editor of *Grazia* magazine."

Madame indicated with a courtly sweep of her arm that Madame Melik was to sit close to her.

"Lovely features," she said. "But oily skin," she added. Madame Melik's lower lip quivered. "Don't let it worry you. Just follow my instructions. But write everything down. Who knows? Some of your readers may be interested."

Out came Madame Melik's pad and pencil. *"Che carina!"*

"First," Madame said, "you must watch your diet. Too much olive oil, too many starches, not enough fruit. Now for the real cure. I'll give you a simple treatment to dry your skin and close your pores." Madame now edged closer to Madame Melik. "You should use my

Skin Exerciser. It tightens the muscles. But whatever you do, don't forget wake-up cream—my first cream! The one I took to Australia with me. Even if I say so . . . it's a miracle!" Madame closed her eyes, as if she had had a vision, and went on to recount, like a guru discoursing on the need for universal love, that wake-up cream was the original "Crème Valaze." The one her mother had endowed her with.

"I swear! If I was shipwrecked on a desert island, it's all I would want, would use. Besides," she added, "it's very economical. I know that people in Italy don't have much money."

Madame Melik sat enthralled. She had filled her notebook.

Lastly, Madame spoke briefly on the necessity of facial masks. "I don't want to recommend too many things. Still, a good mask—like our herbal one—can do wonders for an oily skin. Don't worry, I'll send you the products." She paused dramatically. "You have lovely hands. Here. I want you to have this. . . ." Madame slipped off one of her massive rings and placed it on Madame Melik's forefinger. "Take it . . . take it. For luck!" Madame Rubinstein nodded encouragement. "I bring luck! And it will bring you luck, too!"

Tears of gratitude and admiration welled up in Madame Melik's eyes. She received a further flourish of affectionate pats before reeling out of the room. *Che cara! Che bellezza!* she repeated over and over.

"That was good!" Madame nodded at me. "I've made a friend. Wait and see. She'll spread the gospel." She looked down at her small, vermilion-tipped fingers. "One ring more or less. . . . What's the difference. *Now, let's go home for a bite.*"

# "A Rothschild! Where's My Gold Plate?"

❦ ❦

For the first week, on that first of my many visits to Paris with Madame Rubinstein, the working day began at eight sharp with the inevitable buzz on the house phone, followed by a throaty "Hallo . . ." and entreaties for speed. It was then my job to type and present a list of the day's appointments. "Ha! Let us study my *sche-du-le*." Curled in bed like a greedy badger, Madame snatched my handiwork and read it out loud.

Gathering information for the "sche-du-le" required the guile of a thief and the patience of a sleuth. I did so on the previous day by eavesdropping on Madame's conversations (both verbal and telephonic); by checking every secretary and executive in the Faubourg offices; by attempting to censor her incoming and outgoing mail. "This is private!" She plucked a letter I was about to read from my hand. "If I can't have my secrets, who can?" And, stuffing it in her purse, she bustled out on a secret mission. Madame seldom let her right hand know what the left was up to. She constantly left one meeting to conduct another elsewhere, shot out on quick shopping expeditions, or vanished to enjoy whispered conferences in a dark corridor.

As in New York, I sat in her Paris office with my back to her—typing away. If I stopped, however briefly, she hollered, "Finished? I've got something else for you!" or, pointing to a visitor, "Come over here and listen carefully to what Monsieur is saying." Her French was far from fluent. I was called upon to act as translator, interpreter, sometimes mouthpiece: "Tell him he's a nice man but not practical." She listened, carefully, as I attempted to voice this sentiment to a chemist. "Stop beating around the bush! *Vous êtes* not practical. . . ." Madame first hushed me and then roared at her victim. *"Oui, chère Madame . . . très* practical." The French, with their devious and subtle approaches, floored her. "Chutzpa, I call it!" By six in the evening— the official closing time—she had often worked herself up to a pitch of hysteria; then, noticing everyone wanted to go home, wishing to prolong the working day, she quickly calmed down: "How clever! Most interesting . . . put it down on paper. *Restez!* Let us finish. What's the hurry?" The French are also creatures of habit. Dinner is one of their sacred family obligations. "I'll be damned. Everyone's vamoosed." With a sigh, Madame collected her papers. She led me down three flights of stairs saying: "Don't use the elevator. Set a good example as I do! Electricity is very expensive. . . ." We then settled back in her car: "Let's go home for a bite!"

I dreaded this announcement. Dining alone with Madame Rubinstein, until I knew her better, was a form of torture. I had not yet adapted myself to her peculiarities. I was ignorant of "a transient madness" which struck her whenever she returned to Quai de Bethune. Our evening meals, "the bite," took place in the small dining room whose exquistie hand-painted wallpaper, priceless furniture, and serried opalines were hardly visible in the semiobscurity. Madame believed in conserving electricity. I could barely see the contents of my plate as she sat, facing me, hunched over the Biedermeier table. Her dentures clattered like castanets on crusts of French bread. She nagged and wailed: "Don't drink any more wine"; "I hate Eugénie's soups"; "Paris is some hell!" With this rosary of complaints came a broadside of orders. "Write to my sister in London. Send a wire to New York. Remind me to call up the lawyer tomorrow." Nine o'clock hadn't yet struck from the bell tower on the Île Saint-Louis when, scooping up the papers she was never without, Madame shuffled off to bed. "Stay home! Get a good night's rest. We have lots to do tomorrow!" she called out over her shoulder.

Something's got to give or I'll go bats, I thought. Our dinner of vegetable soup, fried liver, salad, and rock-hard Camembert weighed on my stomach. The evening menu had barely changed since our arrival. "So you don't like the food? Me neither. . . ." Madame often growled, eyeing my plate. "I'm telling you, Eugénie's bills are as-tro-no-mic. For what? For garbage. . . . What to do? What to do?"

What, indeed. It was evidently my job to find a solution. From the nearby kitchen a tantalizing aroma prickled my nostrils: herbs, butter, fish. I went there. With their napkins carefully tucked under their chins, the servants—Eugénie, Marguerite, and Gaston—were guzzling *moules marinières.*

"May I come in?"

"Certainly, Monsieur Patrick."

Eugénie offered me a chair, wine, and a soup plate filled with shiny black mussels.

"Why didn't you give us any of these tonight?" I asked, scooping the last of a delicious sauce.

"*Ah, Monsieur! Il faut* punir *Madame.* I have to punish her. Imagine, with her millions, she allows me five thousand francs a day to feed a household of five." This was ten dollars—two dollars a head. What to do indeed? Eugénie had been Madame's cook—or "*garde,*" as she preferred to call herself—for more than thirty years. She was critical but faithful. Besides, she knew her employer. "*Il faut la punir!*"

"Is there anything I can do?" I asked the tough old war horse. She came from Alsace, where the peasants are known to be stubborn but shrewd.

"*Oh, oui, Monsieur!* Madame Rubinstein is always like this when she first gets here. She thinks she's setting a good example. You're new. She wants to show you. She wants to assert herself. It's the same old story. She bullied Monsieur Titus *Père.*"

Eugénie's bosom heaved with indignation as she went on to explain to me that Madame treated all men—relatives included—as employees, "*Elle les dévore.* She eats them alive . . . even her own sons!" Marguerite and Gaston nodded agreement. "I'll tell you what you must do. First, show her you're independent. Then, do what the Prince does when he's here. Take her out. Get her away from her office. Make her entertain. . . ." I thanked Eugénie, and, wishing to

:[ 113 ]:

show my own independence, skipped out into the night feeling much like a schoolboy playing hooky.

My first objective was Les Deux Magots (in Saint-Germain-des-Prés), glassed-in and steamy, crowded with silent watchers, gossiping groups; I always knew I might meet a friend or two in this congenial atmosphere. It was one of my favorite Parisian haunts. Sure enough, seated at a corner banquette, I caught sight of a familiar ginger head. "Hi! What are you doing here?" Tom Keogh's greetings were always perfunctory—even if I hadn't seen him for months. His wife, Theodora, wrote novels. She invariably did so across the street, on a marble-topped table at the Brasserie Lipp, while Tom preferred Les Deux Magots, claiming that the faces there were more in tune with his work. He was a talented artist. Sketching away, he now cross-examined me as I sipped on a brandy.

"What are you doing?"

"Working for a tyrant."

"That's nothing new."

He had known both of my former bosses—Fleur Cowles and Carmel Snow.

"Who is it this time?"

"Helena Rubinstein."

"Oh, God! You do have a knack for picking them."

Or did they have a knack for picking me? I wondered.

Tom now lived permanently in Paris. He knew the city's night life intimately and told me where I should go if bent on letting off steam—on exorcising my new boss.

"See you soon!"

In quick succession, observing his advice, I tacked from the Place de la Bastille to Montmartre and thence to Saïd's beyond Les Halles. "It's a cozy *maison de passe*-cum-whorehouse," Tom said. "Saïd's wonderful company. He'll find a way of relaxing you!"

In every doorway, blurred faces—or were they Halloween masks?—whispered, *"Tu montes, chéri?"* Crates of vegetables, hunks of meat, early spring flowers, cluttered the sidewalks.

L'Hôtel du Saumon, as Saïd's establishment was called, had the look of a provincial summer boardinghouse tightly shuttered for the winter months. The front doorbell tinkled with the derision of a shop-girl's laughter. A man wearing striped pajamas let me in. His dark, speculative eyes glowed incongruously from under the rim of a beret. *"Attention, aux courants d'air!"* he cautioned. We entered a vicarage waiting room filled with overstuffed furniture.

"Are you here to watch or to participate?" he asked without pre-liminaries. My heart was beating at the level of my tonsils.

"To chat."

*"Un cérébral."*

I explained who had sent me and that I was in the process of "unwinding" from the pressures of business.

"That's what they all say. Proust used to come here to take notes on the décor; and Cocteau to escape from his telephone. Unwind, you said?"

Saïd had started life as a manservant and pimp to the Infante Don Luis of Spain and when, as he told me later, "the poor little dwarf copped it from mixing cocaine with kief, he left me *une bagatelle* in his will. . . . So, so what else could I do but become a madam?" He not only catered to *la pédale,* but also to a group he labeled "kinky senators." "They like to feel they are being seduced by nuns. I keep a wardrobe to satisfy their fancies. This is not a brothel, Monseiur. It's the Comédie Française."

The rooms at l'Hôtel de Saumon were like Saïd's parlor where, by day, a few listless creatures, *"mon écurie*—my stable," sat around waiting for customers. At night, arrangements were made "by appoint-ment" unless, as Saïd took pleasure in explaining, "You want to pre-tend to be a *putain*—lots do—specially the society ladies."

Saïd, for the next few years and until his death, was to be my favorite Parisian method of escape from Madame. I even managed to sneak him in to Quai de Bethune. He was insatiably curious. "I'm a sub rosa queen of beauty," he said. "I have to know how my col-leagues live!"

By the time I returned to the Île Saint-Louis—relaxed rather than satiated—the garbage collectors were having their first glass of hot red wine at the corner *bistro.* There was a smell of chicory and coffee in the air. Specks of light gleamed through Notre Dame's flying buttresses. Dawn, in this part of Paris, had a rural quality. Before snatching a couple of hours' sleep, I even heard a cock crowing.

"Hallo!" Madame's voice spelled doom. "You were out all night. Aii! Come quick."

My tormentor's eyes were like a cobra's, as I wove uncertainly into her room half an hour later.

"Where did you vanish to?"

"I went out . . . for a breath of fresh air."

"Until dawn?"

"I don't remember."

"Don't lie to me. I saw your lights. Just like Horace. Just like all the men you were out all night. Wasting your energies. Wasting your time. . . ."

She pointed to herself. It was her time I was wasting. She spluttered, raised a fist. I turned on my heel and, thinking of Eugénie's advice "Assert yourself," walked out. "Coward!" Madame bellowed after me.

Later that morning, Eugénie paid me a visit. "Whatever you've done, Monsieur, it's had its effect. Madame is still in bed. She made me call up the Faubourg and cancel her appointments. She says that she had a terrible shock."

When opposed, however vaguely, and unable to enjoy one of the rows she used as an invalid might a stimulant, Madame collapsed. This decline usually lasted for a day while she lay in bed pondering the next step.

By six o'clock, she had still not appeared. Eugénie, doing household chores, remarked: *"C'est un caprice!* Don't worry. Wait and see. She'll soon be up and about." I was answering mail—mostly my own —when I heard the distant clatter of Madame's footsteps. She appeared through the foliage, across the greenhouse bridge to the office where I worked, like a vision. Was it Messalina . . . Poppaea . . . or Salome?

Madame was dressed to kill and wore an embroidered tunic of fiery orange velvet. It had long, batlike sleeves that trailed to the ground. There were rubies massed around her neck, knotted about her wrists, clustered at her waist.

"Eugénie! Get me a vodka. . . ."

Although Madame usually drank sparingly, she favored alcohol as opposed to wine. Before an interview, particularly if it was with a member of the press whose publication enjoyed wide circulation, she sometimes took a nip of brandy: "For Dutch courage!" At cocktail parties, but never hers, a bourbon-and-soda on the rocks was all she touched: "My doctor says it's good for the heart!" With meals a glass of Vichy water splashed with red wine usually sufficed.

Vodka! Now I'm in for it.

Rattling the ice in her glass, she gave me a sad, hooded look, and queried, "Still angry with me?" Before I could answer, she smacked her lips and said: "Let's go out for dinner tonight. I've ordered a table at La Méditerranée. We both need a change!" And then, "It's my party. . . ."

We drove to the Place de l'Odéon, near the Luxembourg Gardens, in silence. It was only as we were arriving that Madame explained: "La Méditerranée's very swell, very fashionable. It caters only to the best people. . . ."

I had heard glowing reports about the restaurant. Christian Bérard, the painter, discovered it right after the war. He was then at the zenith of his short-lived career when few fashionable Parisian gatherings—whether it was a play, a dress collection, a new hostess trying out her social wings—could succeed without his official blessing. In Bérard's bearded wake came other artists: Cocteau, Vertès, Leonor Fini, and, with them, established personalities, editors, neophytes of that ever-shifting social world known as *Le Tout Paris*.

Jean, La Méditerranée's garrulous owner, gave Madame Rubinstein a table in the main dining room—a small enclave reserved for celebrities. His cries of *"Princesse, quel honneur!"* made her blink with pleasure as necks craned to catch a glimpse of her.

"See, he knows me. I was one of his first customers."

Madame liked being "a first customer," whether it was in a fashion house such as Dior or Balenciaga, a jeweler like Jean Schlumberger, even a restaurant. It gave her a feeling of permanence.

Before she even managed to tuck a napkin over the broad, glittering expanse of her bosom, a procession came by to greet her—evidently vague friends and chance acquaintances—for she kept hissing at me, between mouthfuls of bread: "Who is that? Get his name. Write it down. . . ." She then lapsed into silence, concentrating on cold trout, lobster bisque, bouillabaisse: "This is a fish place. When in Rome. . . ."

Over cheese and a dessert that looked like one of her bowler hats covered in cream, Madame finally relaxed. A full stomach always made her feel gracious, even chatty: "I seem to know more people than I think I do. I wish I could remember them all! See that lovely woman over there?" she said, pointing to a hawk in black. "What's-her-Name . . . Mrs. Fellowes. At least I remember *her*! Very rich."

I knew that Mrs. Reginald Fellowes was one of the original "fashion locomotives." She was given to wearing diamond necklaces with black turtle-neck sweaters when attending English hunt meetings, to appearing at the French couture collections with a red rose in one hand and a rubber cushion in the other. Before the war Schiaparelli considered her "the smartest woman in the world" and coined the word "chic" for her. Eccentric, original, and, as Madame observed, "very rich . . . ," Daisy Fellowes was no longer young, but her sub-dued elegance filled the room with that particular brand of magic that the French like to call "Parisian."

"Who's she with?"

It was then I noticed Tom Keogh in her party, on whose advice I had "plummeted the depths" the previous evening.

An exchange of signals ensued and we soon joined their table. Madame's delight at this extemporaneous behavior exploded in a series of vague invitations. "They must all come to lunch at our place some day . . . find out when."

La Méditerranée was the type of restaurant where good food promotes excessive sociability. Visiting cards were pressed into my hand. It took us ten minutes from Mrs. Fellowes' table to the doorway to cover an equal number of yards.

"I need fresh air," Madame said. "Let's go for a spin!"

"A spin" consisted of driving slowly through the Bois de Boulogne —a dark, wooded area favored by cavaliers of both sexes—with the car windows opened wide.

"What are all those people doing at this hour of the night?" Madame sat bolt upright, fascinated by interlaced couples wedged against trees, outlined in the glare of our headlights.

"Being friendly," I said.

"Friendly?"

"Yes. . . . You know."

"Was that what you were doing last night?"

My defection was still on her mind! She had had time to mull, possibly to plot a counteroffensive. Lydia Lane's warning, "Madame must always come first . . . ," came back to me—an echo in a wind tunnel. "You know, I've been working hard," I said, using my Iago voice. "I sometimes need a change."

"Yes, yes. Everyone does. I enjoyed dinner tonight. We must do it more often. . . . I have a plan for you. *Then you'll get your change!*

"Business you don't yet understand," she said. "But people you do. Public relations . . . that's what you must concentrate on. I'll teach you! And that will be your change!" Madame asserted.

In France, public relations was still looked upon as an American gimmick—a diversion—consisting, for the most part, in dining and wining obdurate clients into a state of pliability. The Paris Rubinstein offices were, as Madame admitted, "Old hat," if compared to those in New York where, under Amy Blaisdell's guidance, beauty editors, feature writers, and journalists throughout the United States were supplied with a stream of information concerning the hundreds of different Rubinstein products on the market. These offices also helped to launch new items with what Madame admiringly called a "stunt." "There's nothing like a clever stunt to get something off the ground," she said, recalling, no doubt, the "Heaven Sent" campaign.

When "Heaven Sent," a Rubinstein fragrance, was first launched in the late 1940s, hundreds of pale blue balloons floated down on Fifth Avenue with, attached to them, a sample of the fragrance and, tied to it, the legend, "A gift for you from Heaven! Helena Rubinstein's new 'Heaven Sent.' " This was a "stunt." It received national publicity. Madame sat behind her desk anxiously viewing the balloons floating by the windows of her office: "Clever?" she kept asking. "Clever!" she finally admitted when sales soared to well over the million-dollar mark.

In France such stunts had never been seen. The Paris office didn't even have a public relations representative. This was where, Madame decided—as a part of her campaign to rehabilitate me—I would "fit in," "take an interest," under her tutelage, of course.

Madame Rubinstein had a flair for public relations. As with advertising, she "felt it in her bones" and knew, instinctively, what was right or "clever." My education started on the day following our row and our dinner at La Méditerranée.

The first lesson embraced "her beauty pronouncements." These, like so many Catherine wheels, flew from her lips.

"Public relations is just blah-blah, but to be really useful the blah-blah has to be merchandised," she said, and, warming to her subject, added: "No use publicizing a product unless it sells. . . . A good free write-up is worth ten ads. . . . But the secret of public relations is making friends with the press; knowing how to use them. A real, clever press release is one way. It can save them a lot of work!"

Madame now set me to writing press releases. She hovered over my typewriter like a strange, impatient bird.

"Let us first write about the cleanser. . . ." This was the product I had witnessed being named in New York—what Madame called "bread-and-butter."

"First we must say, naturally, that it is a cleanser," she emphasized. "And . . . that it cleanses better than *any* other cleanser on the market." Madame's conviction was such that with the word "any" her eyes closed automatically. "It also nourishes, purifies, lubricates. It gives a glow to the skin. It . . . it . . . it's all things for all skins. Now see what you can do with that! Make it personal. Tell the women that I have their best interests at heart. *Make them hear my voice.* . . ."

"Madame Helena Rubinstein," I typed, "is the world's leading beauty authority. . . ."

"Good, good!" She slapped my shoulder blades.

"For more than five years with scientists, chemists, leading dermatologists in Europe and in America, she has worked in an effort to produce the first 'all-purpose' cleanser. It was personally christened by her, 'Deep Cleanser.' This revolutionary product is now ready for women—whatever their skins. And, it will help to solve that most basic of all beauty problems: *the removal of make-up.*"

:[ 120 ]:

"Now, now talk about me again . . . ," Madame urged. Her eyes were dancing with delight.

"Helena Rubinstein, The First Lady of Beauty-Science, considers 'Deep Cleanser' a cosmetological breakthrough . . . one which will save women both time and money while assuring them new promises of youthful beauty!"

Without knowing it, I had coined the sentence, "The First Lady of Beauty-Science." It was later to be used in all Madame's American advertising, and although she wasn't given to overt praise, when others tried to take the credit she snapped: "Patrick thought of it . . . with my help!"

When I had retyped the "Deep Cleanser" release, Madame Rubinstein read it through with the concentration and care she lavished on any written word—even a telegram. "It all costs money!" She shortened a sentence: "Better! Quicker . . ."; underlined her name, "That's what we are selling," and said, "We'll work on it some more tomorrow." Nothing, in her mind, was ever finished. Everything could stand improvement. "Now, let us study the literature!"

Wherever she operated a business, sold her products, a mass of "literature"—as Madame called the booklets, package stuffers, "flyers," and other detailed instructions on the use of her products—was to assist and to inform the sales staff, the retailers, and, finally, the customers.

"The literature," throughout the world, was traditionally printed in English and in the language of the country where it was used. When, some years later, Madame Rubinstein opened factories in Israel and Japan, she was beside herself trying to decipher Hebrew and Japanese. "It's all Chinese to me!"

We now studied the French "literature." There must have been more than fifty booklets that, characteristically, she kept filed in an old shoe box.

Two hours later, after she had corrected many of them, lavishly annotated others, torn up quite a few—"They're outmoded!"—she said, "Now, let us next look at the 'Sales List.'"

The "Sales List" featured every Rubinstein product available in each of the countries where it was printed, with pertinent information on sizes, prices, discounts (usually forty per cent), and other related details. What often confused Madame was the fact that many of her products bore different names in different countries.

"We're a house divided!" she wailed.

This cry, even if sincere, was window-dressing. She now unfurled a massive document—the French sales list—and whistled. "Pfft! Look at all the dreck . . . too much. When I first started, I made a fortune on one product. A year later I added four more, then six, eight, ten. . . . That's the curse of this business. It's like Topsy! D'you know who's Topsy?" I didn't. "Topsy's someone who kept getting bigger. She couldn't stop. That's the beauty business. What does an average woman need?" she asked me. "She needs a cleanser, a night cream, a stimulant, a mask. But now, *look*! We have forty-two different make-up items in France alone. Twenty specialties . . . deodorants, depilatories. Aii! Besides all the creams, perfumes, soaps. I tell you . . . the Sales List will be our downfall!"

Madame rocked. "What to do, what to do?" She sounded like a fire engine in the night, but quickly recovered.

"If that's what they want. . . . Okay by me."

Such moments of *Angst* were short-lived. Madame was always pliable concerning her business. She knew it to be a gold mine. "Look, here's a lovely new product." She pointed to a circular plastic box. It could have been a miniature lavatory seat. "We should push it in France. Wonderful! 'Minute Make-up' powder. Mrs. Cooper, my sister in London, worked on it. She's clever at such things."

Madame then explained that under Ceska Cooper's direction— "Cesh-ka" she called her—English chemists had managed to blend raw silk fibers with powder. "That's what makes it cling! That's what gives it advertising claims! Without claims, you're a dead duck. Here, read this letter from her . . . slowly. Then you'll know." She handed me a piece of paper.

I did. "Minute Make-up" sounded positively edible. "Now, let us see what you can write about it!" Madame was relentless. "Make it sound exotic. Treatment products must sound scientific, but make-up should be so-phis-ti-ca-ted."

I again set to work.

"Five duchesses, twelve countesses, and other members of the English nobility constantly use Madame Helena Rubinstein's unique

Minute Make-up at all Court functions. They unanimously agree that this silk-enriched powder endows their complexions with the 'glow of Dresden.' . . ."

"Dresden is German!" Madame growled. "Make it English!"

"Worcester, Staffordshire, Wedgwood?"

"Too countrified."

"Porcelain? 'A rich porcelain glow.'"

"Nice!"

I had disposed of "Minute Make-up." Madame again studied the sales list looking for another likely victim. She came up with "Waterproof Mascara."

"I swear! If I live to be a hundred . . ." This product had originally been launched in 1939 at the New York World's Fair with "a stunt," she explained, asking me, "Do you remember, what was the name of that water show?"

"The Aquacade?" On my first visit to New York, as a schoolboy, I had spent joyous days at the World's Fair. It was indelibly stamped on my mind.

"Yes. All the girls of the Aquacade wore our mascara. You see . . . it is really waterproof. If I live to be a hundred, I swear," she repeated, "there's nothing like it! Get to work. Write something nice."

When we had finished our session, I had written three releases. Each was of the same length. Madame insisted that two pages of "blah-blah" sufficed. "If you say too much, they get bored!"

"We'll study them tomorrow. It's always good to sleep on words."

We now entered upon Phase Two of my public relations training.

Madame had me draw up a list of newspaperwomen, both French and "foreign" (as she called visiting members of the press attending the fashion collections whom she wanted to see). These collections occurred twice a year. Spring and summer styles were shown by the Paris *couture* houses in late January. Fall and winter took place during the dog days of early August. Many members of the "foreign" press stayed on in Paris for the first two weeks of February and August in order to photograph the models with which they proposed to illustrate their reportages.

"Here! Take my address book," Madame said. "You'll find the names you need listed in it. Pick six good ones. *Vogue*, I have to see.

*Elle* also. . . . Organize a nice lunch. And, while you're at it, try to reorganize my book. The New York butcher's listed under meat and Chanel's a service."

Address books have always fascinated me, from the day I first heard that Elsie de Woolf, the decorator, left hers as bedside reading for her guests ("Far more interesting than pornography and far less harmful to the eyes than television," she claimed.) Madame's must have weighed at least two pounds. It was an ordinary black, loose-leaf binder spattered with colored markers. The first marker occurred (where else?) at "B" for business. This section had more than sixty closely typed pages subdivided into the countries and cities where Madame maintained offices, salons, factories . . . even bank accounts! I flipped the pages until I reached "F" for France, "P" for Paris. The names, addresses, and telephone numbers of the hundred and twelve members of her staff were duly listed with, scribbled in the margins, a few of her comments: "That's *the rubbish* who always wants a raise!"

Beyond "staff" were four subdivisions: "Friends," "Press," "Relatives," and "Services." Sure enough, under "Services," I found Chanel with one of Madame's question marks by her name. She also appeared under "Friends"—Mademoiselle Gabriel Chanel, Hotel Ritz, Place Vendôme. "What's she doing in the Ritz?" Madame had scrawled, forgetting that she slept there.

I now jotted down six names of members of the press culled haphazardly. Most of the names were unknown to me. Fortunately, Madame's address book had clues. In the "Press" section," besides each name and function ("Editor," "Beauty Editor," "Feature Writer"), the magazine's or the newspaper's circulation ("over a million," "small but exclusive," "caters to teen-agers") had been typed! There were also Christmas gift suggestions. The word "money" occurred frequently and beside it, equally frequently, Madame had written, "How much?"

I selected Edmonde Charles-Roux, the editor of French *Vogue*, whom I already knew; Hélène Gordon-Lazareff, the editor of *Elle*; and Countess de la Touche, the editor of *Votre Beauté*—a prestigious monthly devoted to beauty. To balance the three French ladies, I now picked an equal number of "foreign" editors. My task was facilitated, for—as with movie ratings in the *Daily News*—each editor was endowed with a number of stars. Four was top billing. I picked Eugenia Sheppard of the New York *Herald Tribune,* Ernestine Carter of the London *Sunday Times,* and Irene Brin—who not only represented my old alma mater *Harper's Bazaar* in Rome, but wrote for several Italian newspapers whose total circulation was in the millions. "She's very important!" Madame had scratched above her name. "Find out why!"

"Where shall we take them to lunch? Do you want to see them as a group or separately?" I asked her. "Important ones, important ones such as these should all be seen *separately,*" she answered.

Madame always selected restaurants with a theatrical producer's eye for the relationship of the background versus the cast. She first gauged the personality of her guest. "Charles-Roux doesn't care where she eats. She's an intellectual. A good *bistro* will do!"; "Sheppard should be taken to Maxim's. Americans feel comfortable there"; "Brin's a problem—Italians like a fuss, but I hear she only eats salads!" Faced with this dilemma, Madame invariably picked the Castiglione, a small family hotel on the Faubourg Saint-Honoré. "It's close, it's unassuming, it's cheap! Besides," she added, "their food's nice and fresh."

The Castiglione, to which, on Madame's orders, I invited Signora Brin, hadn't been refurbished since the thirties, when leather upholstery, Lalique glass, and stainless steel ornaments were the rage. These fixtures were now battered. The dining room had the look of a tourist-class saloon on a French steamer plying between Marseilles and Madagascar. It must have reminded Madame of some distant milestone in her younger days when she was constantly "on the road."

When Signora Brin appeared, half an hour late, Madame's eyes fairly popped. She studied her like a philatelist a rare stamp. "Pfft! Look at those eyelashes. . . ." Her whispered asides were hardly necessary. I had seldom seen longer ones. Although it was early February, Irene Brin was dressed in a white, fitted suit. Her slender neck supported incredibly fragile features from which, beneath the black-lacquered curtain fringes of her lashes, enormous pale eyes peered with shortsighted intensity.

"Hungry?" Madame asked.

In a precise voice she answered: "I'm never hungry. All I eat is skin!"

"Skin? Why . . ."

"Because, *chère Madame,* it keeps me 'skin' slim."

"Ha!"

Madame's surprise turned to incredulity when Signora Brin ordered: "The skin of a boiled potato, the rind of a slice of Camembert, the peel of an apple. . . ."

"So, that's a new diet?" she asked.

"Yes. My doctor in Roma insists on it."

"Very economical. . . ."

Madame was also mad for diets. She tried many, but seldom stuck to one: "I need my energy!" While Signora Brin nibbled on her roughage, Madame said with slow deliberation: "Did you know I was the first to introduce diets in America?"

"Tell me. . . ."

"It was like this. I used to go a lot to Zurich. They have clever doctors there. When I divorced my first husband, I was sick. Someone said I should try the Bircher-Benner cure." In fits and starts, eating an enormous *steak au poivre*, Madame explained that Doctor Bircher-Benner maintained a special clinic in Zurich where he fed his patients a diet of fruit, nuts, and *Muesli.*

"*Muesli?* What is that? . . ."

"Rolled oats, lemon juice, grated apples, hazelnuts . . . it's a sort of fruit stew. Very healthy. Then, three weeks of rest, plus the *Muesli,* and I swear . . . I was a new woman!"

It was Signora Brin's turn to be wide-eyed.

"A new woman?"

"Yes, but how could I afford to waste three weeks there every year? So, so I said to myself—I'll bring the Bircher-Benner cure to New York. You know . . . ," she continued, "if the mountain can't go to Mohammed! So we launched his diet at our salon in 1938. It was called 'A Day of Beauty.' For thirty-five dollars a woman could get a consultation from a lady doctor, a facial, a massage, a hair style, and . . . a free lunch. . . ." Madame notched each item off the tips of her fingers. "Five things! What happened? American women are *so*

Madame's Paris bedroom on Quai de Bethune "tidied up for photography." *(Vogue Photo)*

One-tenth of Madame's jewelry, valued at a million dollars in 1950 but auctioned in 1965 for less than half. *(Vogue Photo)*

Some of Madame's eclectic "oddments": Venetian and Indonesian chairs haphazardly arranged beneath her Tchelitchew portrait in her New York apartment. (*Vogue Photo*)

Madame's New York living room: "Before the war I could buy Belter furniture for a few dollars."

*shrewd* . . . I'm telling you! They just came for the lunch. You see, it only cost a dollar. *We lost a fortune.* We were forced to close. But, but . . ." she added, eyeing Mrs. Brin's plate, "if we had only to serve skin we might have broken even. . . . No! Think of the waste. What would happen to the inside of the apples, of the cheese, of the potatoes? Let us consider something else!"

Signora Brin, as is the case with most newspaperwoman whose written words are elegant and flowery, spoke in parables. Her English strummed. Her French was like a Mozart recitative. She also liked to answer her own questions.

"What is she saying . . . ? What is she saying?" Madame kept nudging me.

"I don't know!"

But, finally, I managed to piece together Madame Brin's thoughts. These revolved around "Roma" where she lived and her husband, Gasparo del Corso, maintained an art gallery called L'Obelisco. "You must both come to Roma, Princess! Roman ladies need your advice, your products. Roman artists would be so happy to have your patronage. Yes, I'm sure you will not want to disappoint them."

"Yes, yes! I'll come." Madame was ready to travel.

"When?"

"Soon."

"My husband, Gasparo, has an idea for you."

"Good! When can I see him?"

Signora Brin explained that they would both be at the apartment of Marie-Louise Bousquet, whom I had first met some days before with Mrs. Snow at Dior's, that evening—for besides running the Paris office of *Harper's Bazaar*, Madame Bousquet maintained a *salon*. Every Thursday, in the time-honored tradition first instituted in the seventeenth century by the Marquise de Rambouillet, she "received" from six to nine P.M. Truman Capote indelibly described these weekly parties thus: "Lord, the men who have adored Marie-Louise! Signed photographs of her victims, what she calls 'my lovairs,' are thick as Persian flies on the gewgaw-laden tables of her Place du Palais Bourbon apartment. A few specimens may have eluded the net, Oscar Wilde did, Proust and Cecil Rhodes are missing, but the rest, the century's tycoons of art and industry, are richly represented. What song does this Circe sing? The melody is flirty; the lyrics delivered in a jungle-purr from a throat lined with tiger skin, are not always understandable, but always understanding. Her age is uncertain, the validity of her hair color, currently mahogany red, may be queried; but her lasting allure goes unquestioned. If you doubt it, consider the hordes who every Thursday afternoon find themselves climbing four flights of unilluminated staircase to attend her weekly salon. The drinks are bad, the rooms too crowded; but the hostess, ruffling herself like a parrot, banging a gold-headed cane as though it were a gavel, mincing and moueing and making oh horrid mischief, can be forgiven—yes, all."

At seven that evening, Madame—still burdened with her quota of envelopes and paper bags—led me up the "unilluminated staircase," stopping frequently to catch her breath. It was worth the effort. Wedged in a succession of tiny, smoke-filled rooms was a wild human scrimmage. After we had pierced the outer entrenchments—Madame leading the way, a housewife forging through Klein's during one of their annual sales—I first recognized Audrey Hepburn, Stanley Marcus, and then Jean Genet. Miss Hepburn hardly needed an introduction; Mr. Marcus, Dallas's star retailer, introduced himself; while Genet, whose masterpiece *Notre Dame des Fleurs* had just appeared, sat trapped on a tiny sofa wedged between two ladies of fashion whose conversation had evidently numbed him.

Madame Bousquet now emerged from beneath a pair of legs belonging to John Huston. *"Mon Helena!"* she cackled. *"Mon Helena and her lovair!* Helena, come and meet a most important, a most distinguished, a most delightful man. . . ." With each superlative she struck me across the shoulder blades. "This is Monsieur André Malraux . . . one of France's elect!" Madame blinked. She obviously didn't have a clue as to who was "France's elect." While the great author and politician twitched nervously in front of her, holding up a hand to screen his face, I was swept away in the crowd.

*"Bonjour! Oh, regarde! Mais il n'y a pas de whisky. . . ."* The only available drinks seemed to be a weak concoction of canned orange juice and gin. In quick succession, Marie-Louise Bousquet introduced me to Bernard Buffet, Francis Poulenc, and Alice B. Toklas. In my innocence, I was unaware that Monsieur Buffet—tall, phlegmatic, and

distant—was a painter. Nor, for that matter, did I recognize Poulenc, a puffy man who might have been a banker, as one of *Les Six* (the six, self-elected composers who revamped modern music). Alice B. Toklas, I knew, however, from having read her autobiography by Gertrude Stein. She was forbidding, and sported a mustache over dragon lips. While searching for a few pleasant words to exchange with this alarming lady, my sleeve was plucked. I turned and faced Signora Brin. *"Caro!* This is my husband . . ." A bald man with a grinning face greeted me with an old friend's enthusiasm. Gasparo del Corso looked like Friar Tuck done up to the nines by an imaginative Italian tailor. His shirt was of silk. His cuffs sported handsome gold links. An orange bandana handkerchief sprouted out of his breast pocket like a great, tropical flower. We immediately took to one another. Alice B. Toklas, for all I cared, could have been Alice in Wonderland. *"Amore!"* Signora Brin ordered her husband. "Tell our friend of your plans! *Raconte lui tout. . . ."*

Signore del Corso hardly needed a cue from his wife. He explained that Italian art was currently enjoying a renaissance. "Now's the time," he insisted, "to take advantage of the situation! And your Princess should do it."

"Why? How . . ."

"She's so *simpatica. . . ."*

"But how should she take advantage of the situation?" I asked.

He outlined a plan. It was just the sort of publicity "stunt" Madame reveled in. Twenty Italian artists who had never visited the United States would be selected by her and asked to paint imaginary American scenes. This exhibition, under her auspices, could then travel throughout Europe and America. It was an ideal proposition.

"You must tell, you must tell '*La Madame!*'" he insisted.

"You tell her." I was slightly tipsy.

"I have. But she told me to tell you!"

"I think it's great," I answered. I also knew, with Madame, the necessity of striking when the iron was hot. But where was she? It took me ten minutes to find her. She was listening raptly to André Malraux discussing African art with a small, incredibly neat man whose head was entirely shaved. This was the famous photographer

Henri Cartier-Bresson who, as with Malraux, had spent many years in the Far East.

"Ha! There you are. . . ." Madame signaled to me. In an aside she asked, "What do you think of What's-his-Name's Italian art project?"

"Wonderful!"

"Then we'll go to Rome. Tell him."

Madame believed in prompt decisions and quick action. Later, she said to me, "I know a good thing when I hear it. I'm glad you do, too!"

On our way home, stimulated by Marie-Louise Bousquet's party, Madame told me that she had invited "a whole lot of people" for luncheon, but, apart from Malraux, couldn't remember their names or, for that matter, the day she had bid them come to Quai de Bethune. "You'll have to find out. Call up Marie-Louise. She'll help you!"

Two days later, on a Saturday morning, I had discovered the names of the fifteen guests Madame had asked and verified their acceptance for luncheon on the following day!

"Aii! I didn't realize it was that soon," was Madame's only reaction. "We must go to the Moulin this afternoon to stock up. I'll ring up Gervais. She can drive us."

The Moulin was the old mill Madame owned at Combes-la-Ville, a rural village on the northern outskirts of Paris. She had bought it in 1938 to celebrate her marriage to Prince Gourielli, but seldom went there: "He doesn't like it. Too countrified. . . . They grow nice salads and their chickens are lovely."

Gervais, I next found out, had been employed by the Paris Rubinstein office for more than twenty years as a sales representative. Her territory covered the South of France, where she originally came from.

"She's what I call a real doer," Madame said before the lady arrived. "Imagine! She can cook, sew, keep house, sell—oh! how she can sell . . . and she drives a car!"

Madame valued any members of her staff who drove their own cars. She used them to ferry her around, particularly during week ends. "Why not? It saves petrol, and Vladimir—curse the devil—can then take the day off!" Madame disdained owning a car. "The minute you buy one it's gone down in value half of what you've paid for it!"

Gervais' arrival was heralded by a loud, cheerful, voice: *"Alors, ma petite Madame . . . ça va?"* She was obviously on the best of terms with Madame Rubinstein. Of uncertain age, angular appearance, Gervais looked as if she had spent years at sea. During the half-hour drive to the Moulin, while Madame dozed, she informed me: "I may be a 'Mademoiselle' but I'm no virgin!" Her wild monologue only ceased when she proclaimed, *"Nous voilà!"* We had reached a series of vine-covered buildings huddling in a wooded valley.

"Let's go and steal some eggs!" Madame said before I had a chance to admire the rural charm of my surroundings. "And, Gervais, you get the chickens. . . ."

On our way to the poultry yard, I caught sight of the main building of Madame's country property, the Moulin. It was square and lofty, built of rough gray stone, enhanced by green-shuttered windows and a sloping tile roof. "I hate it!" Madame eyed her mill. "Useless. . . ." A stream, at the far end of a well-tended lawn shaded by magnificent evergreens, fed a series of canals. These crisscrossed the property, rose to the level of the house, hemmed it in with clear, flowing water. One of these canals hurtled under the building where, in the past, the miller's wheel had obviously been situated.

Madame led the way into the house. "It's not me!" she said. Whitewashed walls, beams, solid Louis XIII furniture endowed the main living room with feudal austerity. She was right. The décor would have suited a retired philosopher. "We'll have an omelet and then we'll go home . . . back to Paris with some chickens. . . ." As in all of her homes, Madame employed a staff of two at her Moulin. It was a husband and wife team. "He grows the stuff . . . she cooks it."

We returned to Paris loaded down with farm produce. Eggs by the dozen, chickens, potatoes, lettuces, and a few bunches of battered, hothouse flowers. "Ten thousand dollars a year. That's what the Moulin costs me . . . for ten thousand francs worth of food . . . maybe ten times a year . . . that's a hundred thousand—two hundred dollars! I tell you, it's a white elephant!"

The following morning, the Sunday of the luncheon party, I found Madame in the kitchen sipping coffee with Eugénie. Each cradled a large earthenware bowl, such as French peasants use, between her hands. Eugénie wore a white pinafore. Madame had knotted a shawl around her thick cotton nightdress. It was of violet crocheted wool.

"Join us. We're discussing the menu!"

Peace had finally been established between the two ladies. I was struck by how much they looked alike. Madame, without make-up or jewels, had the same solid look as did her cook. Their hair styles, with neatly knotted chignons, were identical. They even sat with the same imperturbable stance of women who have spent much of their lives on straight-backed chairs.

"Eugénie says that the Moulin chickens are scrawny," Madame told me.

"*Oui, Monsieur,*" she banged her fist on the table. "They are not suitable for a hero of the Resistance! For Monsieur Malraux . . ."

"Well," Madame injected, "what should a 'hero of the Resistance' eat?"

"Beef, a fillet of beef!"

"Then buy one. The shops are always open around here. . . ." And Eugénie, warming to the challenge, added, ". . . garnished with peas, carrots, artichokes."

"Garnished, yes . . . ," Madame answered, "but not with too much!"

Eugénie, who had already planned the menu in her head, next suggested: "*Coquilles Saint-Jacques.* What about *coquilles Saint-Jacques* as an entree?"

Madame rose to the bait. "Good idea!" And, in an aside to me, "Eugénie's *coquilles Saint-Jacques* are the best in Paris." This whetted her appetite. Before the powwow was over, Madame had ordered *foie gras,* six different cheeses, and Dom Pérignon champagne.

"*C'est un festin!*" Eugénie threw up her arms. "It's a feast."

Always seesawing between extremes of economy and prodigality, Madame now opted for the latter. True to form, she resisted, fought, staged a series of delaying actions, and then, with a shrug, opulence triumphed over ghetto stinginess.

"Get the bills from Eugénie," she told me, "so that I can get reimbursed by the office."

By lunchtime, as the first guests started arriving, Madame had not yet materialized. It fell to me to greet them. Edmonde Charles-Roux, the editor of French *Vogue,* sauntered in. She always wore trim, braided suits. Her finely chiseled features were those of a woman of intellect. By her side was an immensely tall young man: "de Givenchy," he introduced himself. This talented designer, whose passion was perfection—a perfection that led him to spending three weeks learning how to iron the ruching on muslin—had just opened his own dress house. Short of funds, he displayed the clothes on store dummies instead of the usual models. Madame, unable to remember his name, was to call him "The Tall Gentleman." She lavished similar accolades on three other luminaries of the French couture. "The Connoisseur Gentleman" was Christian Dior. "The Greek Gentleman" was Jean Dessès, while Balenciaga was "The Spanish Gentleman No One Has Ever Seen."

Janet Flanner, whose "Letter from Paris" for *The New Yorker* magazine was written under the pseudonym of Genêt, arrived next. Her looks were those of a wind-swept Disraeli. She spoke, as she wrote, with precision. Her words were carefully graduated and then firmly knotted together—cool, but polished to a high gloss. She had a mischievous glint in both of her hooded eyes, one of which was magnified by a monocle.

"Where's Helena?" she asked me after introducing herself.

"Getting dressed, I think."

"I'll go and give her a hand." I led her to Madame's room, knowing they were old friends.

A few minutes later, Miss Flanner was back. Her satirical features were those of a fox who has just seen the hunt pursuing him and dashes off in the opposite direction.

"Poor darling!" she said. "I found her sitting in her cotton nightie on that yellow battlefield she calls a bed. It was piled high with dresses. 'I'm stuck. Help me choose!'"

As a few more guests trickled in Madame finally made her entrance. I wondered if she had planned it that way? Although it was midwinter, she had selected a floral print of what looked like purple chrysanthemums wedded to shafts of lilac blooms. Her jewels reflected these hues. Rosettes of carved garnets, carnelians, and moonstones formed a tight collar around her neck, nestled in her ears, and even decorated the buckles on the satin surface of the tiny violet shoes she wore.

"Helena!" Edmonde Charles-Roux spread her arms like the wings of an albatross. "You are the reincaration of the Empress Theodora!"

Madame's eyes glazed. "Pfft! Old remnants. . . ."

While Madame was dishing up food and drink, André Malraux, the guest of honor, arrived. "Introduce him," she whispered to me. It was then that we both noticed he wasn't alone. A pale, distinguished-looking man accompanied him. Madame's shoulders rose imperceptibly as Malraux led his friend up to her. "This is the Baron de Rothschild," he said. "Pleased to meet you!" Madame gave her hand to be kissed, and, in a hushed aside, "I forgot! He called. . . . We must add an extra place setting at the table. Eugénie is going to have a fit! Come . . . help me." She dashed out, leaving fifteen guests to their own devices.

After supervising the operation in the dining room Madame smacked her forehead: "A Rothschild! Where's my gold plate?" Eugénie was summoned. "I'm cooking, Madame. Your gold plate is in your safe."

"Come!" Madame led me back at a run, down the length of the apartment, through the main drawing room, where everyone was now guzzling caviar, to her bedroom beyond it. "Thank God!" she said. "Thank God I always keep caviar in reserve. If there's a delay, it prevents people from getting bored!" Later, I asked Marguerite, the maid, where the caviar had come from. "While you were adding a *couvert* for *Monsieur le Baron*, I got it. Madame always keeps a couple of five-pound tins on the window sill of her bathroom!"

Her safe was also in her bathroom. The fixtures—chairs, make-up table, taps—were all of silver. These were designed to resemble dolphins, sea horses, conch shells, and other nautical flora and fauna.

"The safe's in there." Madame pointed to a door behind a large silver oyster shell. I realized, with a shock of pleasure, it was a bidet.

"Here's the combination." She now produced a piece of paper. "I'm too nervous. You open the safe!"

The combination read, " 'H' for 'Helena,' turn right to 'A' for 'Archil,' left to 'G' for 'Gourielli.' Spin and pull." Much to my surprise, this simple formula that combined Madame's first name with her husband's did the trick. The heavy steel door swung open. Madame pushed me to one side. She looked into the safe and froze. "Well, I'll be damned!"

I peeked over her shoulder. I could see the gold plates stacked on the top shelf amid great clusters of jewelry. Piles of bank notes, still held together in the paper binders used when issued in quantity, were wedged in like refuse in a trash basket. There were other valuables: stock certificates, gold cigarette boxes, pre-Columbian breast ornaments.

"I'll be damned!" Madame repeated. "Look!" She pointed to the bottom shelf. Nestling on a plate, surrounded by more jewels and bank notes, was half a broiled chicken!

"Can you beat it?" Madame forgot her haste and her guests while she marveled: "That chicken's been there since I last opened the safe three nights ago! I was eating it—a snack—I couldn't figure out where it had disappeared to." She nibbled on a wing. "Why! It's still fresh. Try some!" Indeed, the chicken was still moist—due, no doubt, to its airtight confinement.

"Hurry! Take the gold plates . . . ," Madame ordered. I cradled a stack that must have weighed twenty pounds. "I'll take the chicken! Why not? It will be delicious tonight with a salad."

The guests were scooping up the last globs of caviar. Some of them, Malraux included, gave us a startled look as we ran by.

"Lunch will be ready any minute, now!" she called out over her shoulder.

We ate in the large dining room. The marble table, covered with Belgian lace, now sat sixteen—seven on both sides and one at each end. Always vague on the subject of protocol, Madame turned to Edmonde Charles-Roux: "You do it!" she said. The latter elected to seat us in the French way, placing the hostess in the center of the table instead of at one end. This gave Madame a chance to listen to the conversation without feeling she was in purdah. On her right and left sat the Baron de Rothschild and Monsieur Malraux. Madame, tongue-tied as was often the case with strangers, first urged these two gentlemen: "Eat! Eat!" It was her way of breaking the ice. I sat facing her with Edmonde Charles-Roux and Janet Flanner flanking me. At first, Monsieur Malraux's muteness matched the title of his famous book, *Les Voix du Silence*. The *pâté en croute* with which luncheon opened helped; he pronounced a few monosyllables, cupping a hand over his mouth to do so. As the meal progressed, his shyness slowly dispelled. Madame was one of those women, due to her own lack of small talk, who somehow managed to relax the shy. Actually, Monsieur Malraux wasn't shy, but he suffered from a speech affliction. I thought he stuttered. No. An old war wound had evidently affected his jaw. He spoke through his hand. It was a filter and a protective guard. The words were clear enough—the thoughts incredibly lucid.

For half an hour, over a series of dishes, this great and subtle intellectual now held forth. His monologue encompassed archeology, make-up; took side trips to describe mortuary arts; then landed in darkest Africa as he vividly etched some of the tribes whose art was so liberally represented in Madame's collection—the Senufo, the Benin, the Dogon.

"Take them upstairs!" Madame ordered me after lunch. "Show them the roof!"

Above the length of the apartment, commanding a view that encompassed most of Paris, Madame had created a roof garden. It was the size of a small football field and could easily accommodate three hundred guests without any danger of a crush. At one end, there was a tiered fountain larger than the average Hollywood swimming pool. At the opposite end, across a hundred yards of marble, a mirrored recess reflected various pieces of statuary through a bower of evergreens.

I led a small procession up a circular staircase adjoining the living room. Malraux's facial twitch, when he reached the open air, mysteriously disappeared.

"*Extraordinaire!*" he kept repeating.

There, beneath us, extending as far as the eye could see, was nearly every Parisian landmark known to the world. In the foreground Notre Dame; to the left, the Panthéon, and in the far distance, shimmering like the icing on a wedding cake, the Sacré-Coeur.

"Where's the Louvre?" Malraux kept asking.

It was barely visible, behind Notre Dame, and quite black.

:[ 136 ]:

Was it then, I have since wondered, that he decided to "clean" Paris?

Madame met us at the bottom of the stairs on our return journey and then conducted her own quick tour of the apartment. Malraux paused in front of a life-sized marble statue of Dionysus. It was Greco-Roman, of the first century, and what Madame referred to as "one of our real treasures."

"See the bullet holes in it?" She pointed to several blotches. "The Germans, when they were here, used it for target practice!"

During the war, Göring had inspected the apartment, Madame went on to explain. But he found a Rothschild house more to his liking—Madame smiled at the Baron, adding: "So he gave our place to one of his generals who messed up the statue and, before leaving, smashed all of our furniture since he couldn't take it with him."

"How did you feel about the Germans when your returned?" Malraux asked her.

"Soldiers are soldiers . . . German, Russian, American . . . even French. They're all destructive!"

"Have you resumed your business in Germany?"

"Certainly! Why not? Business is business. Besides, German money is good money."

"*Quel phénomène!*" I heard Malraux confide to the Baron de Rothschild as they were leaving. "Yes!" he agreed. "But she's also just like my great-grandmother, a *groisser fardiner*, a big bread-winner!"

The next few days whirled by in a dizzying succession of reciprocated entertainments. "Tell them I'm bringing you!" Madame said whenever she was invited out. It was both a new life and a new world for me. Not only did I have to adapt myself to being her *cavalier servant*, her escort, but I was still an employee, almost young enough to be her grandson. This could have produced equivocal situations had we not been such an "odd couple."

At the office I was looked upon as Madame's secretary. Outside—in society, in the fashion world, with the press—my position must have produced interesting conjectures. Marie-Louise Bousquet, impish and naughty, enjoyed suggesting that I was the titular "lovair." Some people believed her, citing the contrasting case of an eighty-year-old actress of the Comédie Française who, in the tradition of a super-annuated Colette heroine, lived with and supported a twenty-year-old youth. It was known that this happy couple enjoyed regular sexual congress. Madame, hearing these rumors, first laughed them off, but later warned: "The Prince is terribly jealous. He will be very angry." She then giggled, almost flirtatiously: "I don't mind what the gossips say, as long as you don't!"

Her early morning telephone calls, her work schedule—the daily "grind"—still continued, but was greatly brightened for me by our new social obligations. These took us, like a pair of honeymooners fearing solitude, uncertain of one another, all over Paris. Eugénie had been right! Madame needed such diversions. She fairly blossomed and even told Mr. Ameisen to give me "a little pocket money."

There was a luncheon at Christian Dior's new town house. Here Madame observed, "He's a good manager. Did you see? He rolled his napkin in a ring so that it could be used again!"

After festive occasions, such as this one, Madame Rubinstein seemed reluctant to return to her office. "Let's go and shop!" she said. "No. First we'll visit a painter." She enjoyed keeping up with artists, as with the world of the *haute couture*, and seemed to be soothed by the physical effort of climbing spiraling stairs to roof-top studios. In her younger Parisian days, through her first husband Edward Titus, Madame had known Modigliani: "A nice but a messy boy"; Picasso, "The devil!"; Matisse, "How he liked to bargain!" but on this particu-lar day, after the Dior luncheon, she had contacted Van Dongen, for she had heard that he was anxious to sell one of his early paintings. Madame always kept up with a series of strange contacts—middlemen —who, at the drop of a hat (particularly an expensive bowler like hers), could produce anything from masterworks of art to "hot" jewelry. It was one of them who had tipped her off about the painting we were about to see.

Van Dongen, although eighty, had a young wife, Madame ex-plained in the taxi while stroking her purse. The young wife wanted to buy a house in the South of France. "She's thinking of when she'll be a widow. So I brought along ten million francs." Madame gave me a sly wink. "To help her think. Seven in the purse. Three in the pockets.

We'll see what happens. . . ." This was approximately twenty thousand dollars in cash. The painting, an early Fauve, was hers, Madame further explained. Van Dongen had not only given it to her, but now authorized its sale.

We were greeted, in a large, cluttered studio, by a bearded and courtly patriarch, whose plump, blonde wife hovered in the background. Madame, knowing she was later going to have to bargain with the lady, ignored her. With slow deliberation, she studied a number of paintings hung on the walls. "Nice?" There were portraits of music hall entertainers whose careers were now distant memories: Mistinguett, in an aureole of pink aigrettes; the Dolly Sisters; Josephine Baker sporting only a string of bananas around her waist. This was the costume she first wore, Van Dongen explained, when she opened at the Casino de Paris in the early twenties. "I remember," Madame said. "We made up her eyes." The patriarch twinkled, "And I made up her nipples!"

He now led us into an alcove and there, on an easel, was a monumental portrait—painted in tones of red—of a lady in a straw hat. "Nice . . . ," Madame said. This time it wasn't a query. "How much?" I sidled away. Madame Van Dongen took my place while Van Dongen followed me into the main room. "Woman's business," he winked, stroking his beard.

A quarter of an hour later, Madame emerged from the alcove. Behind her, counting bank notes, I could see Madame Van Dongen. She looked rattled. "Good!" was Madame's farewell remark.

When we were in the street, she smiled, "I got it for eight. Remind me to send her some products. She has dry skin!"

(Madame had again used a favorite ploy to save herself two million francs. She had switched from the subject of money to that of vanity. Madame Van Dongen had fallen for it. The painting, quoted at ten million francs, had been sold for eight.)

"Yes! Thank goodness she has dry skin. . . . Now let's go to Cartier. I hear they have a wonderful new lipstick container. It might be something for us!"

In addition to enjoying the *soulagement*—her word for relaxation —produced by the purchase of a Van Dongen, Madame also experienced the same elation when concluding lesser deals. In Paris, London, Rome, or even in Detroit, she was an avid shopper. Every department store and specialty boutique had to be visited, besides the antique shops she doted on, the drugstores she marveled at. Even supermarkets were carefully cased: "They're the future," she would say, "mark my words." While in Paris, Madame spent hours marching me up and down the Rue de Rivoli, the Rue Royale, the Faubourg Saint-Honoré, gazing into windows. "That little compact— see? Maybe we can do something with it!" French jewelers, because of their ideas, refinement, and exquisite workmanship, were one of her favorite stamping grounds. "Let us go to Boucheron . . . let us look at Van Cleef . . . I wonder if Verdura has anything interesting. Ideas! That's what we need." She was a masterful adapter.

When we reached Cartier, an elderly manager, dressed in a frock coat, sprang forward. He evidently knew Madame.

"*Chère Princesse!* What can we do for the *Princesse?*"

"Pearls!"

Since she was already wearing eight or ten rows around her neck, I thought that her request was odd.

"Pearls!" The manager savored the word, leading us from one small paneled room into the next. There were fabulous jewels in the vitrines lining every wall.

Red leather boxes appeared. "Pearls!" One necklace alone was worth a hundred million francs. Madame dismissed it with a flick of her glove. "Emeralds!" she now ordered. Huge, shiny green conkers in every shape and form were placed before her. Her displeasure etched on impassive but stony features continued. "Rubies!" One blood-red cabochon the size of a turkey's egg seemed to produce a flicker of interest. Madame held it up to the light.

"Pretty!" she said, "soothing. . . . I'll think about it."

She opened her purse, foraged around absent-mindedly. "I've forgotten my lipstick. I need a good lipstick case."

The manager, murmuring vaguely about the ruby, led her into another room. Here, masses of gold jewelry glimmered under glass-topped tables. Madame's eyes, hooded until then, suddenly flickered (the lights on a pinball machine registering a score?). She pointed left and right at various cases. These were next produced for her closer scrutiny.

I knew that Madame spotted the one she wanted, but her technique required a delaying action. With her right hand, she now toyed with one particular case. It rolled on the surface of the glass-topped table and fell to the floor. The manager picked it up. He groaned from the effort of bending down.

"I'll take that one!" Madame snapped, as if to reward him for his trouble. "How much?"

Price tags are never used at Cartier's. Somehow the sales staff memorizes the cost of their merchandise. The manager was taken aback. Such a lowly item! He fluttered, uncertainly, and finally quoted the sum of eight hundred thousand francs.

"I'll give you seven."

"Whatever the *Princesse* says. . . ."

On our way back to the office, Madame examined her new purchase. It was of fluted gold, tipped at each end with a ruby and a sapphire cabochon. Two lipsticks, one for day, the other for night, were contained in the case. "Clever! A double sale. I'll have it copied. I'm sure it will be a success in America."

(A year later, this lipstick, christened "Nite 'n Day," made its debut. As Madame had foretold, it was a success. More than a million were sold at three dollars each. No one knew how she had found it; no one realized—not even Cartier—that it was an "adaptation.")

"What did I tell you?" By then, I was hardened to her tactics. I nodded agreement. "Pfft! You're still naïve. But . . . but that's what I like about you."

In one afternoon, Madame had purchased a Van Dongen that was to be sold, after her death, for three times what she had paid for it. She had also managed to wheedle a two-hundred-dollar markdown on a sixteen-hundred-dollar lipstick case from the world's greatest jeweler. Yes. I was naïve. Never would I have dared to use her methods. Madame had barely begun to educate me—to introduce me to her ways. There was more to come.

Two days later on one of her sudden impulses, she declared: "We must go to Vienna . . . and several other places!"

# "Little Mother, It's Not His Fault!"

❦ ❦

"I like quick decisions!" Madame's call for action still rings in my ears. "We must go to Vienna . . . and several other places!" This "quick decision" heralded one of the many excursions that we were to take together all over the world—even to Russia—until shortly before her death, when her restlessness finally abated. "You can't live forever. . . ."

After three hectic weeks in Paris Madame was ready for a change. She had "shaken up" her French staff, dispensed "pep talks" to all and sundry at the Faubourg office, and settled a dowry on Stella.

"Spring finery," a new wardrobe, was her final concern. Twice a year, in February and August, Madame regularly bought clothes from several Paris couture houses. Although she favored Balenciaga, Madame still liked to shop around. Armed with paper and pencil, accompanied by her "little dressmaker" (a skilled copyist), she would perch uncertainly on a small gold chair, avidly watching the endless procession of twirling models at Dior, Lanvin, Jacques Fath. Whenever a new house, such as Guy Laroche (and, later, Cardin, Saint Laurent, Courrèges) opened, she was one of the first private customers on the scene. Clothes fascinated her. She collected and treasured them as she did paintings, bibelots, homes: "I owe it to the business."

The "little dressmaker" always tagged along behind Madame in the guise of a maid. While Madame ordered "a few costumes" in each house, this somber-looking lady took careful mental notes of a new sleeve, a hemline, the cut of a jacket or a coat. Later she reproduced skillful copies at a fraction of the price. This was one of Madame's pet ploys. "Everyone does it. . . ," she said. Then pointing to herself, "even some of the richest women."

Since it took three weeks for these clothes to be ready for delivery, there was nothing left to detain Madame in Paris. "We'll travel by train. Get the tickets!" She ordered.

"Two sleepers?"

"Certainly not. If I can sit up all night, so can you!"

But Vienna was still occupied by the military. Each of the victorious allied powers had "a sector." The Russians, as usual, were being tricky. I told Madame we would have to fly. "Pity! I love traveling at night by train. It helps me think. . . ."

Why, I wondered, were we going to Vienna? In midwinter, even by plane, it was an arduous and uncomfortable trip. The city was a shambles. There were only two hotels open to tourists. Gradually, Madame Rubinstein briefed me during the twenty-four hours bridging her decision and our departure. "First, it's the farthest spot we can go in Europe. Whenever I travel on business, I always pick the farthest spot. I can then work my way back from where I started. Saves time, effort, money! Second, we have this agent there. He's a thief. Owes us all kinds of money. I must look for a new one. Third, Vienna was always most important for beauty. They have wonderful doctors, chemists, cosmetologists. . . . Who knows? We might pick up a few ideas!"

To this Mr. Ameisen added a few footnotes. "The agent may or may not be a thief. At present, exchange controls are very strict. The agent does owe us money. I'm sure Madame will manage to get it out of him. Then, there's this countess Madame wants to see. She invented our waterproof mascara. We pay her a royalty. What with one thing and another, she wants an extra five per cent. I'm sure Madame will also manage to placate her!"

In this way, I discovered that many Helena Rubinstein products were not always of Madame's invention, or that of the many chemists she employed all over the world. Her great talent—as I had noted during our visit to Cartier's—was to ferret out "clever novelties," "prestige stuff," "nice bread-and-butter items" and then haggle before adapting and merchandising them over her name. "I could have made a fortune selling paper clips!" Madame liked to boast. She considered her own enormous contributions in the formulation of products secondary to her flair, her sense of timing and drama, and her nose for the contemporary beauty requirements of women. "I'm a merchant! To be a good merchant, you need a sharp eye. Do you think Arden, Revlon, Lauder make their own stuff themselves? No! They use their people cleverly, they push them, they guide them. Like Barnum and Bailey. They are . . . what d'you call it? Ringmasters!"

The origins of "Crème Valaze," with which Madame started her business in Australia, were hazy. They centered around a mysterious Doctor Lykusky. Madame described him in her memoirs, *My Life for Beauty*, as "a Hungarian friend of my mother's who had been introduced to her by the Polish actress Modjeska." How Modjeska, the world-famous international tragedienne, befriended her mother is left to conjecture. Madame hated, unless when dealing with financial matters, being overly specific. "Good publicity doesn't need too many facts!" At all events, Doctor Lykusky's Valaze cream—like the sweet pickles Madame doted on—became a staple in the Rubinstein household. Again in her memoirs, still blithely glossing over details, Madame recounts why she decided to emigrate to Australia. It was because her father—"a strict, thoughtful man from a well-to-do family, more addicted to books than bookkeeping—refused to let me marry a handsome young medical student at the University."

Why did she pick Australia? So distant, uncouth, difficult to reach? Her mother's brother lived there. He was a widower whose only daughter corresponded with Madame. They became "pen-pals." Disappointed at not being allowed to marry her medical student, the young (she was barely eighteen) Helena Rubinstein shipped off to the antipodes "on a visit . . . to my relatives . . . to forget!" No explanation is given why and how these relatives first went to Australia. This was surely due to one of the many pogroms regularly plaguing the Jewish community of Eastern Europe. So Madame set off— explaining that her mother "had sold a piece of jewelry" to pay for her ticket—and adding, "I packed my old-fashioned trunk with all of my possessions, including twelve jars of my mother's beauty cream!"

These, she writes, were "the finger of fate!" It is a modest but accurate statement. They were to be the foundation of an empire which, fifty years later, encircled the globe and gave her the satisfaction of seeing herself referred to as one of the ten richest, self-made women in the world.

In 1958, when we both visited Australia, I managed to piece together a few snippets of Madame's early history there. Again, fiction outbalanced fact. She first settled in a small sheep-ranching community, some eighty miles from Melbourne, called Coleraine. This Gaelic derivative means "land covered with ferns." Her uncle, whom she stayed with, is variously described as "a sheep-farmer," "a merchant," "a landowner." In point of fact, Louis Silberfeld—or Silberfield as he preferred to call himself—was an oculist. Coleraine had only two thousand inhabitants. Trade, for an oculist, must have been slack. My own theory is that "Uncle Louis" managed a general store, ground a few spectacles on the side, and maintained a flock of sheep to keep solvent. Madame disliked him intensely. "He took liberties . . . ," she admitted. But Uncle Louis and his "liberties" were no worse than Coleraine—"the sun was strong, the wind violent . . . and the never-ending sweep of pasture, broken here and there by a blue gum tree, gave me the pip!" Where did Madame learn this nice Edwardian word? It seems that during her first six months in Coleraine she attended an elementary school run by two old maids, the Misses Crouch and de Arroyave. Here, a buxom eighteen, she learned rudimentary English, surrounded by small children poring over their alphabets.

"It took several months to accustom myself to the many changes life in Australia made necessary. . . ."

Still in her memoirs, Madame now switches to the beauty of her skin: "My new friends [in Coleraine] couldn't get over its milky texture. In fact, it was no better than the average girl's complexion in Cracow. But to the local ladies, with sun-scorched, wind-burned cheeks, its city-bred alabaster quality seemed remarkable."

She then briefly recounts her final row with Uncle Louis and "a vision!"

If her skin was so enviable, thanks to "Mother's cream," why not use both to escape from Coleraine? Her thoughts were jumbled. But she knew, instinctively, that Doctor Lykusky's cream was the answer to all of her problems. "I had to get to Melbourne, to a metropolis, where I felt there would be more scope for my ideas and energies. Once more, against the wishes of my elders [randy Uncle Louis'?] I took things in my own hands! I had a friend in Melbourne, a young Englishwoman I met on the boat coming to Australia, who was the wife of the governor's A.D.C. We corresponded. When I wrote to her of my plan to leave Coleraine she invited me to stay with her."

Even as a young woman, Madame admits to being a tireless letter writer, but one who knew how to pick useful friends. She again packed her trunk and set off "to conquer provincial Melbourne socially." And, while doing so, finally resolved her future.

"Over and over, I pondered on the possibilities of my beauty cream; then, one day, I knew what I had to do. I would open a shop. But it would be more than just a shop where my cream would be sold. I would *teach* Australian women how to protect their skins and beautify themselves." She continues: "My lucky star must have been in its ascendancy. Upon arriving in Melbourne, I sought another friend I had met on board ship—Helen Macdonald. I told her of my plan. She encouraged me, repeating, time and time again, 'You must believe in yourself as I believe in you.'"

The upshot was that Miss Macdonald lent Madame two hundred pounds (about a thousand dollars). "It was the only sum of money I have ever borrowed, but I never regretted it. And I repaid her with interest before many months had passed." Madame then describes what she did with this loan.

"With half of the money I ordered a large stock of cream in bulk, directly from Doctor Lykusky in Poland. I purchased jars and labels locally. I hand-lettered them myself. The rest of the money was invested in the rent and the furnishings for a good-sized second-floor room at 274 Collins Street, in the heart of Melbourne. The light was excellent. Immediately I saw the place I knew it was what I was looking for. I divided it into three smaller rooms, painted the walls white."

Now, finally in business, Madame tacks from one subject to the next. She sets up a "kitchen"—a small laboratory where Valaze cream and its successors were concocted—and recalls, "Even to this day, I think of our immense laboratories, of all laboratories, as 'kitchens.'" In fact," she adds, unable to resist the joy of name-dropping: "I once startled the great Madame Curie by asking her to let me visit her own *cuisine,* where radium was discovered." One longs to hear Madame Curie's answer, but Madame rambles on: "I sewed the curtains myself, using the lovely materials of the full-skirted dresses I had brought from Poland. Bamboo and rattan furniture was cheap and decorative. . . . By the time I was ready to open, the three rooms looked light, friendly, and attractive. I was in business!"

A breezy paragraph now reveals yet another of Madame's momentous discoveries. This occurred after she had opened her shop: "The women streamed in, mostly out of curiosity, since a beauty salon was unheard of in those days. I saw to it that they stayed on for advice. Few left without a jar of my hand-labeled cream. . . ." Examining so many skins at close quarters, Madame now realized that skin textures were different. It dawned on her, "That, wonderful as my cream was (and still is), it could not solve every irregularity. I would have to learn how to create new creams and lotions to suit different skin types. I began to classify these as oily, dry, combination, and normal."

Now she knew! Four skin types would require four different products; four products would next have to be expanded into four related lines catering to each skin type. She would need a cream, an astringent, soap—and other preparations—for all of these differently textured skins. The beauty horizons were unlimited! In the meantime, "Sydney's foremost woman journalist, who had heard of Australia's first beauty salon, came and interviewed me. She reported every word I said in her widely read column, adding that my Valaze cream was the answer to every Australian woman's prayer. I was deluged with letters and money orders from every part of the country. I was overwhelmed. I didn't have the stock to fill the demand! I wrote and acknowledged every order by hand, sat up nights to do so, and offered to return the money orders of those for whom I had no cream at the moment. Only one person asked for her money back!"

Small wonder Madame had such a healthy respect for the press! "If one little free write-up sold several thousand jars of my cream, imagine what happened when I started advertising!" Within a few months, Madame's deficit of two hundred pounds owed to Miss Macdonald snowballed into a profit of nine thousand pounds—nearly fifty thousand dollars with twice the buying power of today's money. She was able to summon Doctor Lykusky to Australia, who arrived accompanied by two of her sisters—Manka and Ceska. They were all urgently needed to lend a hand with her expanding business. But here again there is a strange discrepancy. Ceska was some ten years younger than Madame; Manka a few years Ceska's junior. Always vague on the subject of her age, Madame must have been in her late twenties when she was sufficiently solvent to call for help.

This leaves a gap of several years unaccounted for in Australia by Madame Rubinstein in her biography. What was she up to? Her success, the opening of the MAISON DE BEAUTÉ VALAZE in Melbourne, obviously took longer than she cared to admit.

When I was in Melbourne, staying at Menzies Hotel with Madame in 1958, a shabby old man popped into her suite. As with her offices everywhere, the door was ajar. She liked unexpected visits. "My name is Abel Isaacson," he introduced himself.

Madame heard him perfectly clearly. But she cupped an ear and, turning to me, dropped her voice, "What the devil does he want? Money . . . I suppose."

"We first met sixty years ago! You were a waitress at the Café Doré. . . ." Mr. Isaacson announced with no further preliminaries.

"He's gaga . . . get him out of here!" Madame hissed. She seemed alarmed and shot into her bedroom banging the door.

Mr. Isaacson sat down in Madame's empty chair.

"Hasn't changed a bit! High strung. . . . You her son?" he queried rolling a cigarette. Since it was difficult to explain my exact functions I nodded vaguely.

"I've been in Australia since ninety-eight. Lived at one time in a boardinghouse outside Melbourne on Grey Street. Saint Kilda. Run by a woman called Mrs. Stern. The Madame . . . ," he cocked a finger at the bedroom door, "stayed there in 1904. She was one of Mrs. Sensenberg's girls at the 'Café Doré.' Used to give me two helpings

:[ 149 ]:

of fish for the price of one. That was well before she rented a place in Collins Street and started selling them face creams. Some worker!"

Through the corner of my eye I saw the bedroom door open an inch. Madame Rubinstein was listening.

"Tell you something. . . . I'm eighty-four. She must be nearly as old!" Madame rattled the door. Mr. Isaacson went on:

"Without Mr. Thompson—he was the manager of the Robur Tea Company—the Madame wouldn't have done what she did. He helped her. . . . He taught her. . . . He made her! Mark my words, he was the brains behind the little lady!" With that, stubbing his cigarette and pocketing the butt, he left.

"Why did you talk so long to the old fool!" Madame snapped at me after our visitor was out of sight.

"He seemed to have known you. . . ."

"Lots of cranks have known me!"

The subject was never discussed again. Mr. Thompson's identity still remains a mystery, although a few days later an old lady, even older than Mr. Isaacson, materialized out of the blue. Bird of paradise feathers decorated her hat. There was a cameo hanging from her neck and she twirled a white parasol in her hand although it was midwinter. "I'm Mrs. Dedman, dear." Madame eyed her finery.

". . . Remember? I was your neighbor in Glen's Building on Collins Street when you first opened." She turned to me. Her voice was genteel but precise. "We were the only two real ladies in trade. There were twenty-four singing teachers besides us. Very trying. . . . That's how Dame Nellie Melba became one of her customers. After practice, she always popped in for a facial . . . claimed it helped her high C's."

I longed to hear more, but Mrs. Dedman fared no better than Mr. Isaacson. Madame prodded her out of the door, and when she was safely out of hearing, said, "Another nut. . . . Who cares about the past?"

Similar scenes were to be repeated in most of the capitals of the world. Noting my interest, Madame shook a fist under my nose: "Don't waste your time . . . and mine . . . with all these rubbishy people!"

She had invented her past. She wanted to stick to her version of what was finally a dull biography (wherein success was never to be clouded or obscured by any misfortunes) although I often tried, in devious ways, to unearth information. But I was no match for Madame Rubinstein and her sisters. They all stuck to the official script —"The Rubinstein party line."

"What was the meaning of the word 'Valaze'?" I asked Madame, hopeful that she might come up with a glorious anecdote. "Nothing. Just a good word . . . easy to remember."

"But who thought of it?"

"Someone who was probably paid too much!"

For the first fifteen years of her career as a beautician, Madame Rubinstein called her salons in Melbourne, London, and Paris MAISON DE BEAUTÉ VALAZE. It was only after she was firmly established in France, around 1912, that she switched to MAISON DE BEAUTÉ HELENA RUBINSTEIN. By then "Crème Valaze" had been superseded by other products, Doctor Lykusky was dead, and Madame was free to unfurl her own banner: "If Ida Rubinstein can be a success with that name, so can I!"

This was not another "poor relative," but the great dancer who fascinated Europe as a star in Diaghilev's Ballet Russe.

When further queried about "Crème Valaze," Madame, to the end of her days, continued to wax vague. She closed her eyes, pressed a jeweled hand to her heart, and listed the ingredients! "It's made of a wonderful mixture of rare herbs, the essence of Oriental almonds, extracts from the bark of an evergreen tree. . . ."

A few months before her death, while sifting through masses of old papers discovered in the cellar of her Paris home, Madame handed me the original Valaze formula: "Here!" she said. "You may need it one day. . . ." Knowing that such information was guarded by her as a lioness might its cubs, I hesitated to accept the tattered sheet of yellow paper.

"Take it! It's historical. . . ."

There was no mention of rare herbs, Oriental almonds, or the bark of an evergreen tree! The formula listed a variety of common garden raw materials such as ceresine wax, mineral oil, sesame. All that was lacking were the instructions. Without these, the formula was useless. Why did Madame give it to me? Was it to tease, to tantalize, to test my honesty? Later I unearthed other papers concerning Valaze. There was the first advertisement, dated 1904, published in Australia. It read, "Mlle. Helena Rubinstein of 274 Collins Street announces the launching of Valaze Russian Skin Food by Doctor Lykusky, the celebrated skin specialist." I next found another advertisement, dated 1906, with completely different claims. Doctor Lykusky and the word "Russian" were omitted. Instead, in bold headlines, it proclaimed "What women want! A few remarks by Helena Rubinstein." The "few remarks" ran to thirty lines of closely stacked copy. Madame's advertising philosophy, even if the language wasn't as elaborate, was still the same half a century later. What she called "fear copy with a bit of blah-blah!" "The healthy woman with an unhealthy or ill-nourished skin is not doing her duty to herself or those nearest her. Vivacity and personal charm are not enough. We cannot all be ladies of Milo, but we can all be the best possible in our individual cases." A cheerful quatrain relieved this slightly threatening opening paragraph:

Little blots of blemish
In a visage glad
Make the lover thoughtful
And the husband mad.

Then, after several of her favorite "hard sell" lines, the advertisement closed with what Madame called "a bit of humility":

"It is daring of me, but I timidly suggest that a reasonable woman owes some consideration even to her husband. An ill-kempt complexion is really as inexcusable as ill-kept teeth."

I once showed her one of these early ads. It was a tiny five-liner from a Sydney newspaper. Madame snatched a pencil from my hand. "All wrong! I must correct it. . . ."

"But it's over fifty years old." I tried to grab my pencil.

"You'll never learn that way!" She cut two lines.

"See! I could have saved a lot of money."

In the twenties, Valaze was renamed "Skin Food." "Why?" I

asked Madame. "More precise . . . better, clearer." In the late thirties the Federal Food and Drug Administration clamped down on it, claiming that no beauty cream could be dubbed "a skin food."

"Those devils in Washington!" Madame railed. She soon recovered her composure. Sara Fox, never at a loss for a good cosmetic name, suggested "Wake-Up Cream."

"Very good." Madame stroked her arm. "Now think of something equally good to sleep with!"

"I've never found anything wrong with a man. . . ."

"That's always been your problem, dear," Madame murmured.

This friendly exchange led to an early Rubinstein "all-purpose cream," "Novena Cerate," being launched anew and specifically branded as a night cream—*with bedtime claims*. Such simple ideas revolutionized the beauty business. Other existing creams, lotions, emollients, and unguents were now advertised and promoted for use at certain hours of the day and night. As with Madame's early discovery of the various types of skins, this was another chance breakthrough for the beauty industry.

"You've got to be lucky!" Madame insisted. ". . . Take advantage of the situation. Every situation! That, that and hard work." She failed to mention one of her peculiar and particular talents: Situations were produced by people. She knew how to use people, to drain them of their ideas, and then had the skill, the tenacity, the patience to turn these ideas into gold. But, unlike many of her competitors, including Arden and Revlon, she remained faithful to anyone who contributed to her success.

The twelve jars of "Valaze Cream" with which Madame emigrated to Australia grew into the Valaze line of cosmetics, a string of Valaze Beauty Salons, and other products, ostensibly because of Madame's "vision." She might have stayed on in Australia, settled down and married there; for that was where she first met Edward Titus who courted her assiduously. "But my demons drove me back to Europe. I told him to wait for me and if I was successful in London, I would then accept his proposal," she admitted in her memoirs.

Her demons were contrary beasts. Madame had fallen in love with Titus and yet at age thirty she wasn't yet ready for him or for marriage. She wanted to "sleep" over his proposal—to weigh the pros and cons. Flight was her method. And flight fanned her ambitions and fed her energies.

Our departure for Vienna was no less chaotic than when we left New York three weeks earlier. Even on such short hops Madame traveled with a superabundance of luggage. I had to carry my quota of paper bags, books, fur coats, while she clutched her jewel case and wore the same garish outfit she had elected on to cross the Atlantic: "sensible clothes." But she had supplemented them with a strange and opulent addition—a huge sable stole. It looked like an Indian squaw's blanket.

Madame affectionately rubbed her cheek on one of the worn corners of this voluminous pelt. "Bought it secondhand from a poor fairy who once had a rich mother." She winked: "The Viennese will be impressed. . . ."

Three hours later we were being greeted by the agent, his wife, and members of his staff in Vienna's dilapidated airport. Madame seemed to glow like a firefly as she exchanged compliments in fluent German.

In three tiny Volkswagens we drove through the darkened, snow-covered streets, to the Imperial Hotel. Sacher's, where Madame Rubinstein had requested rooms—because "Their pastries are so good!"—was still occupied by the British.

I had never been to Vienna, but my imagination, stimulated by the current success of *The Third Man*, was primed for zither music, romance on the wing, even intrigue. On the plane Madame, always the hungry realist, had licked her lips: "The best thing in Vienna is *Gans*. . . . You know? Goose."

All I could see, through the Volkswagen's frosty windows, were ruins. "That's the Cathedral!" The agent pointed to a Gothic shell. "Please! And now the Opera." We rounded a mass of scaffolding framing some cracked gingerbread.

The Imperial Hotel was also in the process of renovation. More scaffolding propped up the rococo splendor of an entrance decorated with quantities of stucco. Beyond, a blaze of freshly painted white-and-gold paneling made me blink. But the corridors leading to Madame's suite suggested a boardinghouse in Pimlico.

:[ 154 ]:

"*Voilà! Meine gnädige Frau.* . . ." The manager threw open a pair of double doors with a flourish. Madame bounced forward and came to an abrupt stop. Red brocade covered all the elaborate furnishings. There was a full-length portrait of the Empress Maria-Theresa dressed in her coronation robes hanging over an empty fireplace. It was a gigantic mausoleum.

"Only our most important guests are given this suite." The manager pirouetted around Madame who stood rock-still in her sable cloak.

"So?"

"Yes. Even Herr Hitler!"

"Well, if it was good enough for him, it's too good for me."

She turned on her heels. "All I want is one room. . . . Not an Olympic stadium!"

Throughout our travels Madame always insisted on the simplest accommodations. It was not entirely a question of money, begrudging unnecessary luxury, or cutting expenses. She favored compact quarters. "What do I need so much space for? Besides, I'll never be able to find the bathroom!"

Finally, in Vienna, she accepted a smaller suite. The agent reminded her, "Where will you receive the press?"

"In the coffee shop!"

I helped her unpack. Madame's wardrobe could only be described as "theatrical." Her luggage contained a dozen elaborate suits, tea gowns, evening wear. There were five fur coats (including one in monkey fur), twenty-two pairs of shoes, and an equal number of hats. And yet, in all of this finery, I found only two soiled cotton nightdresses, three petticoats, a tattered girdle. . . .

"I'm so clumsy!" Incapable of hanging a dress, Madame now indicated this was my job.

"Can you iron?"

"Why not?"

"Here. . . ." I was given a portable iron. "See what you can do with this skirt." I set to work and reproduced the splendid razor-sharp creases that had once dramatized my uniforms in the Brigade of Guards.

"Beautiful!" Madame gave me a friendly whack. She was obviously delighted to be attended by a secretary-companion-major domo, and . . . ladies' maid!

Our next few days in Vienna had a surrealistic quality due to the unexpected succession of events.

Madame flitted around the occupied city with the energy of a Halloween witch. She held secret meetings with "The Mascara Countess," visited shops stocking Rubinstein merchandise, and finally presided over a mammoth press conference.

Sandwiched between these business activities were a few brief cultural excursions. We saw the Vienna Woods: "Why do I have to look at dead trees in winter?" Schönbrunn: "Pity it's not furnished!" The famous boys' choir at the Hofburg Chapel: "Such screeching!" Besides being tone-deaf, Madame considered sight-seeing a waste of time. "Everything looks so much better at the movies. Still . . . let us buy some post cards. Then we'll let our people know we've been there!"

Vienna's architectural heritage—all monuments—were one and the same to Madame Rubinstein: "Drafty, a waste of good space, nice for people to visit with nothing better on their minds. Get some post cards." she repeated. "We'll do some useful work!"

Madame loved tart messages. "It keeps them on their toes!" These cards were sent to her staff, a few choice friends, important beauty editors, and her family. She wrote over and over:

"Here in Vienna for business. There is much to do. The city's a mess. Am sure things will pick up. Will have much of interest to tell you when we meet again."

To her family, Madame invariably added an angular P.S.: "Am sure you are doing your utmost as I am." Madame stretched her fingers. She had written some fifty post cards. She then handed me the batch. "Here! Mail them yourself at the Central Post Office." I was given Austrian money to do so: "Never trust a hotel concierge! He'll charge airmail and probably send everything third class—if at all! Quick, quick. Don't forget we have a press conference at six and . . . bring back my change."

I sauntered out into the icy streets and with two hours' freedom—a rare luxury—I decided to walk to the Central Post Office. In Paris I could escape, nocturnally, since I knew my way around. But in

Vienna, I had been virtually and virtuously Madame's prisoner. She watched me like a mother hawk. Our bedrooms, at the Imperial Hotel, were adjacent. Frequently, during the night, Madame knocked on the connecting door. "Are you there?" "Yes, I am! Asleep." "Good, go back to sleep."

Vienna reminded me of Rhineland cities I had seen during the war. The ruined buildings—in many cases mere façades—had the look of elaborate, operatic stage sets. I forged on, following my frosty breath and instincts, only to realize after a mile or so, that I was hopelessly lost. It was pitch black by five in the afternoon. The ill-lit streets were sinister. No cabs! No policemen! No one, it seemed, but me, clutching Madame's fifty post cards.

Like some apocalyptic vision, out of billowing clouds of white fog, a jeep materialized. I bounced in its path. The jeep's wheels, as it braked before me, produced sparks. In it, three burly soldiers and an officer stared blankly at me. Their caps were decorated with the Russian star.

"Passport!"

"Good evening . . . *bon soir* . . . *da da*!" I smiled back. The only words I knew in Russian, besides "*da*," were "I love you." Under the circumstances these didn't seem quite appropriate.

"*Papier!*"

I had forgotten my passport at the hotel. I showed the officer my post cards, trying to explain, in pantomime, that I was looking for the post office. The top one, fortunately, by some strange quirk of fate, was of Lenin. Madame had elected to send it to her son, Horace, whose beard always disturbed her.

"Ha! You like Comrade Lenin?" the Russian officer said in hesitant English. He gave me a dazzling smile, all of his front teeth were capped with stainless steel.

"Yes, indeed!"

"I drive you back to Imperial. Jump in!"

By straying into the Russian sector, after curfew, I discovered later that I might well have ended my evening locked up. We arrived as Madame Rubinstein was about to set off for her press conference. She was stomping about the hotel hallway wrapped in her sable cloak. On the crest of one of her favorite bowler hats a large diamond pin of twin eagles, topped by an Imperial crown, twinkled aggressively as did her eyes. This had been the Tsar's cipher. The Russian officer, who followed me into the hotel, eyed it apprehensively.

"Who's the Little Mother?"

"Ha! Where have you been?" Madame glared at me. "I was so worried!"

"The Russians detained me while I was looking for the post office." I pointed to my escort.

"You no-good butterfly!" Madame sputtered and, unable to produce further invective, struck my shoulder.

"Little Mother! Little Mother! It's not his fault. . . ."

The Russian officer stepped between us. Madame looked up at him incredulously. She hadn't, as yet, been aware of his presence. Her eyes popped.

"Where did you find him?"

"He found me!"

"Well, I'll be jiggered!"

Madame always called Russians "beasts!" She had an ingrained fear of them. Even in Tsarist days, she claimed, they had been responsible for all of Poland's woes, for pogroms, for Jewish suffering.

The agent, who had been hovering in the background, interceded. "Madame! You'll be late for your press conference."

"Quick! Quick! Let us go. . . ."

To everyone's surprise, the Russian officer led the way to Madame's car, ushered her in, and followed in his jeep to the Pallavicini Palace where the conference was taking place. This handsome baroque building, on Josefsplatz, currently served as an international meeting place. It had hastily been patched up, after the war, for this purpose.

Madame's arrival, with a Russian escort, caused "quite a stir," as she admitted later, for such was her inborn sense of drama that she ordered the Russians, in a mixture of German and Polish, to follow her up the winding marble staircase into a huge gilded ballroom. The Russians needed little persuasion. Their cheeks glowed with self-importance as they formed a phalanx around the tiny, commanding figure.

"Little Mother. . . ."

The ballroom was filled to overflowing with gold chairs on which were seated row upon row of what looked like cooks, waiting to be interviewed by a prospective employer. When Madame entered, they rose as one, eyed her escort, clapped uncertainly. Was it fear or admiration? The Russians were not popular. Seldom had I seen so many heaving bosoms and large bottoms. Madame tripped up some steps to a dais followed by the agent, his wife, and a group of city officials. The Russians stood diffidently to one side. One of the officials made a speech, the agent another, prior to introducing . . . "Frau Helena Rubinstein, Fürstin Gourielli."

Madame removed her hat with its diamond insignia. At a distance, it also looked like the Austrian Imperial crest. She allowed her sables to drop from her shoulders. Eight rows of pearls, "my good ones," framed her splendid jaw. She wore an elaborately embroidered bodice of magenta and vermilion.

"Ask me questions," she said in German. Her voice was clear, authoritative. "Although I would like to . . . I'm no good at exchanging compliments!"

The mild hand clapping which had first heralded her arrival was now a roar. It made the crystal chandeliers tinkle. She had captured her audience with a mixture of exotic opulence and peasant simplicity.

One of the agent's beauticians translated for me the ensuing dialogue.

"What do you think of Vienna?" someone asked.

"I'm sad seeing the ruins. But I'm filled with hope and admiration seeing you!" was Madame's answer.

"How can Austrian women consider beauty when there are so many other pressing problems?"

"Beauty is not a problem. It's a woman's birthright."

"Why did you come to Vienna?"

"To see and to talk to you!"

"Please! May we have your beauty philosophy for Austrian women?"

"Make your men happy! Be happy yourselves! Never look back!"

As Madame left the dais, a thunder of hand clapping greeted her exit.

"Was I good?"

"Superb!"

"Yes, I know what to say to women. . . ."

Madame gave each of the Russians a lipstick and turning to the agent said, "Now let us have a good dinner of goose. I've earned it." And to me, "We'll go to Zurich in the morning. Lots to do there. A good week's hard work. . . ."

Madame Rubinstein liked to ration her time when on the road—three days here, four there. A whole week was the maximum she could ever stand to spend in any city unless forced to do so or on one of her yearly health cures.

Our departure, at dawn, was not unlike our arrival. There were roses, boxes of chocolate, and other souvenirs. She handed them to me, I shoved them wherever there was space in my supply of paper bags. *"Küss die Hand, gnädige Frau!"*

"Thank God, that's over!" Madame sighed when we were safely on the plane and I had strapped her into her seat.

"Boring people! Still, that's business. I hope you learned something?"

"What did you decide to do with the agent?"

"The money he owes us is in here." She patted her purse. "He still has a two-year contract . . . we will wait. Meantime, I'm sure he'll work harder."

"And the mascara countess?"

"Ha! You know about her, too?" She gave me one of her owlish looks—suspicion mixed with begrudging admiration . . . as if I had been peeking through keyholes.

"I've fixed her. Gave her a long-term contract and three per cent instead of five."

We were met in Zurich by another agent, one whom Madame called "The Shrewd Swiss." His name was Herbert Bauer. He distributed and sold Rubinstein products in Switzerland and in Italy. "That's the up and coming market! . . . Italy! Switzerland's only good for banking."

Mr. Bauer and his wife looked like Tweedledum and Tweedledee after spending a holiday on a Swiss mountaintop. Both were short, plump, and sunburned. They were dressed in matching outfits of heavy tweed.

In Vienna, the official greeting had been, *Küss die Hand*. At Zurich, it was *Gruss Gott*! accompanied by bunches of carnations instead of roses (why not edelweiss? I wondered).

During these ceremonials, I was suddenly aware of a small, blonde woman with a pronounced facial twitch. She kept edging her way forward by Madame's side, who, using an elbow, pushed her back. They occasionally snapped at one another in Polish—sharp short sentences like machine-gun fire. I thought her to be a poor relative. The blonde woman now latched on to me.

"I'm Maeder!" she announced. "And Maeder's Switzerland. . . ."

So this is Madame Maeder! Madame Halina Maeder. "In Switzerland we have this wonderful woman, very strong . . . a real terror!" Madame Rubinstein had warned me.

Madame Maeder was also Polish. She had been married to a diplomat, divorced, exiled during the war. As with many Polish ladies, Madame Maeder had cosmetics knowledge. Impoverished, she used it; in need, she somehow sought out and found Madame Rubinstein. "So I gave her a job!" Madame said. "I told her . . . go and help out in Switzerland."

"I'm Maeder! And Maeder's Switzerland. . . ."

Small wonder Mr. and Mrs. Bauer dodged her too. She wasn't one to be upstaged. While in Vienna, we were met by a fleet of Volkswagens, at Zurich there were several Mercedes.

". . . Travel with Maeder. Find out what tricks she's up to," Madame whispered to me.

We settled in the back in one of the cars, while Madame Rubinstein drove on ahead with Mr. and Mrs. Bauer in another.

"Why are we always met by so many people?" I asked Madame Maeder.

"It's to impress *her*." She pointed to the tail-lights in front of us.

"What will we be doing here?"

"Don't worry! I have an agenda."

Madame Maeder foraged in her purse and produced a roll of papers.

"See! I need your help." She stroked my arm. The gesture could have been Madame's.

"We must build a factory. We must open an office. We must. . . ."

By the time we reached the Baur-au-Lac Hotel my ears were humming. Madame Maeder used an average of three languages to express the simplest thought. I was also bruised. With each successive statement, when not whacking her hefty thighs and pounding the seat, Madame Maeder nudged me in the ribs with even greater insistence than my boss was given to doing.

The following morning when I checked in to Madame's bedroom, at eight A.M., she was still in bed propped up by her usual quota of pillows. Madame Maeder hovered around her. They were sharing a bottle of beer.

"We've been talking shop since seven. If you only knew the problems!"

"Why the beer?" I asked, longing for one. "Maeder swears after hot coffee it's the best thing in the world to clean you out!"

The two ladies spoke in Polish.

"She says . . ." Madame tried to keep me posted.

Finally, the beer and the hot coffee ended their discussion.

"Ha! It's working."

I was told to leave the room. Madame Maeder stayed on. Her piercing voice could still be heard through the double doors.

"She's a real tyrant!" Madame Rubinstein confided later. "I wish we had six of her. . . ." We were driving into the snow-covered countryside outside Zurich to view a tract of land. "Maeder says it's perfect for a factory. I'm going to buy it!" As when we had visited Van Dongen, she stroked her purse. ". . . With good land, these days, who can lose?"

Madame Maeder manipulated the wheel of her miniature sports car like a racing buff and, to give impact to her words, slapped the gears from low to high without troubling herself with intermediary speeds. The engine's groans counterpointed her own excited pronouncements. Madame Rubinstein nodded away by her side while I huddled on the narrow back seat.

Some ten miles outside of Zurich we stopped in a hamlet called Spreitenbach.

"Are we there?" Madame asked. "Let's eat!" As usual, she was hungry—business transactions sharpened her appetite.

In a deserted inn, over an omelet, trout, and a local wine called Oeil de Perdrix, Madame Maeder—who hogged most of the wine—explained why Spreitenbach had a future. It was on the main line linking Zurich with the South—with Italy. There was an ample supply of good water, much needed in the formulation of cosmetics. Lastly, taxes were lower in that particular area, since the government wished to see it developed commercially.

"I'll bet she makes a commission!" Madame's teeth crackled on a trout's head. She spat out a bone. Madame Maeder was telephoning the owner of the land. He appeared while we were all drinking coffee. "Have some kirsch?" Madame suggested, studying his bland features. After a third glass, they colored slightly. "Now let us see the land!" Madame snapped her purse open, indicating she wanted to pay the bill. He noticed, as she wished him to do, that it was stuffed with money. "A bit of temptation always helps!"

Madame leaned on my arm as we left the table, pretending to be old and weary. She might have been impersonating King Lear. With a groan, Madame forced me to help her into the car.

"Is the lady all right?" The owner's complexion varied from pink to amber.

When we reached the field, Madame, gasping for breath, tottered around it.

"Nice view!"

The main road, bordering the property, didn't escape her sharp eye; nor, for that matter, did a tiny railroad station. She nudged me as I held her arm. "Wait and see. In another five years, if we build, this will be a town. I hope he has more than less to sell!"

We returned to the inn. Over another cup of coffee, Madame announced without preliminaries: "Five hundred—five hundred thousand Swiss francs. That's what I'll give you!"

"But the price is six."

"Take it or leave it!"

With that, Madame emptied the contents of her purse on the table. His eyes narrowed.

"Five-fifty?"

"I'm not one to quibble. All right."

:[ 163 ]:

From one of her pockets, Madame produced another crisp roll of one thousand Swiss franc bills.

"Count!"

A bill of sale next sealed the deal.

"What about stamps?" (Stamps were needed to formalize the sale.)

"I'm sure you'll want to pay for them." Madame gave him a sweet smile.

As we were driving back to Zurich, Madame Maeder was unusually quiet. Finally she said, "But you took six hundred thousand francs with you!"

"Yes! So I did. . . ." Madame Rubinstein's grin was that of the Cheshire cat's. "Here's the other fifty." She emptied another pocket. "When buying anything, I always believe in little reserves."

The next few days were spent in discussions with architects, viewing temporary premises in Zurich, interviewing the nucleus of a prospective staff.

Madame did this with her usual thoroughness.

"Nice architect! He'll be the one. . . ."

"But you didn't study his plans!" Madame Maeder twitched aggressively.

"He's built a supermarket, a bank, and his own home. We saw them all. I liked them all. What more do I need to know?"

With prospective applicants for staff positions, Madame Rubinstein was equally decisive. A young man called Charles Zell presented himself. He had been designing packages, advertising campaigns, and creating "publicity stunts" for Juvena—a new cosmetics company based in Switzerland. "They're doing very well!" Madame affirmed. "Too well. . . . I've offered him a raise and small extra bonuses in France, England, and America. In that way he can travel scot free. It's the fringe benefits that matter these days. So, so, Juvena's lost a good man," Madame nodded. "He's very calm. That will balance Maeder's nervousness." Another contract was drawn up. This time Madame didn't quibble about the stamps.

"Now, now let us go to Rome! And this time we must definitely travel by train!"

Madame hadn't forgotten.

"And remember, we'll sit up!"

From Zurich to Rome, with a stop in Milan, the night train takes about eight hours. We left in a blinding snowstrom with Madame Maeder in attendance. She was wrapped in what looked like a lion's pelt and charged up and down the platform until, having dispensed suitable bribes, she secured a first-class compartment for Madame and me to share alone.

Having dismissed Madame Maeder in a flood of Polish, Madame stretched out on one of the twin banquettes. She indicated with her thumb that the other was mine. We had already dined in Zurich. It was midnight. The train slowly rattled forward, gained speed. We were on our way.

Before I fell asleep I caught a glimpse of Madame's features. They were creased with concentration over a book. Her spectacles dangled on the tip of her nose. She reminded me of the owl in Tenniel's drawings for Edward Lear's poems.

Later, I woke up with a start. The train, as it ground to a stop in Milan, almost threw me off my narrow banquette. Madame was still reading. She looked up.

"Slept well?"

"And you. . . ."

"I've been reading. Most interesting!"

"What?"

"The Bible."

"Whose version?" I mumbled. The train again rattled into motion but before I drifted off a second time I heard her say: "The Charlatan's!"

"Never slept a wink!" Madame announced in the morning. "It's nice to be young like you. Sleep comes easy. Let us have some breakfast."

I looked at the cover of her book as she led me out of our compartment. "The Charlatan's Version of the Bible" was Gaylord Hauser's newest diet manual.

"That book's full of common sense!" she informed me over coffee.

"So at least I didn't waste my time!" She sneezed repeatedly. "Damn it! Must have caught cold. . . ."

When the train arrived in Rome we were again met by Mr. and Mrs. Bauer who had gone on ahead by plane. They had forsaken their sensible Swiss clothes for Roman finery. Mr. Bauer's shantung suit glistened in the winter sunshine like a sea lion's pelt. Mrs. Bauer seemed to be gift-wrapped in mink. Eddying in their wake were the usual crowd of photographers, cosmeticians, members of the beauty press.

This was Madame's first visit to Rome since the war. Irene Brin, again in the white she had worn at our luncheon in Paris, embraced her: "Welcome to Roma!"

Bulbs snapped; a crowd surged around us; Madame was momentarily engulfed in a surging mass of arms, flowers, and bobbing heads. When I managed to reach her side she whimpered: "I can't stand it! Quick, let's get to the hotel. . . ." She was shivering and didn't complain, this time, at the vastness of her suite, but shuffled, instinctively, to the bedroom, where she collapsed on a huge Empire bed.

"I'm done in! Tell them all to leave. . . ."

The Bauers, Signora Brin, and the phalanx of courtiers backed out exchanging worried looks: *"Poverina. . . . Che brava!"*

I hovered uncertainly over Madame and tiptoed out as soon as she seemed to be sleeping. At lunchtime I peeped in. She was still fully clothed, huddled in a corner of her bed, wrapped in an eiderdown.

"I'm sick. Get some aspirin, lemon, brandy!"

However ill, even if bordering upon unconsciousness, Madame always managed to give lucid orders. By six that evening her position hadn't changed, although she had somehow managed to remove her suit, girdle, and jewels. These were scattered on the floor by the bedside.

One watery eye nailed me as I picked them up. "Patrick! Better get a doctor. . . ."

A doctor!

I dialed the Bauers' nearby room, tried to reach Irene Brin. No one answered. Even the house doctor had gone off to the opera.

Madame's breathing now sounded like a kettle on the boil. Her

:[ 166 ]:

eyes were closed. Drops of sweat flecked the make-up on her forehead and cheeks.

"Oh, God! What am I to do? What am I to do!"

Finally I found her address book, that sturdy manual, and flipped the pages to "I" for Italy, "R" for Rome. The list of names was long and confusing. It began with Aldobrandini (Prince and Princess—*friends*) and ended with Zzzap (*masseuse*). Madame groaned and repeated the words: "Get a doctor. . . ." It was then that my finger rested on "C" for Crespi (Count and Countess—*friends*).

Friends! I had known Consuelo Crespi in New York when, as Consuelo O'Connor, she first exploded into visual prominence with her sister Gloria as a "Toni Twin." This advertising campaign promoted home permanents. It also raised both sisters from the gentle anonymity of their middle-class background to mild prominence in café society. They were beautiful girls blessed with the soft features of the Irish, and an inborn sense of style. Luminaries of the fashion world, particularly Diana Vreeland, quickly recognized and used these qualities. They both became fashion editors.

Consuelo soon met and married a handsome, rich, young Italian—whose money, it was said, came from the vast Matarazzo holdings in Brazil.

At first Roman society laughed, as they are given to doing, behind the Crespis' impeccably groomed backs. But Consuelo's charm, matched by her husband's flair for publicity, soon established them in Rome's aristocratic jungle where titles meant little without wealth, and wealth was only enshrined if coupled with good looks.

The Crespis had additional weapons in their considerable arsenal. They were backed by powerful American friends in the press. The newly established Italian *haute couture* dressed and courted them: Simonetta, her husband Fabiani, Irene Galitzine, Federico Forquet all created clothes for the countess. She modeled them gracefully, astutely. The count publicized the clothes, their designers, and his wife; everyone benefited.

Madame liked to remind me, "Whatever you do . . . always start at the top!" The Crespis had done this. I dialed Countess Crespi's number, *"Pronto! Pronto!"*

:[ 167 ]:

The Italian telephone service, even at the Excelsior, is anything but prompt. Half an hour later, blurred by the ruckus of a cocktail party, Countess Crespi's voice tinkled at the other end of the line. Her English was subtly veiled by the singsong innuendoes of multilingual Roman conversation. *"Caro!* What a joy . . . how do you say it? *Quel bonheur!"*

"Princess Gourielli, Madame Rubinstein, is desperately ill. Can you help me find a doctor?"

"How divine! Kirk Douglas, Princess Colonna, and John Huston are here. . . . They will be so happy if you can join us."

"But . . . but I need a doctor!" I hollered. The urgency in my voice finally penetrated.

"Oh, dear! Let me see. . . . I'll call you right back."

For further agonizing minutes I tried to synchronize my breathing with Madame's. She was the color of the starched sheets. Her mouth sagged.

The phone rang.

*"Amore!* I've found you a doctor. He's heaven. . . ." Countess Crespi paused dramatically. "His name is Doctor Ovary. Doctor Zoltan Ovary. Hungarian and my gynecologist!"

Beggars can't be choosers! I carefully replaced the telephone by Madame's bedside. Ovary. A gynecologist. Only in Rome. . . .

When Doctor Ovary finally appeared, Madame seemed to have stopped breathing. He bent over her, felt her pulse, produced a stethoscope.

"Leave us alone." I was given a gentle push as he closed the door.

His manner was brisk. I ordered myself a double whisky while waiting for him to emerge.

"Your Princess has pneumonia. She should be in hospital. However, it would be difficult and unwise to move her," Doctor Ovary informed me in perfect English when he had concluded his examination. His lean face and slate-colored eyes registered anxiety.

"How old is the lady?"

"Over eighty. . . ."

"She needs oxygen. I've given her antibiotics. She must also have a nurse. Don't worry, I'll find one. Please order me a whisky while I do

:[  1 6 8  ]:

so!" He eyed my glass. I had told Countess Crespi not to divulge Madame's true identity, fearing the insatiable Italian press.

After several animated telephone conversations, Doctor Ovary said, "I've found a nurse . . . a nice nun." He paused. "Are you related to the Princess?"

"I'm her . . . her sort of secretary!'

"Well, Mister 'Sort-of-Secretary,' we'll be lucky if she pulls through the night! Both her lungs are affected. Her heart isn't too strong. She also seems to have diabetes. . . . Where is her family? They should be informed."

I could feel sweat trickling down my shirt front.

"Doctor . . . the 'Princess' is Helena Rubinstein. Her family is in New York. I wouldn't know *where* to start. I doubt if her husband will be of any help. As for her sons. . . ."

He patted my shoulder. "I knew who she was. I saw her picture in the paper this morning. That face of hers isn't easily forgotten. My advice . . . call her lawyer first. That's what he's paid for. Meantime, I must find some oxygen. Rome, you know, isn't equipped for this sort of a crisis."

While Doctor Ovary was searching for oxygen, I again struggled with the telephone. Madame's lawyer seemed unimpressed when I finally reached him. "She's had pneumonia before." The Prince— Prince Gourielli—was away for the week end; and Albert, the butler, who answered my transatlantic call, banged down the receiver after giving me this information.

It was then that I thought of Horace and recalled Madame's conversation concerning him: "He's in trouble. He's run away. He's in the South of France. . . ."

I rang up Mr. Ameisen in Paris. Always solicitous, he was equally sure that Madame would recover. "She's tough!" he declared while agreeing with me that it would be wise if I talked to Horace. "He's living at Auribau, near Cannes." Mr. Ameisen gave me Horace's telephone number.

I must have sounded hysterical when, dazed by the effort of reaching him, I yelled: "Horace! Is that you?"

"Yes. I believe so."

:[ 169 ]:

"Your mother has pneumonia. She's desperately ill. . . ."

"Where are you both?"

I told him.

"I'll be there tomorrow!"

For all his funny ways, Horace didn't hesitate an instant. I was unaware, at the time, of the extent of his difficulties. "I'll be there tomorrow!" Would Madame still "be there"? I wondered.

I sidled into the bedroom. She was gray. The two circles of rouge on her cheeks had turned to purple.

Doctor Ovary, accompanied by a majestic-looking nun, returned. They were wheeling an enormous oxygen cylinder. It must have been six feet tall.

"This is Sister Angelica." He introduced us. "I couldn't find an oxygen tent. We'll have to manage with this." He produced two long rubber tubes and set to work connecting them with Madame's nostrils.

"Did you call her lawyer?"

I related my brief conversation.

"Lawyers only like corpses. They may soon have one on their hands."

"Fortunately, her son will be here tomorrow!" I said.

"He may be too late!"

Sister Angelica sat down by Madame's bedside and watched the flow of oxygen. She toyed with her rosary beads, mumbling the Ave Maria.

"Well, Mister 'Sort-of-Secretary'!" It was Doctor Ovary's turn to mop his brow. "I've done all I can. Sister Angelica will call me if the Princess takes a turn for the worse. There's nothing more to do but wait. I'll be back in the morning. I suggest you go to bed."

What with a night on a train and a day of such bewildering con-fusion, I was swacked. All I could manage, when I reached my bed, was to kick off my shoes and wrap myself in a couple of blankets. Ten minutes later, so it seemed, my bedside telephone jangled.

I sprang up. The same pale Roman sunlight that had greeted us twenty-four hours earlier flickered through the Venetian shades. It was morning.

"Your Princess is asking for you!" Doctor Ovary's voice hit me like a bucket of ice water. He hung up before I could demand further news. I rushed to Madame's suite. All of the windows were wide open. Doctor Ovary greeted me at the door. He was smiling. Over his shoulder, beyond the drawing room, I could just see Madame. The oxygen tank was still connected to her nostrils.

On the previous night, her cheeks had been ashen. Now they almost matched the pink of her satin quilted bed jacket. Her hair had been freshly brushed. Balanced on the tip of her nose were the familiar tortoise-shell spectacles. They seemed to flash a challenge at the morning sunlight. She was sitting up in bed, reading a newspaper.

"Ah, Patrick!" she called out. "Where have you been? I need you. Abbott Laboratories have dropped twelve points. The doctor here says they make the medicine that cured me—some new sort of penicillin. You must wire The-Broker-with-the-Nice-Wife in New York. Mister . . . Mister. . . . Never mind! Tell him to buy me five thousand shares of the laboratories!"

# "All You Think of Is Money"

"And what are you doing here, Horace?" Madame's greeting to her younger son when he arrived later that morning only intensified his pained expression. He gave his black beard a sharp tug.

"Patrick phoned me to say you had pneumonia."

"So I did. That was *yesterday*. The doctor gave me some wonderful new pills. Now I don't!"

Horace stood staring at his mother, stunned, unable to answer. In all the years I was to know him, his physical presence seemed to reduce Madame's small talk to zero. Their dialogues were little more than questions and answers. Being in bed, hooked up by the nostrils to an oxygen tank, only added to her discomfort.

"So what's new, dear?"

"Nothing . . . Mother."

"So, so why waste the time coming here?"

Her hands clutching nervously at the sheets signaled petulance. "You were stupid to call him," Madame berated me later. "His visit will cost a fortune."

Mercifully, at that moment, the arrival of the Bauers, accompanied by Irene Brin and her husband, produced a diversion. They waltzed in loaded with bunches of flowers, beribboned cornets of chocolates, magazines, and dumped their tributes at Madame's feet.

"You shouldn't! How kind. . . ."

"Dear Princess . . ."

"*Meine liebe Frau . . .*"

Madame, whose appetite, even when ill, could always be depended
upon, wolfed several chocolate truffles while her guests praised God,
Doctor Ovary, and Abbott Laboratories for her miraculous recovery.
During a lull in the animated exchange of chatter, Irene Brin re-
minded her of the Italian art project we had discussed at Marie-Louise
Bousquet's house in Paris. She then tactfully attempted to draw
Horace into the gossiping circle grouped about the bed. He was stand-
ing by a window, staring at the traffic whirling up and down the Via
Veneto.

"So this is your son, *cara Principessa*? He is magnificent . . . like one
of Michelangelo's apostles!"

Madame now stroked her sheets. The oxygen tank echoed her
pleasure. It produced an arpeggio of warm, gurgling sounds.

"Sit down by me!" Irene Brin summoned Horace to share her
chair. He shuffled over.

"*Bene*. . . . Now let us discuss your interests."

"Tell her!" Like a child on display, Horace was encouraged to
speak by his mother. He continued to stare into space. "He likes to
paint . . . to write. He is artistic . . . literary." Madame gaily enumerated her forty-year-old son's talents.

"*Benissimo!*" Irene Brin's voice was like a flute—a high note of
approval, a low note of inducement. "We must get him involved in
our art project."

"Good! Good! . . ." It was Madame's turn to be the child. "Tell us
more . . . describe!" The oxygen tank again burped. Madame was
flushed. Her eyes were wide with anticipation as Irene Brin carefully
recounted, with the slow formality of Italians speaking English, how
a group of young Italian artists were currently enjoying enormous
European prestige. This was because of their talents, she explained,
coupled with the dedicated efforts of her husband, Gasparo, whose
Obelisco Gallery had first introduced them.

"We want your dear mother, the Princess, to be like one of the great
art patrons of the Renaissance . . . a modern Medici."

Everyone but Horace beamed at their own visions of Florentine
magnificence while Madame lay back in her pillows—already bargain-

ing over imaginary commissions. Doctor Ovary now appeared. He was again attended by Sister Angelica who carried, carefully wrapped in the *Corriere della Sera*, what was obviously a bedpan. The doctor felt Madame's pulse. We were all ordered out of the room.

"Irene! Horace! Patrick! Work together . . . I want to be a Medici!"

That evening, Madame had a relapse. All visitors were barred, and another nun, Sister Rosa, was added to the medical staff. It was her duty to stand guard over Madame during the day. "We must protect her," the doctor insisted, "from overextending herself."

"As Madame Rubinstein's son, I heartily concur." Horace liked to be formal when talking about his mother to strangers. He also seemed relieved. His eyes, usually so sorrowful, were a bit brighter. He changed from his black cloth suit into a sports jacket and slacks, and, for the next few days, freed from his mother's badgering, blossomed into a *bon vivant*.

It was his turn to shine. He longed for recognition, admiration, affection. Urged on by Irene Brin, he now took an immediate interest in her projects. These included not only art and artists, but the demands of Roman society, the joys of night life, of entertaining, even of seduction. Horace was in his element.

Irene Brin started the ball rolling: "Let us have dinner at l'Osteria del Orso tonight." This was Rome's most fashionable restaurant. Hungry artists and their wives were happy to be invited, and Horace, with the nonchalance of a professional gambler, signed Madame's name to the bill.

"*Che simpatico!*"

"*Horatio!* Surely the name of a hero . . ."

"*Che bravo!*"

Puffing on a huge cigar, listening to Roman adulation, Horace sat dreamily at the head of a long table. For years Irene Brin had been known as "the Roman Elsa Maxwell," such was the skill she extended in mixing guests. That night there were artists, a papal princess, two popular film directors, several dress designers, and . . .

"*Che bella, la Lollobrigida!*"

Horace shot a timid glance at the extraordinary cleavage. He ordered a magnum of champagne.

"*Caro,* please meet the Principessa Colonna . . ." Irene Brin

:[ 175 ]:

dropped her voice. "She has a Botticelli hanging over her bed and this," she chattered on, "is our dear friend Visconti!" Sad eyes simmering over an inquisitor's jowl; huge, capable hands; a distant smile.

Dazed, giddy, and happy, Horace next played host at Passetto, at Giorgio's, and in a succession of Trastevere *trattorias* hand-picked by Irene Brin. He loved it. I loved it. Even his guests seemed to be enjoying themselves. In the early fifties, Rome hadn't yet been overwhelmed by the Hollywood invasion, by Seventh Avenue, and by what Madame called "rich European dreck."

As dawn broke, more often than not, Horace led me up the Spanish Steps, paused to admire the view, and then said, "Let's have a Vecchia Romana and an espresso before turning in." Later he was to admit, "For once I feel content." I asked him why. He stared into space and pointed, vaguely, at Saint Peter's. "It's so peaceful."

During the daytime, after but a few hours' sleep, we wandered around in Gasparo del Corso's cheerful wake from one artist's studio to the next. Irene Brin stayed in bed. She was typing copy for one of the eight newspapers she worked for. "Run along, my dears . . . but don't forget, tonight we dine with . . ." she raised an engagement book to her nose, "we dine with Giorgio di Chirico!" I have seldom known a woman so organized, yet so vague. Her memory was prolific, but, what astounded me, she never made a carbon copy of any of the thousands of words that passed through her typewriter daily.

"What if your copy gets lost?"

"It will be the messenger's fault and I will write it again."

The fashionable artists of the day lived on the Via Margutta. The hard-working ones favored the Piazza del Popolo. The few with real talent seemed to have their roots in Trastevere. This was still a workman's district, honeycombed with tiny streets, teeming with people.

Horace waxed his beard, ordered slinky Roman suits from Cifonelli, and sent huge bouquets of flowers to artists' wives who might have preferred baskets of food.

In the evening we would check with Sister Angelica. "*Come va la Principessa?*"

"*Molto stanca, poverina.*"

Horace and I, for all of our differences of character and taste, not only made good progress with the Italian art project—what is more important, we became friends. He still treated me with caution, as his "mother's man," and constantly tested my reactions.

"What will Madame Rubinstein say?"

"What do *you* say, Horace?"

His taut, fleeting smile was filled with uncertainty.

"It's for you to decide!" I insisted.

"I'm not used to doing so . . . *for her.*"

Somehow, with my help and encouragement, he now made his final choice of the painters who were to be commissioned and who were to add to his mother's glory as a collector—"a modern Medici." But it wasn't until a year later, in the spring of 1953, that the result of our joint labors was finally unveiled to the public. The exhibition, christened "Twenty Imaginary Views of the American Scene by Twenty Young Italian Artists," first opened in Rome, at the Obelisco Gallery, before being shipped to New York where, with considerable fanfare, it was shown in the private picture gallery of Madame Rubinstein's apartment. Various Italian charities benefited from the event and Madame, much to her consternation, received the Stella della Solidarietà, the Star of Friendship, from the Italian Government.

"What will I do with it?" she said when the decoration was pinned on her breast.

"Wear it!"

"That huge medal?"

"No. A small ribbon. It can be sewn on all of your dresses. Carmel Snow has one, so does Sally Kirkland!"

"Why waste the money?" The Star of Friendship vanished into the filing cabinet in which she kept her jewelry but reappeared whenever Madame visited Italy.

"Some people may be impressed!"

Two years later the Italian exhibition was still traveling around the United States. More than fifty million people saw these paintings in museums, department store windows, and reproduced on the pages of national magazines, Sunday supplements, daily newspapers. For an initial investment of eight thousand dollars ("Without all of those horrible expenses . . ." Madame was thinking of Horace's extravagances while in Rome *and* Doctor Ovary's bill) she received more than half a million dollars of free publicity while the twenty paintings, at the time of her death, were valued at one hundred thousand dollars.

"Interesting!" This was Madame's only word of praise when the exhibition had nowhere else to go but back on the walls of her own apartment.

All of the best contemporary Italian artists of the fifties were included. The list started with Afro, the *doyen* of current abstract art. It included Enrico D'Assia, a talented young prince, the nephew of ex-King Umberto of Italy, who painted stylish, surrealistic landscapes. His contribution, "Somewhere in the West," was an elaborate gouache of a rocky canyon. An empty sardine box was prominently visible in the foreground. "What's that for?" Madame inquired when she first saw the painting. "Tourists always litter," the Prince replied, "and I believe that America is filled with such litter."

"No worse than Italy!" Madame was proud of her adopted country.

Burri, an avant-garde abstract painter, submitted a strangely tattered painting called "Jazz." It was made of burlap. "Can you imagine paying good money for *that*?" Madame was studying the artfully torn canvas. "But it only cost two hundred dollars!" I tried to defend both the painter and his work.

"What's it worth now?" Three years had gone by. "Five thousand!" "Good!"

Bruno Caruso, a Sicilian artist, painted the Brooklyn Bridge with a skeletal ice-cream vendor in the foreground. Gentilini, a hulking Roman, was inspired to interpret his version of this historic landmark.

Mirko, Mosca, Muccini, Music, Fazzini, Clerici, and Vespignani were a few of the other artists whose works Horace and I selected. When we showed the final list to Madame she frowned. "They all sound like grocers. Their names are not very inspiring . . . I don't know one of them!"

Skeptical, never willing to voice her appreciation, Madame couldn't resist needling Horace and me. Besides, he was still under a cloud due to "the scandal with the black girl."

"It cost me a hundred thousand dollars . . . and *more!*" was Madame's only comment. She never revealed any of the details. It was years before I finally discovered what may have been the truth.

Horace, the sensuous dreamer, had been having a brief affair with a black model whose titular lover, a small-time gangster, discovered Madame's identity. He set to work milking Horace, hopeful there would be unlimited funds at his disposal. Horace, on the other hand, liked to show off. There had been dinner parties in his New York town house on East Fifty-first Street, attended by admiring sycophants. These led to drugs, and drugs to blackmail. Horace lost his head. He devised a madcap scheme to frighten his tormentors. The girl and her greedy protector were spirited off to New Jersey by another group of Horace's ne'er-do-well chums. But the job was bungled and the police summoned. Horace was charged. He spent a night in jail. Madame's lawyers swung into action, paid his bail, and succeeded in hushing up the case.

Horace now chose to settle in the hills above Cannes, selecting for his temporary Elba a romantic farmhouse at Auribeau, where he planned to paint and write.

"Wait and see!" Madame's voice was that of Cassandra. She knew, full well, her son's failings. Auribeau was rustic, but the fleshpots of Cannes, Saint Tropez, Monte Carlo were all within easy driving distance. Moreover, Horace's father, Edward Titus (still spry and full of mischief at eighty-plus) lived nearby and enjoyed influencing his son, fanning family dissent. "He was always a troublemaker," Madame said. She had bought him a house at Cagnes-sur-Mer where he amused himself with what she called "his literary interests." These included a new, young, and attractive wife.

"She'll be the death of him," Madame kept repeating.

This event did not occur until three years later when Madame, on hearing the news, quite forgot her second husband, Prince Gourielli.

"What will I do? What will I do?" she wailed. Edward Titus, Horace, and, to a lesser extent, her elder son Roy were the only three men who really mattered in the strange tapestry of her family life. She had been enslaved and then humiliated by Titus. Roy was the result

:[ 179 ]:

of that contrary union. Horace, the child of a brief reconciliations, reaffirmed her love. He became a living proof of the passion she nurtured for Titus—ran from, returned to, and finally spurned.

"The business must come first!" she trumpeted.

"Money's a curse!" she also liked to say. But, with *her money*, artfully, even cruelly, she manipulated each and every step made by her seven sisters, two husbands, two sons, and anyone who crossed her path—including me.

Horace, fully aware of this maternal quirk, developed the skill of a mongoose faced by a hooded cobra. He attacked, retreated, ducked—then sprang forward. "Mother only respects those who take money away from her!" It was to be a lifelong struggle wherein Madame cried out, "He's ruining me!" as she opened and closed her purse.

Even as an embryo, before his birth in 1912, Horace's life was subject to his mother's whims. "Pregnancy in no way prevented me from making plans and continuing with my usual activities," she admitted in her memoirs, concentrating on a description of her new English home rather than on the child who had been born there.

"It was a large, comfortable Victorian house situated outside London, near Putney Heath, and mysteriously called 'Solna.' The park in which it stood had previously been owned by J. Pierpont Morgan, the American banker."

While Roy, her first son, had been born "above the shop," on Grafton Street, Horace first saw the light of day at Solna.

"He was a beautiful child . . . so docile. Until a nurse dropped him on his head!"

For the rest of his life, whenever Horace "acted up," Madame pointed to her head, twirled a finger over a temple, and shrugged. "Horace is cuckoo!"

She failed to realize that Horace's childhood, marred by frequent changes of environment, deprived of maternal affection, had been far from happy.

In 1913, the whole family moved to Paris. Madame was bored with London. "Such highfalutin women! Only interested in flowers and horses. . . ." She rented Solna and justified her sudden desire for change claiming, "It bothered me that I had never properly launched my *Salon de Beauté* in Paris."

:[ 180 ]:

Mala Rubinstein and myself some months after Madame's death in 1965. She is wearing her aunt's "good pearls." (*Photo Wilbur Pippin*)

Myself leaving Australia in an Anzac hat, 1958.

1963. Madame and three of her four surviving sisters:
left to right, Manka Bernard, Stella de Bruchard, Ceska
Cooper. *(Photo Jean-Paul Cadé)*


"Helena! Helena! I adore you. . . ."
Madame with Janet Flanner (*The New Yorker*'s Genêt)
and Marie-Louise Bousquet (Paris Editor of
*Harper's Bazaar*), 1964.

For two years Madame busied herself consolidating her French business but in 1915, driven away by the war, she moved her family to New York, saying: "Edward was an American citizen. He persuaded me to go to America for the sake of our sons."

Horace, barely three, now made his first Atlantic crossing. His mother, who shared the awesome experience, only recalled: "The ship was crowded beyond belief! The sea was rough, and the constant threat of enemy submarines added to my anxiety. . . ." She soon regained her composure.

"We arrived in New York on a bitterly cold day in January 1915. . . . The first thing I noticed was the whiteness of the women's faces and the oddly grayish color of their lips. Only their noses, mauve with cold, seemed to stand out."

Madame's vigilant eyes didn't miss a detail. She was immediately conscious of the size, the wealth, the possibilities for commerce in America.

The Titus family settled in a series of rented apartments on Riverside Drive and Central Park West. "Very Jewish" . . . Madame didn't approve. She set Edward to hunting for permanent quarters, preferably in Christian neighborhoods. He had a flair for what Madame called "good real estate," and soon found a brownstone on West 49th Street. Madame Rubinstein settled her family on the upper floor. Her first American salon was established on the two lower floors. It was here she set to work concocting her powders and lipsticks—to counterbalance "the whiteness of the women's faces and the oddly grayish color of their lips."

Her next purchase was a country house in Greenwich, Connecticut, on Old Indian Chase Road, where she dumped her family while commuting daily to West 49th Street. Roy, seven, and Horace, a toddler of three, were left to fend for themselves—watched over by a series of what their mother called "nice women."

"Nice women" were impecunious ladies. Madame was never short of them. "Less demanding," she claimed, "better educated, cheaper than housekeepers, nurses, maids."

She failed to mention that one of these "nice women" was the cause of her separation from Edward Titus. In 1916 he vanished to Chicago with one of her protégées. Madame, beside herself, demanded a legal separation. She got it, received the custody of the two boys, paid Edward one dollar (which he was later forced to return to her) but continued to see him, love him, occasionally live with him. Edward Titus was always to have a hypnotic power over Madame Rubinstein. He ferreted real estate for her, bought art, antiques, and rare books on her behalf. He advised her concerning her investments. He tortured her and she repaid the compliment by frequently refusing him funds.

With the armistice, in 1918, Edward Titus rushed back to Europe. Madame followed him and soon fell into the routine of sailing back and forth across the Atlantic. "I used to do it four or five times a year . . . most restful." In Paris, Madame chose to live in a small flat above her Faubourg salon while Edward opted for the Left Bank. Here, 4 rue Delambre, he opened a bookshop, published a literary magazine in English, *This Quarter*, and launched "The Black Mannequin Press." Madame subsidized these endeavors, muttering later, "Just like Horace! He started all these things, then soon got bored. . . ."

During the few years of Edward Titus's publishing career he produced a grand list of authors whose prose is still avidly read. He might have continued doing so, had not Madame yanked the financial carpet, so to speak, from under his small, neatly shod feet.

When she was alarmed over the expenses, or bored and at odds with her beneficiaries, Madame cut them off. Despite this, Edward Titus printed several important books and short stories by James Joyce, Ernest Hemingway, D. H. Lawrence, and e. e. cummings. His feeling for sound prose, graceful poetry, was as keen as his eye for real estate, abstract art, African sculpture. He recognized quality in any and all forms. Madame respected this talent.

"How was I to know all those writers were worth a sou . . . I never had a moment to read their books. To me, they were meshugga . . . and I always had to pay for their meals!"

Her recollections of some of the awesome literary figures who crossed her path in the twenties and thirties were fragmentary.

"Joyce? He smelled bad . . . couldn't see . . . ate like a bird."

"Hemingway? Women liked him, but I didn't. He was a loud-mouth and a show-off."

"Lawrence? Nice little man . . . shy. He would sit for hours staring into space while his pushy wife held the stage."

By the mid-twenties, Horace was in one of the several private schools he attended until the age of fifteen while Madame, when not presiding over her New York, London, or Paris headquarters, was in perpetual motion: "Why not? I was still young . . . what's forty going on fifty? Come Friday night, if I wanted a change, I would get on a train and surprise a few people who were taking it easy because it was Saturday."

Madame's relations with Horace, during these years, during his formative years, were not unlike her travels—erratic. She gave, she took, feuded, and made her peace. Horace entered Yale University. He was barely fifteen. At first his mother was immensely proud of him. She soon changed her tune. "Too green . . . it couldn't last . . . he flunked!" She next sent him to a "crammer" in England where, hopefully, he might be prepared to enter Cambridge University. He did. But again, after a few months, he was forced to leave. He next went off to the South Seas: "Wanted to be Gauguin!" Madame was not amused. On his return to America Horace now joined the Art Students League, but he was no Gauguin and soon had to give that up too. It was then he met a girl, a girl whom Madame was to call "the butcher's daughter."

Evelyn Schmitka came from Woodstock. Her father was, indeed, the local butcher. Horace took to this lithesome, carefree, and affectionate girl. They were married in the early thirties, while Madame was in Europe.

"Imagine! Without my blessing! The first news I had was when their baby was born . . . a girl. Toby, Toby Titus. I ask you, is that a suitable name?" Two years later, when Horace and his wife produced a son, there was the first faint hint of a reconciliation. Madame's dynastic feelings were strong. She had to see the child. "A beautiful boy!" Her eyes were moist with pleasure as she remembered and told me the story. "But he, he too, was given an odd name—Barry!"

Madame made her peace with the young parents. She loaded them with gifts, established trust funds for both her grandchildren, and declared: "Now the business will last for three hundred years!" Her optimism was premature. Neither Barry nor Toby Titus, when they grew up, took the slightest interest in "the business"—or, for that matter, in their fearsome grandmother. Horace's marriage failed to last. He was finally forced to work for his mother and did, intermittently, in various capacities, until I joined the company in 1952. It was then that he again fell into disfavor, because of "the colored girl" and was forced to live in the South of France.

Horace's arrival in Rome, as Madame apparently lay dying, relapsed and then recovered, at first did little to improve matters. But as the days went by and her strength returned, when she was again permitted to receive visitors, Horace spent long, intimate, and patient hours by his mother's bedside. He described, in his slow, ponderous way, the Italian painters we had selected, their studios, their work. At heart, he was an artist who had never been sufficiently encouraged, who lacked the essential talent, but whose feelings were sensitive and who yearned to escape from what he considered to be his mother's "commercial machinations." Madame soon tired of art and artists. "Let us really talk shop!" She cut him short.

Horace had been weaned on the beauty business and had grown to manhood fatally enmeshed in his mother's affairs. He did not lack information, opinions, or the ideas Madame fed on.

In Rome, as she recovered, he started discussing the need for a new luxury bath line for Helena Rubinstein. It would have to be glowingly packaged, opulently named.

"Good! Good!" Madame bounced up and down. She was still in bed. "But first, let's see . . . what bath preparations do we sell at present?"

" 'Heaven Scent,' " Horace answered, "is one of them."

"It sells well to provincial women," Madame countered.

"And 'White Magnolia' is another." He made it sound like an antiseptic. "What about 'Command Performance'?" Horace produced his trump card.

"Horrible . . . you're right." Madame sat up shaking both her fists at invisible enemies. "We lose money on that 'Performance.' "

Horace continued to expound on the new line he wanted to launch. He even produced a name for it, "Fleurs du Mal." Madame nodded excitedly. The words, "Fleurs du Mal," rolling off his tongue, were incredibly sonorous. For all her knowledge of French, Madame didn't have an inkling of their real meaning—"Flowers of Evil." Horace, forever intellectualizing, had plucked his bitter bouquet from Baudelaire's masterpiece and Madame, longing for action, swallowed the bait—hook, line and sinker.

A few more days of intense bedside discussions, letters and memo writing went by. Madame now took little walks up and down the Via Veneto leaning on her son's arm, talking, talking. Never had I heard her talk to him so much. They were like lovers exchanging intimate thoughts and confidences.

When Doctor Ovary declared that her recovery was complete, Madame tipped the nuns and, as with the Russian soldiers in Vienna, gave them each a lipstick. "Use it . . . why not? . . . it may help." The doctor's bill was next carefully scrutinized and paid in cash as was the hotel by Madame, who grumbled briefly at the "Ruinous extravagance" of her son.

She now decided that he would drive us from Rome to Maison Blanche, her house near Grasse. "I need air . . . an open car! More air . . . the Midi. We'll spend a week there. That will save me a little money." But the idea of basking in the sunshine, with a solicitous Horace, then made her rhapsodize to me: "He's so sensible in many ways. I always knew that he could be *extraordinary* . . . and, helpful!" She savored the word "extraordinary," but tripped over "helpful."

We set off from the Excelsior early on the following morning, with Horace at the steering wheel of a hired Pontiac convertible. Madame sat by his side, bundled in several fur coats. I was wedged in the back seat with the luggage. Some ten hours later, with but brief stops in Florence, Genoa, and at the French border, Madame cried out:

"Fish! What I want is fresh fish."

She had had a surfeit of fresh air, by then. Besides, we had barely eaten all day such was her hurry to reach our destination.

"I know of a place . . ." I ventured, stiff and frozen from my back seat. "It's some miles up the road: Villefranche."

"Good!" Madame licked her lips, "We'll stop there."

Between Monte Carlo and Nice Villefranche spills down a steep hillside to a huge bay deep enough to accommodate the largest ships. It is a colorful, eclectic place—filled with raucous sailors, easy girls—frequented by impoverished artists and slumming intellectuals. We dined, that night, at the Hotel Welcome. The chef, in his towering white cap, ambled out of a tiny kitchen to take our orders. Within minutes, our table was covered with succulent *pâtés*, cucumber and tomato salads, platters of *saucisson* sprinkled with olives.

"Eat! Eat!" Madame's knife harpooned each dish.

As we were finishing dinner a commotion heralded the arrival of new guests. I looked up and recognized Jean Cocteau. He was accompanied by two exquisitely dressed women and the French movie star Jean Marais. Cocteau, all hands and angular motions, his gray hair standing on end, glided forward.

"*Ma table est prête?*" On his lips this simple query had the ring of a call to arms.

I had first known him during my brief career on *Flair*. He had come to New York to write for the magazine and, since I spoke French and he knew no English, Fleur Cowles singled me out to be what he called, "my Antigone . . ."

I rose and greeted him. "*Ah, mon petit Patrick . . .*" He now raised himself on his toes, spread his arms and buzzed me warmly. Madame blinked. Horace seemed paralyzed. Cocteau next raised his arm like a Roman Centurion and said to Madame "*Je salue l'Impératrice de Byzance!*" Although they were old acquaintances—linked by Misia Sert, the painter Christian Bérard and even "that poor Jew boy," Proust—they had not met for years and it was only when I pronounced Cocteau's name that Madame thawed.

Complicated introductions followed. Cocteau always delighted in dramatizing the simplest occurrences, including chance meetings such as this one. With a conjurer's pantomime, he announced, "This is the Duchesse de Gramont . . . and here is Madame Wesweiller!"

"*Et maintenant . . .* And now I have the honor to introduce you to Jean Marais!"

I was vaguely acquainted with each of these people. Marais had been Cocteau's protégé for years. He was a big, smiling man, with the boyish quality of a young athlete in perpetual training. Only his high-pitched voice came as a surprise.

The Duchesse de Gramont, born Princess Maria Ruspoli, had made her way from the shelter of a tightly knit Roman family of ancient lineage, but small means, to ducal splendor in Paris. This was all a mistake! The duke, many years her senior, had settled for her older sister but when he saw Maria, who was to be a bridesmaid, he changed his mind. He chose her, and sent her sister packing. Maria soon gave the duke a much needed heir. She then settled down to a life of extravagance.

The marriage didn't last. After varied adventures, Maria de Gramont settled at Aix-en-Provence to devote her life to gardening. With Cocteau, Marais and Madame Wesweiller, she had emerged from her gardens, as they had from theirs, to enjoy an evening "on the town," at Villefranche.

Francine Wesweiller, neat, tiny and very rich, was the perfect ploy to Maria. While the duchess fluttered, as Cocteau made his introductions, Madame Wesweiller was impassive.

Later that night, as we left the Hotel Welcome filled with "fresh fish," Madame paused a moment to exchange farewells with Cocteau and "those two grand ladies." Cocteau, "The Poet," she called him, was splendidly formal, fanning the air with his hands, filling it with his compliments. "L'Impératrice . . ." he now called Madame.

"You're a naughty flatterer . . ." she wagged a finger at him. "Let us have lunch tomorrow," Madame suggested—extending an invitation to Maison Blanche.

"No, Princesse . . . you must come to us, to Santa Sospir, to Madame Wesweiller's villa at Cap d'Antibes." Cocteau refuted. Never one to refuse an invitation, Madame gave a quick nod. "We'll be there," and waved good-by.

"Lovely people," Madame affirmed, "important people!" Horace took the wheel while I, exhausted by the food and the excitement, settled down in the niche I had improvised for myself in the back seat. There was still a long ride ahead.

Two hours later, as we bumped along an uneven driveway, Madame woke me: "Everyone's gone out, devil take them!" I could just see the outline of a Moroccan villa. Filmy clouds veiled a crescent moon as, suddenly, every window in the house was brightly lighted.

"Maison Blanche . . ." Madame sat up in the front seat to survey her property. "White elephant . . ." Two sleepy servants now bowed on the doorstep. *"Pourquoi toutes les lumières?"* Madame countered their affable greetings, "Why all the lights?" She trotted into the hallway and the cool, spacious living room beyond.

White and green were the predominant colors. Great bouquets of early spring flowers stood on every table, window ledge, even on the marble floors. *"Pourquoi toutes les fleurs?"* was Madame's next remark. The servants made no reply. Horace looked pained. I examined our surroundings. Madame's personal stamp—the vibrant colors she loved, the juxtaposition of strange, exciting objects, the chaos—was totally lacking. At first glance, the interior of Maison Blanche reminded me of a newly opened resort hotel, luxurious, antiseptic, unlived in.

"I hate this place!" Madame said after a brief tour of inspection. "It cost me more than two hundred million francs to build and I've only spent six nights here!"

On the following morning, however, with sunlight bouncing off every wall, Maison Blanche epitomized Provence. Crickets hummed in the lavender patches growing wild under olive trees. Lizards darted around a swimming pool. The heady smell of early mimosa perfumed the air.

Madame, in a flowered dressing gown, sat on the terrace sipping her morning coffee.

"Ha! Lazy bones . . . there you are." She looked up at me. It was ten minutes to eight. "I've been here since daybreak. Look at the dreck." She pointed at piles of letters, which had been forwarded to her. Some were opened, others not.

"Here. Answer this . . . say 'No' to that . . . be sure to write lots of nice notes." Madame paused. "But first, listen to me. I want to talk about Horace. Is he still asleep?"

I nodded.

"Good! You know that he *can* be wonderful. Still, read this . . . read it aloud."

Madame handed me a lengthy letter written by Oscar Kolin, her nephew, from New York. It outlined, in the careful language of the born diplomat, Horace's latest activities in the South of France. The gist of the document was that Horace, while still drawing a large salary, had spent a great deal of money developing a jasmine farm and a perfume refinery near Grasse.

"Stupid!" Madame's fist crashed on her breakfast tray. "How could he do such a thing! There are experts who grow jasmine in commercial quantities. We buy from them . . . It's cheaper that way. I ask you . . . growing your own!" She almost choked, "Besides, we don't use much jasmine! Our perfumes are cheap! That's the secret of our success . . . cheap perfumes, toilet waters, colognes. Now I understand why Horace wants to launch his . . . his 'Fleurs du . . .' whatever it's called."

"Fleurs du Mal."

"Yes. More rubbish! Horace is a dreamer. He's spent all this money with a friend—with Scott . . . Mister Scott. That Scott is also bamboozling us! Growing jasmine . . . !"

She had hardly said these words when Horace appeared.

"Hallo, dear. I was just talking about all that lovely jasmine you plan to grow. You must tell us about it." Madame smiled. "Go on, tell us."

"Before lunch with Monsieur Cocteau," Horace answered, "I want to have you visit the jasmine farm. You can then see for yourself what we are doing."

"Good." She winked at me.

Later that morning, we drove through Grasse, down winding roads and into the countryside. There wasn't a sprig of jasmine to be seen anywhere.

"Interesting." Madame eyed the furrowed fields.

Some miles farther, Horace braked the car. "We're here!"

"Where?" Madame craned her neck.

"At the Helena Rubinstein jasmine farm."

She glanced over her shoulder at me as if to say, "See what I mean?"

A small stone house stood forlornly to the side of the road. I thought it unoccupied until an angular couple emerged from the front door, surrounded by yapping dogs, and rushed forward to greet us. Horace introduced Mr. and Mrs. Scott. He was guarded, cautious, already sensing his mother's disapproval—aware, too, of how intensely she disliked dogs. The Scotts led the way into a shabby living room and, although it was only midmorning, offered Madame a *pastis*. Another mark against them, I thought. Her aversion for the Scotts was now quite open.

She demanded without preliminaries, "Let us see how you are spending *our* money!" Silence. The unhappy couple looked to Horace for help. He merely stared at the ceiling.

"Very interesting," Madame turned to me.

"Might we visit the garden . . . the jasmine fields?" I asked, embarrassed.

"Pfft!" Madame flicked a glove in my direction.

"Yes, the garden . . . the jasmine fields. They are this way," Mr. Scott said as he led us out the back door.

He pointed to empty fields. "That's the garden where, soon, we hope to have a large yield of jasmine."

"Most interesting!" Madame said and, turning to me, added, in a stage whisper loud enough for everyone to hear, "What did I tell you? They're living in a fool's paradise . . . Horace's!"

Mr. Scott tried, in vain, to fill the breach. "Would you like to see our machinery?"

"*Your* machinery?"

Again, in complete silence, we followed him to a nearby barn. It was a wretched place, built haphazardly, in disrepair. Inside, aligned on blocks of concrete, were several vats and a large boiler.

"Expensive stuff!" Madame stroked the boiler. The Scotts exchanged furtive glances. Horace wandered out, humming to himself.

"Well, we must be on our way." Madame had spent barely ten minutes viewing the property. She now gave the boiler a look of distaste.

"Jasmine is O.K.—for bridal bouquets," were her parting words, "but even they are now being made in plastic. For perfume, synthetics are cheaper!"

Horace's face was of stone as he drove, without a word, to Cannes, thence along the Grande Corniche to Nice. It was only when we reached Beaulieu that he managed to suggest, "We're early for lunch. Let's have an *apéritif* and talk things over . . ."

Madame answered, "Good idea!"

"We'll go to La Résèrve," He had named Beaulieu's most expensive restaurant.

"You're crazy!" Madame barked back.

"Crazy?"

"Never mind . . ."

Horace's face had turned crimson. "You were vile to my friends . . ." he blurted out. "You're wicked. You're cruel. You're a miser. All you think of is money . . . money . . . money!—and now, now you say I'm crazy!" With that, he stopped the car, struggled out and reached for the ignition.

"Here!" He tossed the keys in my lap. "My mother is your problem!"

For minutes on end Madame sat staring blindly at the dashboard. I was equally numb until she turned to me: "It's a good thing you can drive . . . ," she murmured. "Let's go home. You can call The Poet. Tell him . . . tell him I can't come to lunch because I don't feel too good."

# "You'll Be the Guinea Pig"

❧ ❧

"Let's go home!" had been Madame's only reaction when Horace stomped off. Back in the house, lost in thought, she emptied closets, cleaned out drawers, took inventory of her possessions. I stayed clear of her, but telephoned "The Poet," explaining that Madame was "indisposed" and we would not be coming to lunch that day. Cocteau chuckled. "Empresses have every right to be indisposed. It's their secret of survival!" Later he was to tell me: "Madame Rubinstein feeds on human differences, particularly those of her own invention. But beware of her silences! When they occur, she is planning an offensive."

Madame continued to be silent on the following day, as we flew back to Paris. She maintained this stolid attitude, even after we returned to New York a week later. Distant, vague, preoccupied, she went about her business as of old, appeared at the office punctually at nine, ate a solitary lunch at her desk, and returned home in the evening long after everyone had left. To those close to her, who hesitantly asked what was wrong, Madame replied: "I've had a terrible shock."

It was soon evident that my vague status as her traveling companion and secretary-on-the-wing had been greatly enhanced by the mystery shrouding our sudden return. Obviously privy to some dark secret, I was repeatedly pumped.

:[ 193 ]:

"You weren't due back in America for another month!"

"Madame is acting mighty strange!"

"C'mon, tell us what happened . . ."

People who had hardly acknowledged my existence now courted me. I enjoyed their attentions, but kept my mouth shut.

"No one must know what happened . . . yet!" On the plane, flying home, Madame had sworn me to secrecy, solemnly shaking my hand. It was the first of many such pacts.

Even her husband, Prince Gourielli, invited me to lunch. After countless vodkas, he growled in his jovial, clumsy way:

"What eats up Helena?"

"I wish I knew!"

Some days later, Oscar Kolin summoned me to his office. He did so unobtrusively, by having me go there in the evening. But I was unable to give him satisfaction.

Only Madame's elder son, Roy, seemed to know instinctively what had happened. In the men's room, looking at me out of the corner of his eye, over a urinal, he said: "I suppose you're back early because my dear mother had a row with my dear brother!"

Roy had guessed. The cat was out of the bag! He soon spread the word around. The brothers had never been overly fond of one another, and Madame always encouraged them to compete for her uncertain affections.

Meantime, aware of what was going on behind her back, she waited for a few words, a mere nod of contrition, from Horace. Nothing came. She next consulted her lawyer. Well experienced in handling his client *and her son*, Harold Weill gently dodged the issue. "For the time being," he counseled, "the best thing is to do nothing. . . ." This sound advice, like a red cloth waved before a bull, stimulated Madame into action. Within twenty-four hours she blurted out several versions of what had happened between herself and Horace to anyone who cared to listen. Madame even carried a piece of paper in her purse carefully inscribed in her angular hand with what few words she still remembered of his outburst: "You are wicked, cruel, a miser! All you think of is money, money, money!" It was shown to relatives, friends, even to Horace's two children. "See what he thinks of me." Her eyes were moist. What could they say? Their embarrassed silence seemed to give her new vigor; flaying the air she struck whatever was handy—a table, a chair, someone's leg. "Well, what does it matter if Horace said I'm a miser? As for the money . . . if I didn't think of it who would?"

Madame had recovered her old fighting spirit. Her voice, for a time so small and subdued, regained its authority. She pummeled her desk, gave vent to tantrums, clattered up and down the office corridors: "Is everyone working?" Horace had been temporarily dismissed from her thoughts. He was "cuckoo." Life had to go on, and with it the plans, the plots she spun with such skill, lived by, and thrived on.

"What's happening to Gourielli?" Madame asked me one morning.

I now had a proper office next door to hers, and a secretary. "I want you to be real strong . . ." Madame said when she gave me these amenities. Miss Fox, who had been the previous occupant of the small, paneled cubbyhole, was relegated to the fourth floor, and my neighbors, besides Madame Rubinstein, were Miss Hopkins and a new "little girl" with a brash, cheerful voice and a cheeky manner—Nancy Goldburgh. Our corner windows faced Fifth Avenue and from mine I could just see De Pinna's, the department store, and Cartier's. Oscar Kolin, Roy Titus, and the sales manager, George Carroll, all had offices nearby. This was the matrix of the business—the executive suite.

"We must do something with Gourielli!" Madame ordered. "Set up a meeting with Oscar; with the salesmen, with Fox. Who else?" Madame pondered a moment. "When?" I asked. "As soon as possible. Right away!" She trotted out as Mildred Sullivan, my new secretary, began dialing telephone numbers. I was lucky, as I was always to be, in the secretaries Madame invariably selected to work for me. "I'll find you someone," she said, and she did. After one of her forays around the building, Madame one day produced a big, handsome girl: "Irish, like you!"

Mildred Sullivan lived in Brooklyn, where her husband worked as a deep-sea diver for the port of New York. This intrigued Madame, who was always curious to know every last detail about her employees' personal lives. "Fancy," she remarked, "working under water, and being paid for it! I wonder what he finds?"

"Sludge, silt . . ." I answered. Equally intrigued, I had already checked.

"What's that?"

"Mud."

"Mud! So that's what I pay New York taxes for!"

A summons from Madame invariably produced an immediate flurry of activity, and executives, assistants and secretaries, all armed with voluminous files, soon clogged her outer office.

By now, Madame was seated behind her Renaissance desk, all but obscured by it, puzzling over other matters. She had forgotten Gourielli and was studying photographs in *Esquire* magazine.

"See all those nekkid ladies . . ." I glanced over her shoulder at a double-spread. It was of Brigitte Bardot, who had not as yet become a world famous film star. "French girl!" Madame sniffed. "They're always the first to take their clothes off. I wonder what depilatory she uses?"

"People are waiting outside, Madame. . . ."

"Ha? Why?"

"To discuss Gourielli!"

"Quick . . . get them in here!"

The House of Gourielli had been founded shortly after Madame's marriage to Prince Gourielli, in 1938. "I had to do something to keep Atchie busy." "Atchie" was Madame's pet name for the Prince. His background, like that of many white Russians, was hazy. He alternatively claimed to have been born in Tiflis, Sebastopol, Saint Petersburg. This all depended on how much vodka he had drunk. After the Revolution, Archil Gourielli somehow reached Paris and first survived there by reputedly driving a taxi. When Madame met him, he had gravitated to earning his living playing bridge and backgammon —two games at which he excelled. These gave him an entree to some of the best circles.

Many of her friends had been urging her to remarry, although she was of an age when most women are content caring for their grandchildren. "What do I need another husband for?" Madame, although tempted, kept repeating. What she failed to add was that she had fallen in love. Phyllis Digby Morton, an English journalist, recalled that Madame endlessly discussed the pros and cons of this alliance. Gourielli had just formally asked for her hand. She fled to London. "I must think it over." The two ladies were walking around Berkeley Square and after the fourth time round, Mrs. Morton wearily suggested, "Helena, every woman needs a husband . . . if only to get her a taxi." This sound advice appealed to Madame. "You're right, you're right!"

But she still hedged, and, before taking the final step, demanded proof of Gourielli's lineage. According to an article in *Confidential,* an American magazine devoted exclusively to gossip, Gourielli presented her with the *Almanach de Gotha.* He had, so the story went, ordered a special page printed and inserted therein, which gave full particulars of his heritage. Satisfied, but still cautious, Madame summoned a team of lawyers. She instructed them to prepare a carefully worded marriage contract specifying that all of the moneys she might give Prince Gourielli would revert to her, should he die first. This may have seemed odd. Archil Gourielli was fully twenty years her junior. Yet in the long run, Madame proved her foresight. She outlived him by ten years. When the Prince died, in 1955, he left half a million dollars. She was the sole beneficiary.

"Gourielli stinks . . . the bookkeeper's just told me it has lost us a packet this year . . . ," Madame cried out as the meeting convened. But, before she could say more, George Carroll queried: "Was it ever meant to do anything else?"

He was a large man, with a hearty manner and a Southern drawl. His conversation invariably tacked between sly confidences and overt pronouncements.

"Fool!" Madame banged her desk. "Do you think we pay your salary out of a loss?"

Mr. Carroll gave his Countess Mara tie a tentative tug. "Madame, honey, I always thought it was a nice tax loss for *you-all.*"

"*You-all* are quite wrong!" She sprang to her feet. "And Mr. Carroll, the only honey I know of comes in a jar!"

Oscar Kolin, the family mediator, said, "Madame, Madame . . . we're all here to help."

"That," she blasted, "obviously doesn't include him . . . *honey!*"

"Mr. Carroll means well."

"He means *too* well. Forget it! Let's really talk shop . . . about Gourielli. I'll start!"

Speeches were a rarity in Madame's life; but when she made one, her staccato sentences rose and fell, with barely a pause.

It was Juno speaking with the voice of a Polish hawker. Blustering invectives followed whining pleas. Madame banged her desk, clutched her breasts, raised both arms, then dropped them, as if smitten speechless by a terrible tragedy. And still she talked on, "We must . . . we must . . . !"

The gist of her passionate monologue, which froze everyone into a dead silence, was that Madame had had one of her "visions." It wasn't exactly original, and she admitted to depending upon her staff to make it appear so. "We must do something for the men!" she said. "I want Gourielli to be our new men's line. It will be the finest on the market. You will all benefit. I will benefit . . . even Patrick will benefit." Everyone in the room turned to where I sat, partially hidden by a massive cupboard. They gave me encouraging smiles. Madame went on. "I swear, we'll make millions. The time is ripe. We have the know-how, the facilities, even . . . ," she nodded at Mr. Carroll, "the salesman."

Madame then dismissed the gathering and, as everyone filed out, called after me, "Patrick, stay! I want to talk to you. Alone!" I closed the door and stood at attention before her.

"So what do you think? Bring a chair and sit down here, next to me." She shifted her weight so that we almost huddled together, licked her lips and said, "I'm telling you . . . this can be the greatest thing for all of us. It's not that I need the money or, for that matter, care a fig for the extra business. But we can't afford to sit back. I swear, a Gourielli men's line will be a huge success. Besides, we have to diversify. We need new customers. I depend on your help two hundred per cent!"

It was now my turn to extend my arms. What was to be my role in this new endeavor?

Although we were sitting side by side, Madame cupped her hand over her mouth and lowered her voice. "No one knows. . . . I've already hired a wonderful woman for Gourielli."

"Then why will you need my help?"

"To help her! By helping her you will be helping me. And then the *others* won't be jealous . . . of us."

Another of Madame's ploys—a subplot. She well knew that sooner or later resentment might grow throughout the company if she continued showing me too much favor. So I was to be palmed off on Gourielli, to help "The Wonderful Woman."

Madame was the first person I ever met who could foresee every step she had to take when faced with a combination business-and-human jigsaw puzzle. She forced the pieces into place, and if a few were missing, she knew instinctively that they would be found in time to complete the job. At the time, the principal asset of the House of Gourielli was a fine stone mansion next door to the St. Regis Hotel, on East Fifty-fifth Street. Madame had purchased the building just before the war, and leased it, as she did the Fifth Avenue offices, to her business. "Why not? It's a nice extra income."

"The House of Gourielli"—Madame had elected this name to compete with "The House of Matchabelli," another perfume business started by a White Russian—had the look of a thrift shop specializing in discarded colognes. Its windows were seldom clean. Their contents were haphazard. Dusty bottles, powder boxes with equivocal names— "Something Blue" ("For the bride . . . something new, something old, *Something Blue*") were wedged between strange gift items "Suitable for a week-end gift for the hostess who has everything." These included bottle openers, pill boxes, hand warmers, each swathed in yards of tulle and decorated with an artificial flower and a ribbon bow.

Inside the building there was marble everywhere, some real, most of it simulated. A graceful curved staircase with an elaborate wrought-iron balustrade rose to the second floor where, amid tufted sofas and numerous display cases holding more useless gifts, several genteel ladies spent their days wrapping "creations." These ladies were a choice group of Madame's favorite "poor women"—widows, the superannuated, the partially retired—who eked out a living doing unnecessary work.

The ground floor boutique was equally depressing. It had been subjected to many transitions and "improvements" during the past decade. As a result, a "Bride's Corner" vied with one entitled "Perfume Notions," and another named, "The Apothecary Shop." Behind a long marble counter sat several more of Madame's lethargic "nice women," invariably tatting or knitting baby garments, which they tried to sell to their rare victims. Venetian vitrines, terra cotta caryatids, gilded pagoda lamps added further exotic notes to these dusty, jumbled surroundings which, under the name of The House of Gourielli, were also used as a depository for some of Madame's decorating mistakes.

Madame now attempted to describe to me "The Wonderful Woman" she had hired to put Gourielli back on its feet. "She's a real lady, you know, and a good businesswoman . . . she was the beauty editor of *Harper's Bazaar*. Nice, distinguished, clever . . ." Madame now snapped open her purse, foraged inside it and drew out an old restaurant bill. "Look on the back . . . read it aloud! You'll find out her name." I did. "Eleanor McVickar—H.B.'s Beauty Editor. V. clever. Under twenty."

I studied the scrap of paper and noted that the luncheon had taken place at The Colony, where Madame wouldn't have set foot if she hadn't nurtured high hopes—and that their meal had cost only twenty-six dollars. Eleanor McVickar was evidently a small eater, or a shrewd psychologist. What did the "under twenty" mean? I asked Madame. "None of your business!" she said. "Still . . . you might as well know. All she wants is eighteen thousand dollars a year." Since I only now earned a meager eight thousand a year, it fascinated me to hear my new post described as "the greatest thing for me."

"And where do I fit in?" I asked.

"You'll be the guinea pig," Madame smiled coquettishly. There was a pause while she seemed to take a sudden interest in the texture of my skin. "Could be better, could be worse. Still, you're presentable. You'll be the Gourielli man!"

Some days later I moved from the Rubinstein office on Fifth Avenue to the poky third floor of the Gourielli building with my secretary, Mildred Sullivan. Sure enough, many of my co-workers claimed I had fallen from favor. They were hard-pressed to find reasons to substantiate this gossip until, without warning, Madame produced another acolyte to fill my shoes. Gloria O'Connor, whose twin sister Countess Crespi had recommended Madame's savior, Doctor

Ovary, in Rome, was installed in the space I had vacated. She was far less experienced than I had been six months previously, when Madame hired me, but her smile, lilting voice, and refined manners evidently fired Madame with great enthusiasm. "Such a high-class girl . . . knows only the smartest people . . . I'll probably take her to France when I go next time."

Was I supposed to be jealous? On our return from Europe, Madame had given me what appeared to be a position of some importance, or so it seemed to me when I was put in an office next to hers. Now, equally suddenly, I was being banished to Gourielli. Was I to fear for my future in her company? In those early days, thoughts of insecurity seldom crossed my mind. I merely shrugged and decided to enjoy the respite.

With the passing years, I learned that this strategy was typical of Madame's curious policy of "build them up, knock 'em down—then make them work harder." Edward Titus, Horace, Roy, even the Prince (not to mention innumerable others) had all suffered similar treatment. So I went my way, to Gourielli, where I soon came to enjoy every stolen moment away from Madame's forceful and demanding presence.

Until Mrs. McVickar appeared, my duties were vague. Madame occasionally phoned. "Busy?"

"Of course."

"I'll bet."

My office could have been that of a theatrical agent on his uppers. The pink paint peeled off the walls, and the cinnamon carpet was dark brown with age. The furnishings, here, consisted of two battered desks and a clutter of discarded upholstered armchairs that regurgitated their springs. But I was happy, for the corner drugstore coffee was excellent and friends constantly popped in on me to chat. "Midtown is so convenient!"

This state of euphoria didn't last long. Three weeks to the day, and Mrs. McVickar descended upon us. On learning of her arrival, Madame proclaimed: "Good! Now the honeymoon is over for Patrick."

Without an introduction from a single Rubinstein executive, Mrs. McVickar just walked in of a Monday morning, and announced: "I'm Eleanor McVickar. How in the hell can you stand it here?"

Impeccably groomed, blessed with decisive speech, this stubborn lady lost no time in assaying the situation. "Well, better roll up our sleeves and get to work. I can see there is plenty to be done in this funeral home!"

Mrs. McVickar taught me a valuable lesson or two. After a quick visit through her tumble-down fief, and an examination of the accounts on which it had somehow survived, she set down on paper an itemized list of her requirements. She next put me to work formulating a plan to reduce expenses, and had me ask the Rubinstein accounting department for a proper budget. Such a thing had never existed. It failed to materialize. Mrs. McVickar bided her time for forty-eight hours. She then picked up the telephone, advising me: "When you want action, go straight to the top!"

I heard her ask for Madame Rubinstein. The echo of a guttural "Hallo" was followed by "What's new?" Mrs. McVickar, whose carefully controlled temper could be judged only by her unusually precise enunciation, strung out her reply.

"What's new? *Nothing*, Madame. What's more, I don't believe you hired me to tell you this! I sent to your management memos, itemized budgets, ideas. . . . No answers have been forthcoming. I am still waiting in this limbo called the Gourielli Building for directives."

An angry roar reverberated over the telephone. Then, silence.

"She's on her way over. Let us go down," Mrs. McVickar's voice was firm, "and meet Madame Rubinstein when she arrives."

Within minutes, Madame charged in through the front door, trailed by a number of her executives. Her bowler hat was askew and her eyes blazed.

"Good morning, Madame," Mrs. McVickar smiled. "I'm glad to see you've come with reinforcements."

"I don't need them!" Madame spat. "But I can't do without them. Now quickly, let us see what is to be done."

For the next hour we all toured the six decrepit floors of the Gourielli Building. Serenely, Mrs. McVickar pointed out appalling deficiencies. The elevator didn't work; the heating system produced uncertain blasts of steam followed by loud hammering which, somehow, set in motion the air conditioning; there was thick dust everywhere. With a fingertip, Madame traced the word "Clean" on several pieces of furniture and signed each notation with her initials. This was her way of getting action from the cleaning staff.

Since there was no room in the building where such a large group could be seated, we ranged ourselves in the stair well, where a shouting match ensued—until Rubinstein's packaging director, who was also in charge of decorating and arranging the Gourielli displays, was summoned. He was not one of Madame's favorite employees . . . "too slippery . . ." so she blasted away at him. "This is how you spent all that money prettying up the place last year *and* the year before?" To avoid her sweeping gesture of disdain, he was forced to take two steps upward. Few people could understand his strange accent, least of all Madame, and the rush of his words was wasted on her. With an impatient, "That's enough! I can't understand your English *or* your German," she ordered him to be quiet. No one dared tell her that all the while he had been speaking French.

As in many such impromptu gatherings presided over by Madame Rubinstein, nothing was then accomplished concerning Gourielli. Disgusted, she pushed everyone out of her way, tripped down the stairs, and there spied the "nice women" seated behind the counter knitting. "Beautiful. . . . Look, they're so busy! We should turn this into a Maternity Shop—perfumes for the mother-to-be . . . little garments . . . gifts. Aii, I swear, there's a fortune to be made!"

But she hadn't taken into consideration Mrs. McVickar who, without a moment's hesitation, stepped forward. "Madame . . . Gourielli, if you will recall, is to be a Men's Shop. There will be no more brides' gifts, apothecary corners, or knitting done on the premises while I'm around!"

"Good, good! You're right. But couldn't we have just one little corner . . . for babies?"

"No, Madame."

"Then do as you please. I'll see to it that you get all the help you need."

Within a month the ground floor was transformed into a handsome Men's Boutique—one of the first in New York, for in those days, almost twenty years ago, such specialized emporiums were rare. The décor, to conform with the oddly proportioned rooms, was of white marble enhanced by steel, brass, and glass fixtures. It was quite contrary to Madame's taste. There were none of the gold vitrines, purple curtains, pink mirrors that gave such a feeling of exotic, Middle-European opulence to the Rubinstein salons. Everything was cool and linear. "Looks like a hospital!" Madame could scarcely disguise her disapproval when she first saw the airy, uncluttered rooms.

While work progressed on the Gourielli Men's Boutique, Mrs. McVickar produced her trump card. She set about transforming the second floor of the building into a self-contained barber shop. There were cries of anguish from Madame. "You're mad! A barber shop . . .!" Words failed her—particularly when Mrs. McVickar countered with: "If you can have hair salons at Rubinstein, why shouldn't I have a barber shop at Gourielli?" Prince Gourielli, who had just returned from a winter holiday playing backgammon in Palm Beach, added fuel to the fire. "Prince, Russian Prince, cannot run barber shop . . . is not dignified . . . what will friends say?" Again, Mrs. McVickar had a ready answer. "Prince Romanoff owns a very successful restaurant in Hollywood and all his friends go there to eat. Your friends, I hope, will come here to have their hair cut!" The subject was dropped.

By now, Mrs. McVickar had learned the tortuous ins and outs of the Rubinstein organization. Like any other big, successful company, it was a maze packed with loopholes, through which she maneuvered contracts and purchase orders without having to listen to Madame Rubinstein's repeated cries of ruin. These, now, were almost stilled for good. One day rumors reached us that Madame had been rushed to the hospital. The next day we learned that she had been operated on, and the third, that she was dying. Madame had cancer.

In this atmosphere of terrible uncertainty, Gourielli and the Gourielli Men's Shop were forgotten by top management. They were more concerned with the contents of Madame's will. Undeterred, Mrs. McVickar forged ahead. She ordered barber chairs, sinks, hair dryers, all of the paraphernalia needed for a barber shop. I had never dreamed that anything could be so complicated. Endlessly we tested shampoos, hair dyes, tonics, even face creams—adapted from Rubinstein formulas. "What works on a woman's face should be equally beneficial to a man." Mrs. McVickar loaded me with samples. "Try them out! Report!" I fairly bloomed, occasionally broke out in a rash, then bloomed again.

Meanwhile, reports of Madame's illness began to filter through the barriers of censorship imposed by her family. Horace returned from exile in the South of France and was once more forgiven by his mother. We heard, via the grapevine, that there had been a touching bedside reconciliation which did much to hasten her recovery. Her cancer of the cervix had, hopefully, been arrested, but for several weeks it was touch and go. Only the closest members of the family were allowed to visit her. Then, one Saturday morning at eight, I was awakened by the jangling of my telephone.

"Hallo, is that you, Patrick?" Her voice, instead of being commanding, was sweet and muted.

I'm a wretched conversationalist on the telephone, especially early in the morning. I was touched to the quick hearing her again, and, for a moment, quite speechless.

She wanted to see me. I hurried over to the Polyclinic Hospital where I found Madame swaddled like an Indian squaw, in a hospital blanket, lying on top of her bed. Her usually jet black hair was flecked with gray. I was startled. She had never looked so frail, so old—not even during her recent illness in Rome. She must have been very close to death during the preceding weeks. I was unable to express my emotions. I knew to what extent she hated sympathy.

"What wonderful flowers, Madame . . ."

"Such a waste!" She flipped a hand at a huge, formal bouquet on her bedside table. "People should send them when I go home! Then I could really enjoy them . . . pfft! You didn't come all the way here to talk about flowers!" Madame propped herself up. "What I want to hear about is Gourielli!"

For the next two hours, I tried to fill her in on what had been accomplished. Madame sucked on her thumb. She listened, but she showed little reaction. I described the Gourielli Men's Shop—the boutique, the clothes, the accessories—adding that it would undoubtedly be the first place in the world to incorporate all of these things with a barber shop, massage facilities, even a sauna. She never said a word, but simply kept staring at me until I ended my spiel with:

"We're even going to have a ticker-tape machine. Imagine! Our clients will be able to get the latest stock market quotations while they have their hair cut!"

"Better a broker," Madame said, dryly. "His commissions will make more money for the shop than the ticker-tape machine."

After my first Saturday hospital visit with Madame Rubinstein, she urged me to see her regularly: "Come over at night when the office closes, on Saturdays, Sundays!" Besides her anxiety concerning Gourielli, she was lonely. The hospital routine bored her as did many of the members of her family who tried to show their devotion. "I know they feel that they have to see me. But they never tell me a thing of interest!" To keep her distracted, extra telephones and a typewriter, with relays of secretaries, were installed by her bedside. Madame's husky voice now greeted us almost daily as we arrived at work. Mrs. McVickar and I soon learned to dodge her questions with cheerful chatter. She listened, "Yes . . . Aha . . . Ha!" until one day, when I was describing press plans for the opening of the Gourielli shop, she interjected: "It's all up to you, Patrick! You must now be strong and do something really worthwhile. I've already talked to Mrs. McVickar. You must handle the publicity for Gourielli."

With these few words, Madame launched me on a long, sometimes erratic, but always entertaining, career as her personal publicist. She had first sensed I had a flair for this vital aspect of the cosmetics business in Paris—when she set me to writing releases. Now, she said: "People like you! To be successful in publicity people have to like you." In the past, Madame had employed practically every expert in the field including Benjamin Sonnenberg who was reputed never to accept a fee of less than a million dollars (usually in stock options) for publicizing what Madame called "Nice little accounts. . . ." Pepsi-Cola, Pepperidge Farm, Unilever. "But for me," she was quick to add, "he helped . . . as a friend." Few people knew better how to take advantage of their friends. In publicity, this included Igor Cassini, Marianne Strong, Eleanor Lambert.

While Madame maintained her own P.R. offices, within the structure of each of her companies, she was always open to suggestions and outside help. "Who knows *who* has good ideas . . . even a nebbish can have good ideas!" The publicity staff at Helena Rubinstein, while held together by a faithful nucleus, included at one time or another a number of Russian and Polish expatriates, free-lance writers—anyone, in fact, on whom Madame took pity. "The poor thing needs a job . . . put her in publicity!"

It was an expendable department. And yet Madame had her own personal ideas concerning publicity. She had to be the center of attention. "Start at the top!" To emphasize this, she pointed her hands to herself: "After that it's all luck, contacts; or people like you, Patrick, who know how to spread the gospel . . . *my gospel.*"

Although I knew little or nothing about publicity, Madame's basic ground rules proved invaluable. "First you must have a good story to give. Next you must know how to give it. Last, call up the best women's editors on the most important newspapers in New York. . . ."

"There are seven, Madame!"

"Call them all."

"Which . . . comes first?"

"The one with the largest circulation. *Tell her I'm opening a Men's Shop!*"

"And then?"

"Call up the others! And don't forget to ring up the *Wall Street Journal*. I'm sure they'll be interested in the silly ticker-tape machine. The stock market's down. What else can they have to write about?"

I followed her instructions. The *Daily News* then, as now, had the greatest circulation of any newspaper in the country. When I asked to speak with their beauty editor, a clear, tripping, Irish voice announced, "Antoinette Donnelly." She listened, patiently, to my sales pitch and said, "Dear boy, Helena's an old friend. I'll do anything for her. But why should I brave the hazards of New York traffic when you can describe everything on the phone?"

My next victim, Virginia Pope of *The New York Times* readily accepted my invitation to come and view the Gourielli premises. Pat Lewis of the *Journal American*, Ann Yates of the *World Telegram*, Alma Archer of the *Mirror* were all equally patient and amiable, while I fumbled; "Would you, could you, might you be interested in the new Gourielli Men's Shop?" Only Eugenia Sheppard, of the *Herald Tribune*, gave me a tough time. "Gourielli. . . . What's that?" Several phones were jangling away in her office. I realized I had to be precise. When she returned to my line, I said, "Madame Rubinstein, Helena Rubinstein, is opening a Men's Shop. It's the first of its kind. When would you like to come and see it?"

"Why didn't you tell me at once?"

"Inexperience!"

"You're the first press agent who ever admitted to *that*! I'll be over tomorrow morning at noon."

Some days later she ran one of her breezy columns under the headline: "Young Irishman helps launch new men's shop for Helena Rubinstein!" I was described as being impeccably dressed. My glib sartorial philosophy borrowed, for the most part, from Beau Brummell, was quoted: "Clean linen, country washed! Handsewn shoes honed with flat champagne! Well-worn tweeds often rained on!" It made me sound like a smug young pup; but it was entertaining and it did put Gourielli across, for Miss Sheppard next carefully enumerated the services available in the shop: "Jerry, a star among barbers, believes in only using straight razor blades to contour the head!" "Tired executives will love Ischian mud packs" and "Special snacks are prepared by the St. Regis Hotel chef at no extra cost!" All of this was true, except for the "Ischian mud," which was actually manufactured in Madame's Long Island factory. But these heady words inaugurated a trend of good grooming care for men. Until then, de luxe barber shops were a rarity, while men's cosmetics were limited to after-shave lotions, colognes, and deodorants. They were looked upon as effete. Madame's unpredictable nose sensed the enormous potential of this new business and had she not grown bored and given in to Prince Gourielli, who objected to his name being linked with "a common barber shop," Gourielli could have survived triumphantly.

When Madame read Eugenia Sheppard's write-up she was furious. I was "stealing" her thunder. From her hospital bed she stormed at anyone who would listen: "Fancy wasting all those words on *that* boy! Why does Sheppard write about him? *I swear*, he must be building himself up for another job!" Again, she was jealous. It took me years to live down this article and from that time I dodged reporters, side-stepped their personal questions, ducked out of camera range for fear of rekindling her wrath. I had learned the basic lesson which no public relations person can afford to overlook—especially if working for a woman of ego—*Never get your name in print even if it does help the client*. Still, had it not been for Eugenia Sheppard's enthusiastic words, *Life*, *Time*, *Newsweek*, and most of the women's service magazines, besides the daily press all over the country, might well have overlooked the Gourielli phenomenon. "Publicity starts at the top," Madame had said and Eugenia Sheppard was the top. Other journalists copied her, sought and found ideas in her column, were inspired by her. This was another invaluable lesson. One really good write-up can start a chain reaction. *Life* magazine produced a three-page photographic essay on the Gourielli Men's Shop and had it not been that the Pope was near death, my own sinner's face, heavily disguised with Ischian mud, might well have appeared on their cover, instead of his saintly one. When Mrs. McVickar sent Madame an itemized list of the publicity we had worked so hard to get—underscoring that in the terms of paid advertising it was worth around eight hundred thousand dollars—she immediately returned it with, scribbled in the margin: *"It should have been a million!"*

Even though the shop was fully stocked, the barbers busy barbering, and clients storming the doors, these articles preceded the official opening—the press party proper. It was Madame's opinion that the first wave of publicity was always needed during "the dry run," when the staff was busy familiarizing themselves with their work, and that the press party then produced a second flurry of publicity. As usual, she wasn't wrong.

As the opening date approached, I was aware, through secretarial rumors, that Madame had issued orders from hospital to every member of her family, including the reluctant Prince Gourielli, that each was to be present at this event. I now knew, instinctively, that whatever I did, and however successful, someone was waiting in the wings to take a pot shot at me and to criticize my efforts. Miss Arden, Elizabeth Arden, liked to call the Rubinstein family "A Polish Mafia." She was right. They did stick together, but it wasn't always for their mutual benefit. What they feared most was the head of their clan's invective.

Although this was the first of the many social functions I was to organize for Madame Rubinstein during the next twelve years, I faced the ordeal with all the glee of a host on the make. Why not? First, I recalled the advice of my grandmother, who believed in mixing people freely: "An acrobat, a conjurer, a few chorus girls . . . are manna to any party!" Next, I thought of my mother who was more of a gourmet and a horticulturist: "The hors d'oeuvres must be piping hot, the drinks icy cold, and the flowers . . . the flowers as profuse as at a christening that occurs only six months after the wedding!" Observing women friends and ex-employers added further fuel to my Emily Postery. Carmel Snow said: "Keep all of the windows open. Draughts produce motion." Fleur Cowles also opted for movement, human movement: "Don't let anyone sit with anyone else for more than ten minutes unless you're sure they'll ultimately end up in bed together." While I once heard Tallulah Bankhead observe that her parties were always a success because she made it a point to appear nude as soon as most of the guests were present, I dismissed that interesting snippet but, armed with these few invaluable tips, I organized, planned and plotted. My guest list of more than two hundred people was a mixture of personalities currently in the news and, of course, the press. When I submitted it to Madame, she immediately deleted about a third of the names, saying: "Too much trash Why should I feed them all?"

She was equally severe about the food and refused to let us serve smoked salmon and champagne. "You can have one or the other, but not both!" She next cut down on the hot hors d'oeuvres, particularly the runny ones, saying, "They'll mess up the carpets." Notwithstanding such arguments, since we were now well under our official budget, I secretly ordered both the champagne and the salmon. I was to employ this dodge for all of Madame's parties. She was informed; she vetoed, cut down. I then added. It was another of our little games.

The Gourielli party was set for a Thursday. Again, from her hospital bed, Madame selected this particular day, saying: "Midweek is always best. Most smart people give their servants Thursday night off. . . . So they have nothing better to do than go to parties."

I posted myself at the front door with Mrs. McVickar as the crowds surged in. By six-thirty the shop was filled to overflowing. There were three Gabor sisters present plus Gore Vidal *and* Truman Capote (to get them both to come I had told each, separately, that the other was to be there). Euphoria soon set in as I introduced Salvador Dali to a surviving Dolly Sister as "Madame Dolly." He understood "Dali," grabbed her and vanished into the crowd.

It was then that my eyes nearly popped out of my head. Was I seeing things? I detected a purple bowler hat bobbing up and down in the center of a cluster of people. Could it be Madame or one of her sisters—Stella, Manka—who, at a distance, might easily be mistaken for her. No! While her family copied her taste in jewelry, baroque furnishings, even hair styles, they drew a line at bowler hats. But only on the previous day, I had seen her on a hospital bed. How could she have had the strength to get up, brave the cold, dress herself to the nines, and then face an unruly New York cocktail mob? I pushed my way toward the bowler hat. It was now engulfed by arms, hands, heads, trays. It reappeared, briefly, out of this human scrimmage. Sure enough, there was the glitter of a familiar emerald and ruby brooch caught in the center of the hatband. I could now see the stony profile with its tapered brow, gimlet eye, firm chin line. Yes! It was Madame—and what's more she wore a new dress, at least one I had never seen, cut like a Russian peasant's blouse. I slowly edged my way toward her and, at a complete loss as to what to say, gently kissed her cheek. I had never done this before. She turned, looking rather angry, and whacked me on the shoulder with surprising strength.

"Ha! Patrick . . . surprised?" Although her cheeks had sunk during her illness, the smile she gave me made her look like a happy girl—one who has successfully pulled a fast one.

"But . . . but Madame, should you be out of bed?"

"Had to see what you were up to!

"Besides . . . ," Madame pointed left and right to a gray-haired man and a small woman. Both seemed to be supporting her. "I've taken my precautions. . . .

"That's my doctor and she's the nurse.

"Nice party!" Madame now nodded. "But the doctor says I should be getting back to the hospital. Before I go, see to it that I get a plate of smoked salmon. The food in the hospital is terrible. . . ."

She left, some ten minutes later, cradling a plate in her arms.

For the next few months, my business life was centered entirely around the Gourielli Men's Shop. No sooner was she out of hospital than Madame complained: "You should be involved in other things . . . with Rubinstein, *with me*. Gourielli, mark my words, is a losing proposition." What was I to say? I was kept busy and found it difficult to divide my time between the Rubinstein headquarters on Fifth Avenue and my office on Fifty-fifth Street. In her own way, Mrs. McVickar, my actual boss, was just as demanding as was Madame Rubinstein, my titular boss. "Stay away from Madame!" she kept advising me. "Keep clear of that little old lady. The more time you give her, the more time she'll want! Besides, I need you here."

It came as a relief when Madame announced that she was off again to Europe for the summer. "Pity you can't come with me!" And then, brightening, added, "I'm taking Gloria What's-her-Name . . . the little Irish girl." Madame couldn't resist this jab. She wanted to test my reflexes. "Gloria O'Connor is a wonderful choice," I answered. "I know she'll be just as useful to you as I hope I was." "Maybe . . ." was Madame's only comment.

At regular intervals, during the months that followed, she sent me a mounting collection of post cards urging me to work hard, to report regularly, and to take "good care" of my health. Sprinkled in these short messages was always a line saying, "Gloria sends regards . . . ," "Gloria lost her passport . . . ," "Gloria goes out even more than you do!" I realized, with a glow of mild satisfaction, that I was missed.

A week before Labor Day Madame announced her impending return to the United States. She had had "a beastly summer." A broadside of letters preceded her arrival. "Venice," where the Prince, Prince Gourielli, had forced her to spend the month of August, "was some hell! It smells of stale fish and wherever I set foot it cost me another ten thousand lire."

She longed to be back in her New York home and was sure that many problems awaited her, adding, in one of her notes to me, "I know what happens when the cat's away." What a cat! I could see her curled up on her huge mother-of-pearl bed in Paris, thinking, plotting, seeking new ways to distract herself by exerting her power. Several telegrams now confirmed her plans, canceled them, reiterated her original schedule. She wanted Mala Rubinstein to meet her at the airport, to see that her house in Greenwich was ready for the long holiday week-end. She was returning alone! The Prince planned to follow by boat at a later date. Gloria O'Connor, with whom she had first gone to Europe, wasn't mentioned. What on earth had happened to her? Madame's final telegram said: "Have Patrick come Greenwich Sunday lunch."

On my way out, I puzzled as to why I had been summoned. Some of the mystery was dispelled the moment I arrived when Madame, harpooning slabs of Polish sausage and feeding them to me on the end of a knife, said: "The little Irish girl stayed on in Venice. She deserted me!" So now I knew. "Yes, she found herself a beau. I should have taken *you* to Europe! Besides . . . I'm going to close down Gourielli. The whole thing was premature. What's more, I made a mistake this summer. Gloria's a nice girl, but what I need is a man who can type! Who knows my habits . . . who, who . . ."

The Gourielli Men's Shop closed before the end of the year. There was one last stormy meeting. Oscar, Roy, the Prince, and the "bookkeeper" were all present, as was Mr. Carroll, the sales manager. "The place is full of pansies . . . ," he said, puffing out his chest. "Their money is as good as yours!" Madame answered. "Yes, but we lost fifty thousand dollars on the barber shop. Besides, overhead and the wholesale operation killed us." Madame didn't hesitate. "All right, have a nice Christmas sale. Then, then you can close." Gourielli, as Madame admitted, was premature. It also taught me another lesson—such specialty shops run by large companies seldom succeed.

In November 1955 I was back in favor and in Paris with Madame Rubinstein. The telephone awakened me in the middle of the night. It was a call from New York, from Harold Weill, Madame's lawyer.

"How's everything?" he asked.

"Fine. We're all asleep."

"Madame, too?"

"Yes."

"You'll have to tell her, in the morning, that the Prince is dead. He had a heart attack."

I glanced out of my window at Madame's, across the courtyard. There were no lights.

"Yes. . . ."

The phone clicked.

In the morning, yet another of those crisp days when Parisian sunlight seems to be of spun gold, I called Mr. Ameisen and told him the news.

"I'll be right over."

For some unknown reason, or possibly because it was a Sunday, Madame slept late. When Mr. Ameisen arrived we were able, with Eugénie, to discuss our tactics. Madame had been married to the Prince for close to twenty years. Although her junior by twenty years, she had loved him, in her own way, with a possessive passion. Theirs had been a happy relationship after the first stormy months when she watched over him like one of her profit-and-loss statements. He was a simple man with the appetites, the manners, the rough humor of a peasant smiled upon by good fortune. And yet he had managed his role as Prince Consort to a Beauty Queen with good nature. "My wife very rich, very clever Jewish *Hausfrau!*" He liked to roar a toast, from his end of the table, to Madame who sat winking at hers: "Atchie, don't drink too much. Atchie, don't say silly things. Atchie. . . ." Yes, she loved him. She was proud of him. She enjoyed his clumsy compliments. He was one of her better possessions.

"No use beating around the bush," Mr. Ameisen opted. "Madame's a realist. We'll have to tell her straight out. Besides, she knew he had a weak heart and that he was drinking too much."

The kitchen buzzer rang. Madame was awake. This was her signal that she wanted her breakfast. Eugénie prepared the tray.

"I'll take it," Mr. Ameisen suggested.

"No, Monsieur, let me. It will scare her. . . ."

Eugénie returned, some moments later. There were tears in her eyes. "*Pensez donc* . . . imagine, Madame just told me she had had a terrible dream and saw the Prince dead, in a beautiful coffin lined with white silk. She wants you, Monsieur Patrick. I didn't tell her Mr. Ameisen was here!"

"Give me a glass of brandy."

When I reached Madame's bedroom, at the other end of the apartment, the door was ajar.

"Patrick! Is that you?"

"Quick, quick, come in! I've had an awful dream."

She was propped up by her pillows. Her dyed black hair intensified the circles under her eyes and the blue veins throbbing at her temples.

Notwithstanding the warming effects of the brandy, I was seized with panic. At such moments, my manners become alarmingly formal. I stood uncertainly by her bedside. Trying to disguise my emotions has never been one of my skills. Madame knew.

"So, my dream was true. *Atchie is dead?*"

"Yes, Madame."

"Aii!" Her thin howl of pain could have been that of a bird except that it was repeated and, with each repetition, grew stronger until, summoned by these cries, both Eugénie and Mr. Ameisen appeared. Madame had now covered her head with the satin sheets. Beneath their glossy surface, she continued to wail, to rock and cry out. Eugénie rushed off to concoct a tisane. Mr. Ameisen tiptoed from the room intent upon phoning a doctor.

Madame suddenly whipped the sheets off her head.

"What to do, what to do?"

"He died painlessly and suddenly. . . ." I sat by her side, stroked her hand, and tried to mouth the right words.

"Yes, I know . . . *but what am I to do?*"

Madame wiped her eyes. She blew her nose in the sheets, as was her habit when preoccupied, and again asked, "What to do, what to do?"

"Do you want to return to New York for the funeral?" I asked.

"He's dead. What good? Why waste the money?"

My eyes, wide with surprise, seemed to temper her icy logic. Fresh tears ran down her cheeks as she said: "I'm old. It will soon be my turn. Think—the shock, the effort. It might kill me!"

"Yes?"

"I won't go to the funeral. We'll send a telegram. You, you must tell them in New York that I am . . . I am prostate."

"Prostrate?"

"You know? Brokenhearted. . . ."

She grabbed a pencil and paper from her bedside table and laboriously wrote a series of drafts.

"Here! This is the best. Read it out, read it out loud." I did so:

"Your mother not fit to travel. Please make all suitable arrangements and send flowers on her behalf." It was addressed to her son, Roy Titus, and Madame had signed it with my name—my full name!

"Change 'not fit to travel.' Write 'too sick to travel.'"

I did. She again snatched the paper from my hands, read it carefully, cut and adjusted several more words.

I started to walk out of Madame's room. Her face was no longer stained with tears. The black circles under her eyes had mysteriously vanished. She seemed to emanate a strange defiance. Death, her husband's death, had given her strength.

"Come back!"

"Yes, Madame?"

"He's dead. There's no hurry! See that you send it night letter!"

This halved the cost.

# "*Picasso's a Devil!*"

"Shocked" isn't a word I'm given to using. It has such a sanctimonius ring. Moreover, I can't remember ever being shocked by anything said or done to me. Dismayed, surprised, even angered . . . yes. But it was not until faced by Madame's extraordinary behavior at the news of Prince Gourielli's death that I was consciously shocked. I even felt a little sick as I left her room. A second brandy soon settled that problem. Nice little waves of Irish rage replaced those of British shock. The selfish old witch!

"What happened?" Mr. Ameisen intercepted me.

"She wants to send a telegram to Roy—*a night letter*!"

"A night letter?"

"Yes, the rates are cheaper. Madame doesn't want to fly back to New York for the Prince's funeral."

"That figures."

"What do you mean?"

He gave me a sad little smile. "You must understand there are certain realities, such as death, that Madame refuses to acknowledge. By ignoring death, the Prince's death, she's pretending it hasn't happened; and by not going to the funeral she's delaying her own reactions. That's her way of surviving. Now, wait and see, she'll think of a diversion."

"A diversion?"

"Something to do, something to keep her mind occupied."

Word of Madame's bereavement soon made the rounds. Relatives, friends, members of her Parisian staff, as is customary in France, came by the apartment, leaving their visiting cards and small bunches of flowers. I was kept busy exchanging futile words, listening to equally futile expressions of sympathy, and explaining that Madame was closeted in her bedroom—*prostrate*.

"*Pauvre chérie!*"

Occasionally I looked in on the *pauvre chérie* to see if she was all right. After eating a solitary but hearty lunch—"I must keep my strength up!"—Madame kept herself busy emptying closets, taking inventory of her jewels, counting her money. These activities were similar to those I had witnessed in Grasse after her fight with Horace. It helped her reach yet another startling decision. By nightfall, she called me back to her bedroom.

"Come, I want to show you some dresses."

"Dresses?"

I thought I was about to be treated to a preview of the "widow's weeds" she had elected to wear. Scattered on the unmade bed, hanging from the doorways of her closets, draped on every available chair, was the most extraordinary assortment of embroidered evening dresses, elaborate opera cloaks, Spanish shawls I had ever seen. Only the predominant shades of magenta and purple seemed suited to the occasion.

"Well, what do you think?"

"They seem . . . rather festive."

"Aach, you don't understand. I'm going to have my portrait painted."

"Your portrait?"

"Yes. Picasso has finally agreed to paint me. We'll fly to Cannes tomorrow. That's where he lives. Marie Cuttoli arranged everything when I rang up to tell her, to tell her about . . . the Prince."

There was a slight catch in Madame's voice but she soon recovered her composure. "Now, help me make the final selection. Picasso wants me to wear something really ex-tra-va-gant!"

"But . . ."

"But what?"

"Shouldn't you rest, look after yourself, stay home for a few days?"

"How can I? If I don't keep busy, I'll go mad."

Mr. Ameisen was right. Madame had found a diversion.

For years, I had heard from her that Picasso wanted to paint her portrait; but she could never find the time to sit for him. "Either I'm busy, or he is. Besides, he's a law unto himself, the beast! He wants to paint me when *he* feels like it; not when I do." Now, on the very day after her husband's death, it had finally come to pass. I couldn't help wondering how Madame had accomplished this amazing coup.

On our flight to Cannes, when I asked where we would be staying, she cleared the mystery. "We'll stay at my sister Stella's flat. Marie Cuttoli is a real jewel, I'm telling you. She finally forced Picasso, told him God would reward him with a long life, that . . . that he owed it to her!"

In such snippets, Madame explained that her old friend Marie Cuttoli had helped Picasso countless ways—setting up his museum in Antibes, assisting in the production of his ceramics, supervising the weaving of his tapestries. "And besides," she added, "I believe they were once sweethearts. So you see—one favor deserves another!" What wasn't mentioned at the time was that she had all but promised Madame Cuttoli the first vacant apartment at Quai de Bethune for a friend of hers, and that that friend was the future President of France —Georges Pompidou. Marie Cuttoli, who had once helped Madame collect some of her paintings, not only liked having artists indebted to her, but people in powerful positions as well.

Stella, "The Pill," met us at the airport. Her lipstick was askew. She looked nervous and distraught as if expecting to be bullied by Madame. Her marriage to the Count de Bruchard was on the rocks. She had retired to Cannes where her days were spent playing bridge in a tiny apartment on the far end of the Croisette—the fashionable thoroughfare facing the beach.

"What's wrong, Stella?" Madame inquired.

"I only have two beds."

"Patrick can sleep on a couch."

"I don't have a couch."

"He can sleep on a couple of chairs!"

"No, I can't . . ." I chipped in.

"To hell with both of you!"

Stella's flat (a couple of small rooms on a side street that faced a railroad track) matched Stella's appearance. The furnishings were ramshackle, although from a small terrace the Mediterranean was just visible, sparkling between two neighboring buildings.

"Isn't it lovely!" Madame enthused. She immediately appropriated Stella's bedroom.

"I'm going to look for a hotel," was my only comment.

"Make sure it's a small one. Get a weekly rate. You can eat your meals here . . ." Madame rattled off, handing me a few soiled dollar bills.

Living with Stella and Madame, for the next few days, made me think, in retrospect, of what life in a Crimean resort mysteriously transplanted to a tenement on the Upper West Side of New York must have been like—or, a Polish ghetto. Meals were makeshift with, invariably as a main course, a huge platter of greasy sausages dished up with red cabbage, French fries, herring, pickles, and Camembert all served massed, on the same plate. Madame doted on these disgusting picnics and always wore a selection of the finery she had brought with her to pose for Picasso. At lunchtime there were aigrettes planted in her hair; for dinner she might appear wrapped in several Spanish shawls or draped in an exotic Japanese kimono. Stella, wishing to entertain her sister, invited groups of Russian and Polish exiles to play bridge. They arrived after lunch and seldom left before midnight looking, by then, ever more battered after the effort of sitting around a small card table for ten hours.

"Where in the dickens does she find them?"

Madame eyed a departing group and, suddenly remembering why we were in Cannes, asked me: "What news of the devil? Why haven't we heard from Picasso?" I described my daily telephone calls when, in the morning, a gruff voice invariably answered: *Monsieur dort!* ("Monsieur is asleep!"); by afternoon, another voice proclaimed: "Monsieur is swimming . . . Monsieur is at a bullfight . . . Monsieur has gone to Paris!" Then there was a pause. The voice would change. From a muted falsetto, it turned to a mellow bass.

"Who is it?"

"Madame Rubinstein!"

"Ida?"

"No, Helena . . ."

"Call back tomorrow."

I pantomimed these conversations to Madame. "Ida Rubinstein's been dead for thirty years. Picasso's a devil. He's playing tricks. We'll drop in on him tomorrow." What I didn't know was that the different voices I had been hearing, for all of his loathing of the telephone, were Picasso's.

"La Californie," where he then lived, is a sprawling community in the hills above Cannes. First developed at the turn of the century to house champagne millionaires, Indian maharajas, and their well-kept women, only a few of the elegant Edwardian villas, set in semitropical gardens, survived amid clusters of high-rise apartment buildings.

"Very Jewish . . . ," Madame said as we drove there in a taxi, whose driver, a jolly fellow, asked me *sotto voce* after looking Madame over, "*Qui est la tireuse de cartes?* ("Who's the fortune teller?"). Under an opera cloak quilted in shades of orange and lemon with calla lilies and sprigs of mimosa, Madame wore a medieval tunic of acid green velvet.

"Get out and ring the doorbell!" she pointed to a massive iron gate. Beyond it I could just see an equally impressive porte-cochere. It led into a house that well might have been the setting for an Offenbach operetta such was the quantity of *art-nouveau* glass windows set in undulating stucco. The bell clanged; it produced a villainous-looking; porter.

"No one's at home!" he spat through a Gauloise cigarette. At that moment Madame decided to get out of the taxi. *"Mon dieu!"* He gave her a horrified look. "I must call Madame Jacqueline . . ."

I knew that Jacqueline Roque, who was later to become his wife, had been Picasso's mistress and faithful protector for a number of years. The gate now swung open as a solidly built woman of about thirty came running out of the house.

"Madame Rubinstein! Helena . . . *quel honneur!*"

They fell into each other's arms.

*"Venez!* Come . . . Pablo will be happy! We are just having an *apéritif.*"

I followed them up the stairs, through an empty hallway, into a huge room cluttered with canvases, rocking chairs, and enough flotsam to furnish a thrift shop.

"Pablo!"

"Helena . . ."

Picasso was smaller and stockier than I had expected; even so, Madame all but vanished in his arms as he gave her a bear hug. For once, she seemed to enjoy this attention and even winked at me. Picasso now grabbed her arm and led her out onto the terrace calling out to a group of people sitting there, "Look what I've found!"

It was my turn to blink. Among the guests that included Picasso's daughter, Paloma, and his dealer, Kahnweiler, there stood a tall, lanky man who not only looked like Gary Cooper but who was Gary Cooper.

He bowed formally over Madame's hand, and helped her settle down in the only chair that seemed to be all of one piece.

"I know you from somewhere . . ." Madame looked up at him.

"Of course you do, sweetheart!"

Their brief dialogue was interrupted by Picasso who had vanished and now reappeared dressed as a flamboyant cowboy, firing two toy pistols. Gary Cooper rose to the bait. For the next few minutes he ducked and dodged, recreating every role I had ever seen him play. Picasso's energy—he was then nearly in his mid-seventies—seemed inexhaustible as he charged around like a small boy until Jacqueline Roque gently put a stop to the antics by announcing that lunch was ready. We were all led back into the house where, at one end of the huge ground-floor room, a table had been set with cold cuts and bottles of red wine.

"*C'est un pique-nique!*" Picasso proclaimed as he slit a baguette of French bread, buttered and stuffed it with slices of *saucisson* and, with a gesture worthy of a headwaiter at Maxim's, presented it to Madame.

"You look like a marvelous transvestite—'*un travesti*,'—dressed for the *Bal des Quat-z-arts*," he said as she gnawed away. Fortunately she didn't understand him; and only the word "marvelous," "*merveilleuse*," penetrated her brain.

"I dressed specially for you. When do we start?"

"Start? What?"

"The portrait . . ."

"Tomorrow! Tomorrow at six . . . the light, then, is just right. Besides, I never work until six."

"Six in the morning?" Madame was quite ready to be there at that hour.

"*Merde, alors!* What do you think I am?"

"A very hard worker, just like me!"

Picasso sent us back in his own car, an ordinary if antiquated Citroën.

"Can you beat it?" Madame said. "All of his money . . . sandwiches for lunch and now this battered old thing!"

I felt like reminding her we had come in a taxi and that life at Stella's wasn't exactly luxury—for all of *her* money.

And so, for the next three evenings at six, Madame sat for two, sometimes three hours, as Picasso sketched. He worked at the dining-room table where we had eaten our *pique-nique.*

"*Je vais faire des notes policières!* I'm taking down a dossier . . . a few police notes!"

"Good! Will they make a nice portrait?" Madame asked.

"Who says I'll paint a portrait?"

"The devil . . ."

I wasn't allowed to watch; nor was Jacqueline or any other member of the household which seemed to include, besides a number of small children, half a dozen old retainers and the slovenly porter who doubled as a chauffeur.

While Picasso worked I sat on the terrace with Jacqueline reading movie magazines, of which there was an ample supply.

"Pablo loves them," she said. "To him Gary Cooper is one of the greatest men in the world. He likes to study photographs of his heroes. Then, then they are real to him because he seldom goes to the cinema."

Through an open window we could hear Picasso's grunts of satisfaction as he sketched, as well as his occasional remarks. Madame posed, bone still, like "an Assyrian monolith!" he was to say later.

"You have big ears, Helena."

"So do you, Pablo!"

"You know what that means? We'll both live forever, like elephants!"

Jacqueline, who wished to keep me entertained after we had exhausted the supply of movie magazines, took me for short walks in the garden. "Come and look at the sculpture!" Under every tree were massive bronzes made by Picasso. "This is his *garde-meuble* . . ." she said, "his storehouse. The first cast of every important piece of sculpture he has ever made is here . . . Look, that's the famous goat that's in Saint Paul. And this is me! Picasso wants to have it recast as a forty-foot statue." Jacqueline's Tanagra features had been strangely distorted to give them three dimensions. The statues were a preview of those which now embellish, of all places, a public square in Chicago and another in Greenwich Village.

"Now I must show you Picasso's 'Treasure House.' But don't breathe a word of it. He would never show it to Madame Rubinstein . . ."

"Why?"

"He knows her too well. He says that her only interest in art is acquisitive."

"Why is he doing her portrait?"

"He won't. He's just sketching her as a reference for a series of lithographs. He likes to use real people and Madame, Madame Rubinstein, is . . . larger than life."

This was a revelation. Was I to tell Madame she had been out-maneuvered? That she was hoist with her own petard? No. She was enjoying her "diversion" too much and, even if nothing came of it, I felt, she had used Picasso as much as he was using her.

"How old are you, Helena?" I once heard Picasso ask her.

There was a long silence.

"Older than you, Pablo . . ."

And then my conversations with Jacqueline were also revealing. She always referred to Picasso the man as "Pablo" or "Don Pablo," and only used his family name when talking of the artist or the artist's work.

"Come. Come and see Don Pablo's Treasure House!"

I was led to a room off the main studio. It was a large powder room with a lavatory in one corner, but stacked against the bare whitewashed walls were more than a hundred unframed canvases.

"Look!" Jacqueline said as she quickly turned a few for my inspection. "Cézanne, Renoir, Degas . . . and here, his favorites, Le Douanier Rousseau!"

These paintings alone, to my untrained, uncommercial eye, must have been worth millions. They were all masterpieces that any museum or collector would have sold their souls to acquire.

"How did he get them?"

"He exchanged them, when young, for his own paintings. He knew . . . even then."

"With the artists?"

"Sometimes, but mostly with Ambroise Vollard."

I knew that Vollard—who was called *"Voleur,"* "Thief," by his less able colleagues—had been the greatest dealer of the era preceding World War One.

Jacqueline led me to another stack of paintings.

"These are Picasso's own . . . the blue period, the pink, the first of the early cubist . . . and now his current work. This represents every decade after the war, until I came along." The last canvas, and they were all of superb quality, was of Jacqueline in profile. Picasso had only used three basic colors to achieve a likeness. There she was— incredibly cool, vaguely aloof, lovely.

"How many sittings did it require?"

"He did it from memory, in an hour, one rainy day when I wasn't feeling well."

"Was it to show you how much he loved you?"

"No. But maybe how much he needed me. On the following day he asked me if I would feel better married to him."

"What did you say?"

"I said my feelings for him wouldn't change one way or the other."

"And then?"

"And then he said, 'We'll get married soon. There's really no hurry!' "

"How old were you?"

"Fifty years younger than he was!"

She looked at me with her wonderful deep-set, understanding eyes. "Don't you want to ask me what it's like living with an old man?"

"No! It never occurred to me."

"Well, it's wonderful! He's the most considerate, sensitive, elegant person I've ever known and—besides being a genius—he's the only lover I've ever really wanted!"

As we left the "Treasure House," Jacqueline murmured, "Picasso always keeps what he considers to be his best work for himself. He doesn't believe in the stock exchange, land, commercial values . . ."

"What does he believe in?"

"Paintings. His own . . . or gold, in bars!"

"Has he provided for you?"

"What do you mean?"

"If he died . . . then, what happens to you?"

"Who cares?"

That evening Picasso said to Madame, "No more sittings. I have all I want." More than ever he looked like a cruel schoolboy.

"And the portrait?"

"*Qui sait*? Maybe it's a posthumous work."

"Posthumous?"

"Yes. Either you die first or I do . . . Either I paint it or I don't . . . Either you get it or you don't!"

"The devil!" Madame spluttered again in the taxicab. She shook a fist at Picasso's house. In dismissing Madame, Picasso hadn't even offered his car. "He's playing tricks again." We had come in a taxi, and we were leaving in a taxi.

The Picasso portrait, for all of Madame's ferocious persistence, or maybe because of it (she bombarded him with inquiries, journeyed to Cannes repeatedly, used many intermediaries to lobby for her) was never finished. Nor did she ever see him again, nor ever see the drawings he did. These, according to John Richardson—a mutual friend, art critic, confidant of Picasso's—were extraordinary. Picasso showed him more than forty sketches, filed in a neat folder. Richardson subsequently told me: "You know, they're amazing. But the odd thing about them is that although there are careful studies of Madame's hands, her rings, her neck and chin, even her mouth, there's not a single complete drawing of her—none of them goes farther than her nostrils!"

He then said: "Picasso is convinced that if he ever finished a portrait of Madame he will die before her!"

"Curse him!" were Madame's last words on the subject.

"But," it suddenly struck me, "was a fee ever discussed?"

"Certainly not. What would he want the money for?"

Less than three years later, in April 1958, Madame and I were again in Paris and the horrendous scene following my announcement of the Prince's death was repeated, almost to the last detail. This time the victim was her beloved son Horace. While driving at high speed across a bridge on Long Island he had a slight accident and, although unharmed, suffered a heart attack later that evening. His heart had never been strong; he had had rheumatic fever as a child. He was hospitalized for observation. Two days later, before word could even reach Madame in Paris of his accident, a massive coronary killed him. He died, as he had lived for most of his forty-six years, alone.

"Aii!" This time when I told Madame that the only person in the world she truly adored would no longer be around to delight and plague her—she collapsed, completely, and for days lay in bed in an almost catatonic state. She turned her face to the wall, refused food and the visits of friends, and even when I attempted to read to her the hundreds of letters of sympathy that poured in—for Horace had been dearly loved—Madame again covered her head in the bed sheets, refusing to listen. "Later, later!" she cried, "I'll want to hear later. But not now!"

It was my turn to take the initiative—to produce "a diversion."

While Madame agonized, suffered, puzzled over her wretched but insoluble relationship with her dead son, I telephoned her friends, wrote letters, sent telegrams to people all over Europe thanking them for their words of kindness. This kept me busy, although, once or twice Madame still had the strength to surprise me. "I know I'm useless," she said "but I hope you're not wasting your time."

Then one morning, ten days after Horace's death, a letter reached me from Cecil Beaton in London. He expressed his sympathy and, as a faithful old friend of mine, somehow guessed that the moment was ripe for him to come to my rescue: "Graham Sutherland," he wrote, "would like to paint a portrait of your boss. It's a chance in a lifetime. From being an important landscape artist he has turned into a superb portrait painter. If you want further ammunition mention to Madame Rubinstein that his portraits of Somerset Maugham, Winston Churchill, and Lord Beaverbrook are masterpieces . . . I know that the old trout dotes on publicity. If he paints her she'll get loads. She'll be the first woman he's painted."

I swung into action—veiling certain details (I knew Maugham and Churchill had loathed their portraits).

"Madame!" I announced as she continued to lie comatose in her satin sheets. "There's an important artist in England who wants to paint your portrait, and you must have it done."

"Not now!"

"But Madame—he's painted Maugham, Churchill, and Lord Beaverbrook and he has never painted an important woman!"

This was my trump card.

"An important woman?" She propped herself up on an elbow. "Tell me more."

I elaborated. Madame didn't hesitate.

"Horace always loved England. Let us go there tomorrow! Call Mrs. Cooper and tell her; tell her we're arriving. Make all of the arrangements."

Mrs. Cooper, "the English sister," had a high, hysterical voice. She lived in terror of her older sister's rare visits to London.

"Nothing we ever do seems to please Madame!" Mrs. Cooper screeched. As did all the family, even she called her sister "Madame."

"Ah, yes," I answered, "but this time she's not coming over for business. It's a private visit. Madame is thinking of having her portrait painted by Graham Sutherland."

"Who? Never heard of him."

Such was the size of the English business (it grossed several million pounds but was subject to enormous taxes and the specter of ultimate death duties levied on a private owner's estate), that it had been made into a foundation. Madame, unable to benefit from these

:[ 228 ]:

"Paris is some hell!"
Madame in her Paris office, 1952.

"Nice? Expensive? Keep quiet. I'll do the bargaining!" Madame and myself in Bangkok. *(Photo Brian Brake, Magnum)*

"I swear . . . if I live to be a hundred there is no better cream!" Madame expounding the qualities of Wake-Up Cream, 1964. *(Photo Jean Mermet)*

profits, often lamented, "England brings me nothing! But it's a nice place to visit!"

Madame enjoyed visiting England chiefly because of Mrs. Cooper's principal business associate and manager, Boris Forter, a wily White Russian whose acute financial brain, patience, and tact balanced Mrs. Cooper's many eccentricities. Madame admired him. "He's . . . he's so solid!" He needed to be.

Mrs. Cooper loved details and small sums of money. "Ceska's penny wise and pound foolish!" Madame liked to say. One of her favorite occupations, although she was the titular head of the business, was sitting beside the London salon's cash register. Here, looking like the rich owner of a flourishing delicatessen, tastefully dressed and bejeweled, she checked the receipts while nibbling on a pastrami sandwich.

"Ceska can be very wise . . . when she wants to," Madame half-queried. "But I only wish she didn't think she was running a grocery store!"

Of Madame's four surviving sisters, apart from the splendid Manka who had retired, Ceska, for all her occasional hysteria, was probably the favorite.

"We talk very good shop, when she's in the mood."

Ceska's moods were mercurial. It was only because of Boris Forter that these were contained. "He's so wise! So patient! I could never put up with Ceska for very long," Madame said. But what really pleased her concerning Mr. Forter was his generosity and unfailing gallantry. He never stinted, he entertained her royally in all of the best restaurants. He forced her to stay in a princely suite at Claridge's and, what truly enthralled her, always slipped an envelope crammed with several hundred pounds—"For your expenses . . . it's tax-free!" —into her welcoming hands. Madame failed to realize that this was her money. She was like an employee receiving a generous bonus from a benevolent boss.

We arrived in London and were met by both Mrs. Cooper and Boris Forter.

"You look well, Ceska. Where did you get that mink coat?"

"Wholesale! Mr. Forter knows a nice man . . ."

Mrs. Cooper had fluffy hair and a permanent look of anxiety which

:[ 229 ]:

contrasted sharply with Mr. Forter's cool elegance. He was tactful without ever being obsequious. As had Horace, he firmly believed in milking the fatted calf, but he did so with infinite subtlety. While Madame received her thick envelope stuffed with five-pound notes, I was given lesser baksheesh. "*Amuse-toi, si tu peux*! Have fun, if you can!" Mr. Forter patted my hand abstractedly. It was all very civilized, as was our reception at London Airport, where two rented Rolls-Royces awaited us.

"Fancy!" Madame cooed. "How extravagant."

"In London," Mr. Forter bowed, "you are looked upon as a Queen."

"I've always liked London." Madame nodded approval as she hoisted herself next to the driver of the first Rolls.

"But, Madam!" The chauffeur was appalled.

"Don't worry. I like to see where I'm going."

"As you please, Madam."

Claridge's, in those days, was the most punctilious of hotels. It managed to combine extreme formality with English cosiness. The vast marble hallway, for all its grandeur, had the intimacy of an English home furnished in the twenties. There were masses of flowers and a real log fire burned in a splendid fireplace.

Mr. Van Thuyne, the manager, met us at the front door. All formalities, such as registering, were waived aside.

"Princess!"

Madame preened as she was ushered into the elevator.

There was a slight delay.

"What's keeping us?" she asked impatiently.

"Royalty! Princess . . ."

Mr. Van Thuyne's impeccably manicured hand wafted to one side as he bowed low to Prince Philip, who hurried into the crowded machine. He was wearing full evening dress and was attended by an equally splendid equerry. I respectfully bobbed my head.

"Who's *that*?" Madame gave me a mighty nudge with her elbow.

"Prince Philip, the Queen's husband," I whispered.

The Prince smiled uncertainly at us.

"Nice looking! She chose well. . . ."

Unlike Picasso—who enjoyed "playing tricks"—Graham Sutherland immediately asked Madame Rubinstein to come and visit him at his country home when he heard she had arrived. He and his wife lived near West Malling in a converted farmhouse. We drove there for lunch on the following day. "I love the English countryside," Madame purred before falling asleep. She had again elected to sit next to the driver of another hired Rolls-Royce. "It's so relaxing." Seldom had I seen her in a better mood. Horace was not mentioned. The business seemed forgotten. She had spent an hour before setting off at Fortnum and Mason's buying ginger and cashmere sweaters for herself and the Sutherlands. "Artists have a sweet tooth and their houses are always freezing."

An hour or so later we reached a small, compact white house. It was covered with evergreens. "So unassuming!" Madame woke up smiling as the genial Sutherlands rushed out to their gate to meet her. "Nice woman, elegant man . . ." she kept repeating as they led us into the house. "Very cold! Just as well I bought two sweaters," Madame said giving one to Mrs. Sutherland and draping the other around her shoulders. She was wearing a cloth coat: "Ceska said I should have put on my mink. Why make poor artists envious?"

What Madame didn't yet know was that Graham Sutherland's landscapes fetched several thousand pounds apiece while his full-length portraits were reputedly priced at ten thousand pounds. He was then a man nearing fifty and had the distant, rather sad, but impeccable manners of a Foreign Service career diplomat who had been superseded by brasher colleagues. His wife, Cathy, seemed to fuse impulsiveness with caution. She immediately asked Madame to analyze her skin.

"Dry!"

("When in doubt always tell them they have a dry skin . . . particularly the English," Madame liked to say.)

Mrs. Sutherland cuddled up at her feet.

Adulation suited Madame. She had just spied Graham Sutherland's drawings of Maugham and Churchill that, strategically displayed, were hung on the wall facing her.

"Nice! Strong . . . So you've never painted a woman?"

"Not a great woman with an inspiring face!"

"Are there *that* many?"

Lunch, an exquisite but rural meal, consisted of a huge cottage pie followed by masses of garden vegetables. This simple fare further stimulated Madame. "Sensible food, sensible people," she said, spooning a second helping of greengages and clotted cream.

"When do we start?" she asked as port and cheese concluded the meal.

"Start?"

"The portrait!"

Mr. Sutherland wasn't one to be jostled. "I must think about the pose, help you decide what clothes you want to wear, and then . . ."

"And then?"

". . . discuss the fee!"

"Mr. Forter will take care of the last arrangements. In the meantime let us all go back to London and look at my clothes. I'll give you dinner!"

The Sutherlands were swept out of their house before they even had a chance to refuse; and, such was the success of the evening (for Madame used her secret resources of charm to surmount artistic procrastination) that sittings began in her suite at Claridge's on the following morning. These continued for a week. Graham Sutherland was the most thorough and painstaking of artists and, after sketching Madame's face, hands, and body from every imaginable angle, he declared:

"I need a rest. The commuting is very tiring. I must think."

"Good!" Madame, by then, had also wearied of sitting for several hours on end in a heavily embroidered dress, even though she was enshrined in cushions and her feet rested on all four of the London telephone directories.

"When do we next meet?"

"In a week or so . . ."

"Come to Paris! I'll pay."

Travel restrictions for British citizens wishing to visit the continent were still at their zenith. The Sutherlands accepted with alacrity. But, before parting, Graham Sutherland cut a wisp of Madame's hair, several square inches from the hem of her dress, and took samples of her lipstick, rouge, and eye shadow.

On the Saturday that the Sutherlands arrived in Paris, Madame, to make up for the time lost due to her collapse after Horace's death and the week she had spent in London, rose at six in the morning. She had been going religiously to her office on the Faubourg and working there for twelve-hour stretches without a decent lunch: "I must lose a few pounds, otherwise he'll make me look fat." Chronically constipated, Madame, that Saturday morning, swallowed half a bottle of mineral oil, several senna pills, drank her glass of hot grapefruit juice and two cups of strong black coffee for breakfast. This, not surprisingly, produced a violent explosion in her system. She fainted, fell, and struck her head on one of the bronze legs which upheld her elaborate bed. Moments later, quite alone, she regained her senses and, without troubling to call for help, took a hot bath. It revived her, but, by noon, when the Sutherlands appeared, she had two black eyes. In order to disguise them Madame used quantities of rouge below her bruised eyes and green shadow above them. The effect was extraordinary. She appeared for lunch in the elaborately embroidered Balenciaga dress looking like Theda Bara cast as Count Dracula.

"Her make-up is sensational!" Graham Sutherland could hardly contain his enthusiasm.

I never let on to the true story.

Graham Sutherland and his wife spent a week in Paris. He had decided to start again from scratch; to eliminate the series of drawings done in London: "She's a completely different person. It's amazing what really dramatic eye make-up can do!"

The following fall Madame Rubinstein and I made a quick trip to London, on hearing the portrait was finished and ready for her inspection. Graham Sutherland and his wife had tactfully retired to Venice, leaving a vague message that six months of hard work might be viewed at a framer's, Alfred Hecht's, on the King's Road. We set out there on a dank, dark November day: "I know I'm going to hate it!" Madame's mood was not one of optimism.

Besides Madame, Mrs. Cooper, Mr. Forter and me, our group consisted of Miss Simmons, who headed the advertising and publicity departments of the English Helena Rubinstein Company; and Eric

Garrott, a genial P.R. man turned advertising tycoon. Madame, unable to remember his name, always called him "The Man Who Sends Me Expensive Flowers."

"I know I'm going to hate it!" Madame repeated as she led the way into a tacky little shop. And then she froze.

At the far end of the shop, propped up against a wall in a small alcove, dramatically lit with twin spots, were not one, but two life-sized portraits. We had traveled some four thousand miles to view them before they were officially unveiled to the public in London's Tate Gallery.

Madame asked for a chair, then for a cup of tea.

"Oh, my God!" She rocked uncertainly, staring at herself.

The two portraits were almost identical; in one she was seated while in the other she stood. Both depicted her left profile—"My *bad* side." A gimlet eye glared at imagined foes, a hooked nose seemed to be sniffing to an unpleasant smell. In each portrait Madame looked like a vengeful autocrat. The weight and richness of the embroidered dress she wore, detailed with pre-Raphaelite skill, only served to intensify the vivid but uncompromising likenesses. Her neck, looped with huge strands of pearls, was blue with age—scrawny as a buzzard's. Her jowl and chin, jutting firmly into space, gave an impression of ferocity equaled only by the crimson slit of her mouth; while the forehead, although smooth and untouched by the ravages of age, was a delicate shade of mauve. It curved into an uneven hairline. This seemed to have been yanked back with fury. A huge bow covered Madame's famous chignon.

"I'll have another cup of tea!" she said, still studying herself.

"Do I . . . do I really *look* like that?"

Each tried to soothe her.

"All great portraits are interpretations."

"Artists see people differently."

"These are masterpieces. They will endure!"

She got up, a trifle unsteadily.

"I hate them, Besides, they'll be bad for business!"

"For business?"

"Our business, you fool, my business . . . the beauty business."

"Yes, the business!"

"Look at me." She turned her back on both portraits, ". . . so old! So savage . . . a witch!"

Mr. Forter couldn't resist adding, in my ear: "But a very rich old witch!"

Some days later the two portraits were exhibited at the Tate Gallery. Madame had elected not to be present, refusing to believe that this was a great honor. The Tate Gallery is a public institution (second in prestige to the National Gallery) that can only be compared to the Museum of Modern Art in New York—although it prides itself on being not quite so frivolous.

Here, hung side by side in a small room, the two Sutherland portraits electrified the public. They were viewed by more than a hundred thousand people and the critics, unanimous in their praise for Sutherland's skill, also commended Madame for her courage and vision in submitting herself to the ordeal of such daring and harsh brush strokes. She carefully read and hoarded every review. Soon the folder of clippings marked, in her own hand, "Hideous Sutherland portraits," grew to such proportions that it required a filing cabinet. This impressed Madame:

"Fancy, who would have guessed?"

"Guessed what?"

"Guessed that people are that interested!"

What pleased her even more were further articles to the effect that the Queen and the Queen Mother had viewed the paintings.

"I wonder what *they* thought!"

The upshot of the Sutherland portraits was that Madame again became known and admired in England. Until then, living in New York, visiting London but rarely, she had always been looked upon as an almost fictitious personality. Overnight, the British press, seldom generous in their attitude toward American tycoons, cherished her. They rediscovered her past, her Australian beginnings, her early English triumph when she opened what was actually the first modern beauty salon in the Western Hemisphere. There were feature articles about Madame Rubinstein's long life as a pioneer of beauty, as a distinguished art collector, and as an international fashion influence. These appeared in magazines and newspapers with huge circulations, were reprinted all over the world, so that the "Hideous Sutherland portraits" cabinet grew into two, and then three. Finally, Madame was asked to write her memoirs and when told that they would be purchased by the London *Sunday Times*, she asked, "For money, for real money?"—before setting me to work on a vague pastiche, her official biography, entitled *My Life for Beauty*.

The seated portrait, imported to New York some months after it was unveiled in London, now hung in her Park Avenue penthouse.

"Like it?" she inquired, uncertainly, of admiring guests: "I don't! But people seem to. . . ." Madame knew, better than anyone, that part of the mystique of publicity was controversy. When asked, "Then why do you hang it so prominently?" she answered: "Empty wall space!" When she was told that the standing portrait had been bought by Lord Beaverbrook for his new museum in New Brunswick, she immediately wanted to know, "Where is New Brunswick?" Informed that it was in Canada, Madame feigned relief: "No one will see it up there!"

Sutherland, a tireless worker, had also produced several studies of Madame's head. One of these found its way first to the Museum in São Paulo and then to the new Presidential Palace at Brasilia: "I'm well represented in the sticks!" she snorted. Her eyes seemed to shrink. "He's done very well out of me! Four sales that I know of . . . must have made at least thirty thousand pounds!"

"Think of the publicity," I answered, somewhat on the defensive, of all "poor" artists.

"I'm thinking of the dress."

"The dress?"

"Yes, I gave it to Mrs. What's-her-Name, the artist's wife. I gave her the beautiful embroidered dress I posed in."

"But, Madame, that was surely an 'incidental.' You can charge it to publicity, as a gift."

"My dress! An incidental!" Madame glared at me.

"Yes, an incidental."

"Then, you, too, are an 'incidental,'" she said, snorting angrily. "Who do you think pays for your salary, your expenses, your . . . your own incidentals?"

"Your business does."

"*I am my business.* Don't ever forget that . . . 'incidental'!"

# "So What's New?"

"Let us go to the Orient and a few other places. . . . I want to consolidate!" Madame suggested to me in the fall of 1958. With the death of Prince Gourielli and Horace my role as her favorite traveling companion took on new, global dimensions. We were to go round the world together. I had ceased to be an "incidental."

"Consolidate?"

This was a new word for her.

"Yes, tie up loose ends."

Madame was bored. She needed a change, a radical change, and the stimulus such a change generated. At first, I was hesitant to accept her offer, until I realized it was a command. The word "No" didn't exist in Madame's vocabulary. Going round the world, even with her, seemed enormously tempting. But wasn't I assuming an enormous responsibility? Madame then still admitted to being only eighty, but her passport, which I handled daily, listed the date of her birth as December 25, 1872. In point of fact she was eighty-six.

Who else, at that age, would have dared to undertake such extensive and, sometimes, grueling travels? Who else could endure the rough and tumble of one-night stands, the dubious comforts of strange hotels—and, not least, the fear of sudden death, which, at her age, must have constantly been lurking in the back of her mind? Yet Madame persisted: "I want to consolidate." So, once more, I was to act as her traveling companion, secretary, maid, and escort during more than sixteen enervating weeks—one hundred and thirty-six days in all of constant attendance without a single day off.

How did I do it? Truth to tell, Madame was a different person "on the road." Stoic, fatalistic, amiable—sometimes even rather cozy—she nourished my protective instincts. Besides, I was obviously a gerontophile. Old age, in all of its aspects, intrigued me—but what intrigued me the most was Madame. (Indeed, she had "hooked" me . . . hook, line, and sinker.)

Our first stop was Los Angeles, where Madame Rubinstein—as was her habit—dutifully visited store presidents, entertained salesgirls and cosmeticians, and made her usual pronouncements to the press.

We next flew to Tokyo. It was at the end of this flight, which, before the advent of jets, lasted some thirty-six hours with many exotic stops, that Madame, who had barely spoken to me, although I was sitting by her side, turned and said: "So what's new?"

"We're landing in Tokyo!"

"Good luck."

Our arrival there was confusing. I was not, as yet, acquainted with Japanese formality. My knowledge of this marvelous country, limited to translations by Arthur Waley of Lady Murasaki, of a few Samurai films starring Toshiro Mifume, and of the odd generalizations signed by the Brothers Goncourt, was totally insufficient to prepare me, and Madame, for the strange manners and even stranger business procedures we encountered.

Haneda Airport, where we landed, seemed eerie if compared to Western counterparts. It was so neat, quiet, and organized. Small groups of soberly dressed people, smiling and bowing, greeted us. They might have been members of a ritualistic ballet.

"What do they want?" Madame stared at their banners. These proclaimed, "Welcome to Tokyo, Lubinstein-San!" Her name was spelled with an "L" (the Japanese find "R" a difficult letter to pronounce). Several elderly and distinguished-looking men detached themselves from the chorus of lovely ivory-colored faces, again bowed, and, uttering a few unintelligible words, led us to a string of limousines.

"Who are they? What do they want?" Madame repeated.

:[ 238 ]:

It was not until we reached the Imperial Hotel that our escorts informed us they were all hopeful candidates for the Rubinstein concession. Rubinstein was not, at the time, represented in Japan. It was a wide open market. Madame was aware of this. Consolidate? She was pioneering!

"That's what *they* think . . . ," Madame snorted when I informed her. "Still, find out if they'll take us to dinner. Why not? It will be interesting to hear what they have to say besides saving us some money."

Being entertained by polite and assiduous, but competing, factions is an interesting experience which we encountered repeatedly in the Far East. Madame, who had a lot of trouble understanding what was being said, played her favorite game of pitting rivals for what appeared to be "a show" and "a place" in the Rubinstein stakes. There were no winners, nor were there to be, for as Madame confided to me, belching slightly after yet another superb dinner: "Oscar will have to come out and decide who gets what and how *after* he has checked their credentials."

"Credentials?" I wondered what she meant.

"Bank accounts, silly!"

The next few days were a whirlwind of strange, protracted meetings, interspersed with colossal meals, stranger activities. We were never quite sure of our host's identity. Was it the gentleman with thick eyeglasses? Or the one with all the teeth? No matter. Bravely we ate raw fish, exchanged toasts with hot sake, bowed.

I could see Madame's patience was wearing thin.

"Let's go to Kyoto and do some sight-seeing," I suggested, hoping to create a diversion. Madame wasn't overly enthusiastic, but she finally capitulated. "Have it your way. . . ."

It was bitterly cold as I led her from temple to temple and then back to Kyoto's Miyako Hotel, where, on our last day, one of the most exotic sights we were to encounter in all of Japan materialized out of the blue.

"Two very fine English ladies waiting for you in bar." The concierge sibilated, eyes popping, adding: "Both dressed like gentlemen."

Intrigued, I propelled Madame into the bar where Cecil Beaton and Truman Capote rose to meet us. Cecil had doffed the wide Thai straw hat he had been wearing; but, still swaddled in a number of happy coats, scarves and other unrelated garments, he did present an unusual sight, while Truman had also removed his raccoon fur cap and a voluminous ulster of bold design. It was not until they rose to leave and put on all of their strange finery, that I relayed the concierge's remark.

"I really think the Japanese are *too* peculiar!" Cecil giggled, not entirely pleased.

I had first met Cecil after the war in London. We became friends. Upon hearing I planned visiting America, he warned me: "Don't stay too long. You'll never leave." His prophetic words proved true and when I later announced I was working for Madame Rubinstein, he was dismayed: "She'll run you ragged. Make yourself indispensable and then resign every six months. That's the only way you'll ever get paid properly."

His liberal broadsides of shrewd, worldly advice were always peppered with humor, warmth, and kindness. "I really think . . ." In a slow, calculated drawl he kept tabs on the progress of my career in the cosmetics industry. Hearing that after ten years I was only earning about a thousand dollars a month, Cecil urged me: "Make the old trout pay up. She'll respect you all the more!"

Truman, also, was an acquaintance of long standing, but vaguer footing. Cecil had described him, in his youth, as "looking somewhat like a wombat peering out from under a flaxen fringe." But while Cecil watched over and coddled those he had elected to be his friends, Truman was given to attaching himself only to the very rich and the highly successful. His fame, so firmly anchored on accomplishment, often seemed wasted by this love of society. And yet, was it not a put-on? After the famous masked ball he gave at the Plaza Hotel in 1966 for "five hundred and forty of my most intimate friends" ("The guest book reads like an international list for the guillotine," muttered one observer), Cleveland Amory, author of *Who Killed Society?*, said, "Fond as I am of Truman, I think we can say that society is not only kaput—it is Capote." Others had their comments, appreciative, admiring, bitchy. But it took still another author, Glenway Wescott, upon first announcing, "I don't like this ball. Too many intellectuals!" to gauge what Truman was really up to. "I think he gave it with Proust in mind. . . . He wanted to find out what it was like being the Duchesse de Guermantes."

And so there they were in Kyoto—an unlikely pair in an unlikely place—working their way, so to speak, around the Far East. Madame took them both in her imperturbable stride: "Intellectuals can dress as they please!" But, learning that they had visited many of the places on our itinerary, she immediately set to work milking them for information.

"Tell me, what's Hong Kong really like . . . ? Any little bargains to be found there?"

Cecil, always a tease, urged her off her path into the jungles of Cambodia. "You must not miss Angkor Wat. The temples are magnificent . . . each of them is decorated with endless sculptured friezes of the Duchess of Windsor seen in profile."

"I don't think we'll go. She doesn't interest me much."

But due to this chance meeting, when we returned to New York in the early spring of 1959, Madame, never one to miss an opportunity for a publicity stunt and remembering that Cecil had been instrumental in getting Sutherland to paint her, took to my idea that Cecil redecorate the picture gallery of her Park Avenue apartment, "in the Japanese manner. . . ."

"That should create a furor," she nodded happily.

The final designs were not completed until some months later. Cecil, who had scored a triumph with his costumes for *My Fair Lady*, was riding the crest, one of the many crests of a long and splendid career.

"What do you think of them?" I asked Madame after she had examined a series of immaculately painted gouaches.

"You know," her hand fluttered uncertainly, "the good, the bad. . . ."

"What's the bad?"

"He's charging me ten thousand dollars, *without* labor. And I can't even bargain with him. He would gossip! *That's the bad.*"

Gradually the huge and severe Gothic room that served as a make-shift picture gallery on the top floor of Madame Rubinstein's penthouse home, metamorphosed under Cecil Beaton's lighthearted touch into a verdant, pseudo-Japanese winter garden. The walls were covered in bamboo; the ceiling suggested an open sky seen above a trellis; and, in addition, there were white wicker chairs, Chinese garden seats, and clusters of other fanciful Victorian furnishings for, as Cecil confided, "We must try and lead the eye away from the pictures Madame Rubinstein has selected. I'm afraid she's again been chintzy. I've only been allowed one second-rate Picasso!"

An intermittent struggle had raged between them. Madame refused to allow her "best" pictures to be relegated from her living room and dining room, where there was more traffic, "to that stage set your friend is doing upstairs!" She was unable to understand that Beaton was producing an airy folly. She resented all of the plants he had ordered placed in window boxes beneath the paintings. "Who'll water them?"

When the gallery was finally finished, Madame viewed it. She looked sour. "Not rich enough!" Cecil, knowing that this was one client he could never satisfy, beat a hasty retreat back to England. "Tell your boss that it's very difficult to make a silk purse from a sow's ear," were his final words to me.

The room was doomed from the start, for Beaton's taste, and Madame's, were poles apart. But the final irony only occurred months later when it was discovered that Japanese beetles had invaded the bamboo walls. These had to be taken down and fumigated. The insatiable beetles were devouring everything in sight—even the second-rate Picasso.

"See!" Madame pointed an accusing finger at me. "One must never do business with friends. Besides costing a fortune, they bring in bugs."

Although Madame had failed to "consolidate in Japan," she had bought bushels of pearls, yards of silk, and seemed satisfied as we proceeded to Hong Kong.

At night, first seen from the air, Hong Kong is the most glittering city I have ever looked down upon. Even Madame murmured a tentative "Pretty?" as we circled over what looked like a huge roller coaster carpeted with sparkling violet, green, pink, and white lights. "I know I'm going to like it here," she said.

We stayed at the Peninsula Hotel, on Kowloon. In order to reach Hong Kong Island proper, a ferry trip is required across the bay. These brief sea interludes gave Madame great pleasure ("The air is so . . . refreshing!") as did the food, the shopping, the incredible atmosphere of feverish activity which she adored. Again, there was to be little "consolation," but plenty of activity and shopping.

One night as we returned to Kowloon after a feast given for her by one of the local magnates, Madame insisted we walk back to the hotel from the ferry slip. "I must digest . . . ," she said grabbing my arm to steady herself. We tottered forward, for besides eating two helpings of every course (and demanding a half a duckling to take home) Madame had tippled liberally, from tiny cups, the delicious but murderously strong mulled wine.

Truth to tell—we were both feeling no pain.

The distance from the ferry to the Peninsula Hotel is only a few hundred yards skirting the waterfront. By day, the wide roadway flanked on one side with tatty arcades suggested an exotic suburbia. But at night, these solemn Victorian buildings, lit with pastel neons, exploded with merriment: each one hid a bar, a dancing palace, or a massage parlor, and the narrow lanes linking them led into a further maze of pulsating side-streets from which wafted vibrant sounds and spicy smells.

"Let us look closer. . . ." Eternally curious Madame swayed slightly in her efforts to view a rollicking barroom scene. She stood on tiptoe gazing, enraptured, through a bamboo screen.

"Let us go in!" she ordered, unable to see quite enough. I hesitated. The usual quota of jewelry sparkled on her neck, hands and arms, while the sables, draped about her shoulders, could hardly have been mistaken for rabbit.

She prodded me through the swinging doors. Our entrance was greeted with catcalls and whistles from several groups of English sailors, whose pink complexions, tousled hair and innocent blue eyes reassured me. " 'Allo, luv!" one called out, while another waved a bottle of San Miguel beer. "Have a snort, grand'ma." Without a moment's hesitation, Madame flopped on the nearest plastic banquette and, pulling me down by her side, announced, "Beer for everyone!"

A roar of approval echoed above the pounding sounds of a huge jukebox and produced a flurry of graceful, undulating Chinese girls anxious to join in the fun. Madame, now flanked by two of these chirping creatures, patted their hands, admired the flawless texture of their skins, and then zeroed in on their cheong sams.

"I call them beautiful dresses," she said to one. "Stand up, dear! What's your name?"

"Miss Smooth and Fragrant."

"Lovely name. And yours?" She turned to the other girl who, burying her nose in Madame's furs, murmured in a husky voice: "I'm Miss Lotus of Love."

"Most unusual."

She now carefully studied the "beautiful dresses." Cheong sams endow practically any figure with coltish grace. The high, rather stiff collar gives poise to neck and shoulders; the clinging, simple lines afford the body just the right suggestion of curves; while twin slits, extending from the hem of the dress upward, reveal the sex appeal of even a dumpy pair of legs. Madame, for all the mulled wine in her system, realized this . . . and more. She saw in a cheong sam, to be sure, slightly altered and remodeled, the perfect uniform for her daily needs. It was graceful, economical, and obviously required very little maintenance. The two girls, due to these lovely garments, were endowed with style. They could have passed muster, anywhere, as "ladies," although Madame was quick to observe their true occupation —"soiled doves" she was later to call them. For our companions were B-girls, which, in the East, amounts to prostitutes.

"She . . . a *Madame*?" Miss Lotus of Love's eyes bulged with surprise hearing me refer to my aged companion by this honorary prefix.

"Yes," I quickly nudged her, "but quite a different kind from any you may have known!"

"What-you-mean?"

"She a Grandmother Madame. In America, instead of calling old ladies 'grandmother,' we call them Madame!"

"Very strange."

Still, this seemed to satisfy her curiosity. Madame Rubinstein had completely seduced (if that is the proper word) her smiling companions. After a few whispered words she squeezed each girl's arm, waved a hand at the sailors, distributed a crumpled bill here and there and then shuffled out amid general applause—leaning heavily on me for support.

"Lovely girls . . ." she said as I opened her bedroom door and helped to unzip her; "they're both coming here first thing tomorrow morning!"

"Really?" I was astounded.

"Yes, we're all going out shopping together!"

Miss Smooth and Fragrant accompanied by Miss Lotus of Love duly appeared at nine on the following morning. They were both immaculately fresh and they led us, giggling profusely, to a complex of yard goods shops filled with incredible brocades. "So cheap!" Madame sat down on a rickety chair, drank a cup of tea, while the girls modeled the fabrics that had caught her eye. "Beautiful! How much?"

"Very clever lady . . . ," the storekeeper wiped his brow as we left loaded with merchandise which had cost a third of the quoted price.

"I love to bargain with Asiatics," Madame smiled happily. "They are . . . they are so understanding." She had spent barely a hundred dollars and bought enough material for at least a dozen cheong sams.

Our next stop was Miss Lotus of Love's personal dressmaker, who lived in one of those gigantic concrete buildings that had risen vertically, because of a shortage of space, all over Hong Kong and Kowloon. Madame had to pause to catch her breath at every landing as we climbed eight flights of stairs that were crawling with humanity.

The dressmaker, a diminutive little Chinaman whose hair was artfully painted with silver streaks, greeted the girls effusively and then turned to Madame bowing almost to the ground.

"Much honored!"

His professional name was Madame Rose.

I was forced to stand in the doorway, surrounded by curious moppets, as the ladies unraveled the yards of sparkling fabric we had all carried up. The apartment, a tiny box, boasted of but one piece of furniture—an ancient Singer sewing machine. Measurements were taken and a fitting was promised for the following morning at the hotel, since, as Madame Rose sadly observed, a full-length mirror was beyond his means.

"How can he make a dozen cheong sams overnight?" I asked Miss Smooth and Fragrant when we were back in the street.

"Very easy. All the neighbors help."

With the delivery of Madame's cheong sams made for her by "Madame Rose of Kowloon" (so read the labels), there was nothing left to delay us in Hong Kong. We flew on to Bangkok and thence to Australia.

"What about 'consolidation'?" I asked Madame on the plane. This was where most of our serious business discussions invariably occurred.

"Easy!"

"What do you mean?"

"We only stock English-made merchandise in Hong Kong. It's shipped from London. As you know, the English company's a foundation. I don't see a penny of their profits. We'll now send everything from Switzerland."

"So what's the advantage?"

"Stupid. . . . If we ship from Switzerland there are no taxes. Swiss francs are better money than English pounds. The merchandise is the same. But, the most important thing—I get the money! And," her knuckles crashed on my knee for further emphasis, "that's consolidation!"

Madame was given a tremendous welcome in Sydney—particularly by the press—and this was repeated in Melbourne, Adelaide, Perth.

"Fancy! They remember me."

There were editorials to welcome her, banquets to honor her, speeches to laud her.

"I swear. If you live long enough, everyone loves you."

Still, she adamantly refused to visit Coleraine, the small sheep-shearing town some eighty miles beyond Melbourne where she had first emigrated to from Poland, armed with her twelve jars of face cream—the twelve jars her mother had given her of "Crème Valaze."

"No! No! I don't want to go back there. For what? I was hungry, lonely, poor in that awful place. I worked twenty hours a day, every day, including Sundays. I swear, if I had to do it all over again, I would sooner kill myself."

This sudden outburst was soon dispelled. Madame called for a drink and said, "I've promised to visit Palestine! We'll leave tomorrow."

Our itinerary didn't call for such a detour. In fact, we were due to fly directly to Paris from Australia.

"Why Palestine?"

"Family business."

Madame wasn't yet in the mood to tell me and although I knew that she had relatives there, I also knew that visiting them wasn't exactly a form of therapy she enjoyed.

But on the last lap of our long flight, as we were over the Red Sea, Madame confided: "I'm going to build a museum and a factory in . . . in? Not Jerusalem, but the other town."

"Tel Aviv?"

"Yes, that's the place."

We were to visit Israel repeatedly together and yet Madame never learned to call this plucky, if puckish nation anything but "Palestine," or "You know, where the Jews now live."

"A museum *and* a factory?" I found the combination odd.

"Yes, both. Can't build one without the other."

"Why?"

"It's a deal. They want a museum and I want a factory."

"Tit for tat or 'consolidation'?"

"Both."


We were greeted, in Tel Aviv, by an enormous deputation which put the Japanese *and* the Australians to shame.

"Who are they?" I asked Madame as she straightened a perky "summer" bowler found in Bangkok and made of woven straw. "Probably beggars!" she answered.

They were hardly that.

Junior government ministers, journalists, and members of her family (now settled in Israel) mingled in a happy group carrying welcoming bouquets of honeysuckle, lilies, and wild jasmine. She was nearly engulfed by their warm, unctuous bodies.

"Get me out of here!" Madame pleaded. "I'm suffocating!"

The Dan Hotel, where we stayed, had the look of a provincial French Casino. It was modern and smelled of carbolic soap.

At first sight, Israel and its population seemed to combine the free-wheeling license of Arab nations, the cynicism of middle Europeans, and the opportunism of every nation that is essentially on the make —or trying to survive. But in those days, it wasn't yet a question of survival.

More than ten years ago all was peaceful endeavor and healthy prosperity there, in a setting of great pastoral beauty. However, Tel Aviv, our headquarters, seemed brash and ugly. Architecturally it reminded me of Casablanca and some sections of the upper Bronx. Its tall, modern buildings were already dilapidated. These accentuated the drabness of streets filled with semidetached villas and apartment houses. It was only when we visited Ayelet Hashahar, north of the Sea of Galilee, Caesarea, and Shaiku Zion that I felt liberated from the cloying but kindly efforts of an army of well-wishers who were anxious to make Madame feel comfortable.

They kept popping up, urging us to see "fantastic" sights, listen to "fantastic" concerts, almost begging for "fantastic" words of praise. Their fierce dedication to this land they had reclaimed, often violently, then lovingly nurtured, was indeed "fantastic." It was to remind me, when Madame and I later visited Russia, of the Intourist guides who constantly asked us to join in the chorus of their praise for the accomplishments of "Comrade Lenin."

"Crazy people!" Madame kept repeating. "But dedicated." She changed her tune somewhat when we visited Mrs. Weizmann, Ben Gurion, and Golda Meir.

Luncheon with Mrs. Weizmann might have occurred in Mayfair instead of her house at Rehovot. She received Madame Rubinstein in a well-proportioned library filled with masses of flowers, Chippendale furniture, autographed photographs of world leaders. Churchill glared at us between Balfour and Smuts; while Wilson, Roosevelt, and Eisenhower were kept on a separate table as were three successive kings of England and the Emperor Haile Selassie.

Mrs. Weizmann was Israel's "grande dame." She had a quiet serenity and pale features that were Anglo-Saxon rather than Slavic. At first she made me think of an English peeress forced to receive members of an American garden club. But when Madame Rubinstein, resplendent in one of Madame Rose of Kowloon's cheong sams, captured her full attention, she became just another aging woman interested in beauty.

"Dry skin?" I heard her ask.

"Don't worry," Madame answered with professional bluntness, "I have just the right product for you!"

I knew little of Chaim Weizmann whose bronze bust by Jacob Epstein had the place of honor on a vast desk, and was surrounded by a further posse of famous men. Later, Madame was to fill me in. "He invented some sort of explosive. It helped with the 1914 war. In return, he didn't ask for money . . . ," her lips curved downward at such stupidity, "but he wanted the Jews to have a homeland. Their own homeland. Palestine! He got it. He was a Zionist and became the first president. The founder. I wonder if it was worth the trouble?"

Our next visit was with Ben Gurion, the prime minister, who gave a luncheon in Madame's honor. There were scads of other officials milling around in shirt-sleeves. This seemed to be their favored uniform as is a Mao jacket in China. The food, when served, came up blandly kosher. Mr. Ben Gurion sat facing Madame in the center of a long table. I was at one end wedged between two buxom ladies whose conversation tacked between sewage and coeducation.

The French claim that at twenty minutes past the hour, if there is a silence during a meal, an angel has just passed. There was a silence —and I remember thinking of an anecdote concerning Jean Cocteau who, lunching with a Parisian hostess renowned for her lack of conversation and disgusting food, suddenly declared: "An angel has just passed!" Everyone looked surprised. Cocteau then added, "Quick, let's eat it!"

I must have been smiling to myself at this recollection when I caught Ben Gurion's eye. He was obviously bored.

"Who's your goy?" I heard him boom at Madame, pointing in my direction.

"My goy?" she peeked uncertainly down the table at me.

"*The only goy here,*" Mr. Ben Gurion emphasized.

"That's Patrick!" Madame beamed. "And . . . and, yes, *he is my goy!*"

Golda Meir, our last official visit, was then in charge of foreign affairs. She seemed to be interested only in Madame's possible contributions to Israel. Nothing had as yet been settled concerning the museum and the factory.

Two tough ladies, whose origins were not very different, now faced one another in a small, uncluttered office.

Mrs. Meir seemed brusque but kindly, while Madame was on the defensive. She wasn't used to dealing with such women, unless they were underlings, and couldn't help whispering to me: "Can you beat it! No make-up!"

"Madame Rubinstein, what do you think of our country?" Mrs. Meir asked.

"If I plan to build a factory *and* a museum, I must think highly of it."

"Which do you think is the more important?"

"The factory!"

"I agree."

The Helena Rubinstein Pavilion, when officially unveiled, preceded the opening of the Helena Rubinstein factory by almost three years.

Alas, the Pavilion, the Helena Rubinstein Pavilion in Tel Aviv, proved to be a disappointment—particularly to Madame.

"What a ramshot place!" she said after having nearly been crushed to death by the crowds during the opening ceremonies. Madame meant "ramshackle." "No carpets, funny lights, bad pictures!" Modern architecture seldom appealed to her and the Helena Rubinstein Pavilion could have been grander. But Madame hadn't been told at the time by those concerned with building it that it was merely one wing of an ultimate assemblage of buildings, each hopefully paid for by and dedicated to a rich American. As such, it could pass muster, although the paintings displayed for the opening were hardly stimulating. Madame had given two Utrillos from her collection and a fearsome portrait of herself by a Brazilian painter of little repute.

"What more do they want?" It was obviously hoped that after her death all of her collections would find a permanent home there. They didn't.

"I call it a racket!" Madame snapped some months later when further funds were demanded of her. "Why, it's almost blackmail!" What she didn't admit to was that American tax laws favored such arrangements and that, without them, many museums all over the world would never have existed, been endowed, bequeathed with vast and impressive collections gathered by tycoons such as herself—at minimal expense.

And yet her basic mistake was always holding back. If, instead of half a million dollars, she had given two or three million to Israel, the museum in Tel Aviv might have been equal in splendor and scope to that built by the late Billy Rose in Jerusalem. Of course, he did this to house his collections. Madame had no intention of leaving hers to Israel or, for that matter, to anyone.

"My underwear's all worn out! It's time we went home," Madame said to me some ten days after our arrival. By then, as we left Israel, we had been three months "on the road." But our return to the United States was still protracted. We had to stop in Athens (where Madame shopped for worry beads, carpets *and* a new agent) then in Rome, Paris, and London before our final return to New York in the spring.

This pattern of travel, "for consolidation," was to continue unabated until Madame's death. I was in constant attendance but, as she grew older, a series of nurses was added to our traveling entourage. Three months after we had returned to America from our round-the-world trip, in the summer of 1959, we flew to Moscow, for the opening of the American Fair. Whether it was because of memories of Russian grandeur instilled in her occasionally romantic imagination by Prince Gourielli before his death, or for commercial reasons, Madame approved investing nearly a hundred thousand dollars in the building and stocking of a Rubinstein beauty kiosk within the fairgrounds. Only two American cosmetics companies were represented. Hers— and Coty.

"One day," she said, "maybe we do business with the Russians. Better they know first about us . . . than The Nail Man."

Madame's party, on the Russian expedition, was a large one. Besides herself, a trained nurse, and me, there were Mala Rubinstein, her niece; Mrs. Cooper, her "English" sister; and four cosmeticians who all spoke Russian and preceded us. They were to remain in Moscow for six weeks—the duration of the Fair.

"I wonder if it's all worth it?"

On this doubting note, we flew from Paris in a Russian jet accompanied by a group of American VIP's involved in various aspects of the Fair.

Certain superficial aspects of Moscow and the secretive but proud deportment of its citizens, reminded me of what I had earlier seen in Tel Aviv. But while Tel Aviv was physically a battered modern city, Moscow still retained (notwithstanding ghastly gingerbread buildings erected during the Stalin regime) some of the splendid vestiges of a historical past. There was the extraordinary sweep of Red Square with, as a backdrop, the wild, Byzantine madness of the cathedral, the miles of crenelated walls surrounding the Kremlin, and the façades of nineteenth-century buildings such as Gum's the department store, and that of our own National Hotel.

"Moujiks!" Madame hissed furiously. "Peasants!"

We had just arrived at the National Hotel and were informed that Intourist had reserved three single rooms there—for Mrs. Cooper, Mala, and myself—but that Madame and her nurse were booked into the Leningrad Hotel.

There was no arguing. Smiles, soothing manners, even the suggestion of a tip, failed to sway the concierge's frozen features.

Madame and her nurse, an impassive Irish lady with big feet, were forced back into an Intourist limousine.

"See you tomorrow!" she screeched out of the window. ". . . for breakfast."

At seven-thirty in the morning, on the dot, a loud banging on my door woke me up. Was it the dreaded Secret Police? Nude but for a towel wrapped about my middle, I opened the door with a flourish.

"Hallo!" There was Madame dressed in an imperial purple cheong sam and wearing her favorite diamond brooch of twin Tsarist eagles plumb in the center of a matching bowler hat. Her nurse stood protectively by her side clutching a rosary.

"Time you got up!" she winked at me. "I'll be waiting for you in the dining room."

The dining room, at the National Hotel, offered a sensational view of the Kremlin walls and little else in the way of comfort and décor. Madame had appropriated a large table set in a window and covered every chair, to signify that these were reserved, with various of her belongings.

"The service is very slow!" she announced when I arrived. "But I've given each of the girls waiting on us a lipstick. That should help."

It did, repeatedly.

"The Fair opens tomorrow, *Gott sei Dank*! We can then leave and go back to civilization," Madame said after four days spent visiting "the sights"—four exhausting days.

The Fair started as a nonevent. At least, it seemed anticlimactic for all of the preparations, efforts, and, as Madame kept reminding us, expenses involved—that is, until we witnessed the argument which took place between the current Vice President of the United States, Richard Nixon, and the current Russian Premier, Comrade Khrushchev.

At first, it was a friendly discussion with the Vice-President lauding, as he pointed to the appliances in what was billed as "a typical American kitchen," American ingenuity, workmanship, living standards.

But with the crowds surging around them, television cameras whirling and flash bulbs exploding on all sides, Mr. Nixon couldn't resist the call of publicity over that of good manners. He wagged his finger under the Soviet Premier's nose, intensified his claims, hammed it up. Mr. Khrushchev's crafty eyes narrowed. His pink features flushed a deeper shade. Mr. Nixon, thinking of the votes back home, continued his harangue. He was obviously attempting to steal the limelight. By now, words were immaterial. What mattered was sound. The sound of angry voices enhanced by gestures—since how could such an argument, conducted in English and in Russian with attending interpreters trying to translate the dialogue, amount to anything? This was patently obvious to all present. What we were witnessing were two housewives clearing their lungs for the benefit of the neighbors.

"Silly men . . . ," Madame said, "but sillier people who take it all seriously."

That evening, at an American Embassy reception, Madame was introduced to Mr. Nixon. She talked to him for some minutes.

"What was he like?" I remember asking her.

"Of the two, I prefer the Russian," she answered.

"Khrushchev?"

"Yes. He's much more direct! Still, I wouldn't trust either one or the other. They're both out for *themselves*."

It was a relief to leave Moscow where, for a week, we had not seen a newspaper or heard any news concerning the outside, the "Western" world.

"Was it worth the effort?" I asked Madame when we were back in Paris.

"What do you mean?"

"Was it worth the effort of *your* going to Russia—and, before that, Japan, Australia, Israel?" By then I was tired of traveling. I felt like a middle-aged chorus boy in a road company for I had just celebrated my thirty-fifth birthday and was ready to settle down, even if briefly.

"Does all this travel really mean anything? Does it help the business?" I insisted.

"It helps me. And *I am* the business!"

"How does it help you?"

"It helps me to survive."

# "You're Nothing
# But a No-Good Bum!"

❦ ❦

"It helps me to survive!"

As usual, as always, Madame was thinking entirely of herself. Her ego, her selfishness, grew with age but, fortunately, like the circulation in her limbs, both ebbed and flowed uncertainly. Sometimes Madame was all smiles and small kindnesses; at others a raging termagant, whacking her desk, hollering at her staff and demanding constant attention. We all had to put up with her moods. It wasn't easy, particularly for me, since I was in her direct line of fire.

Often I wondered how I survived. Was I that dumb, faithful, plodding, and insecure? Or merely masochistic? Certainly not! I was a creature of habit and, in my own way, devoted to the tough little tyrant whom I served.

"You must give more, not less!" She kept reminding me.

"And what will *I get out of it*?" I answered back in one of my rare moments of revolt.

Madame was silent.

Upon hearing that various members of her American company were being given stock options, I asked her for a few shares.

"What do you need them for?"

"Don't I deserve them?"

There was another silence.

"The family and more important people than you have taken them

:[ 255 ]:

all. . . . But," she paused dramatically, "I'll buy you some, myself, with my own money."

Before I could thank her Madame was quick to add: "You'll have to reimburse me, of course, little by little . . ."

I accepted with a great show of heartfelt gratitude, for I had seldom had more than a month's salary before me. A few days later Madame presented me with three hundred shares of Helena Rubinstein common stock. The gift was accompanied by a sheaf of promissory notes, equivalent to the current cash value of the shares, for me to sign. Madame was the beneficiary. Since the stock was high the shares amounted to more than fifteen thousand dollars and the notes were payable at a rate of twenty-four hundred dollars every year.

"Without interest . . ." Madame's lawyer benignly assured me.

He had engineered the deal for her.

Every Christmas, as a promissory note fell due, Madame tore it up and presented me with the scraps. This was her private bonus, her personal yuletide gift. I naturally thanked her copiously until it dawned on me, when I asked for a raise and she refused, that the arrangement was a brilliant ploy. "What do you need more money for? A third of the year you travel with me, a third of the year you live with me in Paris—that leaves a third when you're on your own. Besides, you have those shares I gave you. Why, you're very well off!"

I was too staggered to say anything. But I realized that I was trapped by my own insecurity. Seven years would have to go by until my debt, as she canceled it, was finally paid. She died before that, and when she was no longer around to tear up the promissory notes, her "Estate" and lawyers claimed the money I still owed.

While Madame knew full well that she held me fast on sentimental grounds (although this was never discussed), she made doubly sure of it by using money as her principal weapon. She gave me small handouts if and when I became moody. My expenses were no longer questioned by her. But there were no raises.

Until her death we continued to visit Europe twice a year together, with a nurse in attendance. This somewhat curtailed our global travels although it didn't prevent Madame from visiting Scandinavia, from repeatedly touring Italy, and "discovering" Spain. I persevered.

Habit is strong wine, but affection is an even stronger brew. I loved my life with Madame . . . except, except. Where, where on earth, I often wondered, did it lead to?

One day in early 1961 while with her in Paris, I was called up by the Baronne Guy de Rothschild. She had been a friend of mine long before her marriage to the head of the famous banking family, long before I began to work for Madame; in fact, we had known one another when, as Marie-Hélène Van Zuyland, she first lived in New York. Always blunt, she came to the point without preliminaries.

"Do you know Georges Pompidou?"

"By name, of course."

He was then an up-and-coming politician who had worked for the Rothschild bank (where his only contribution, reputedly, had been the installation of computers) and who was now attached to General de Gaulle's staff. It was even whispered that he was being groomed, by his irascible boss, to become Prime Minister of France.

"You must help him!" Marie-Hélène, in her "no-nonsense" voice, urged me. "He wants an apartment at Quai de Bethune, in Madame Rubinstein's building. Please talk to her . . ."

I reported my conversation to Madame. She was vague but finally admitted: "I believe he's coming to see me tomorrow. Marie Cuttoli, Picasso's friend, arranged it. Fancy." She looked me up and down, as when we had first met so many years before on Madison Avenue and at Fleur Cowles'. "You know the Baroness de Rothschild?"

"I have lots of odd friends."

"You can say that again!"

Madame was always surprised by the diversity of my friends and acquaintances—as was I, occasionally—but while I took it in my stride, she pondered. It was pleasing to her, yet disturbing. Would I not, one day, take off; take off for greener pastures? If I could have only told her the answer was "No," many of our subsequent problems might not have occurred. But then, Madame was Madame—defensive, watchful, eternally suspicious.

Mr. Pompidou walked in, on the dot of noon, for his appointment. I received him in the salon. His bluish jaw line, bushy eyebrows and

:[ 257 ]:

prominent nose intensified the cold but knowing glint in a pair of eyes that were never quite at rest. He had the look of a country farmer, very much on his guard, at a cattle auction.

Some minutes later, wearing one of her favorite quilted dressing gowns and a pair of matching bedroom slippers, Madame shuffled in. She was cradling a box of ginger. Before I could effect a formal introduction she offered a piece to the future Prime Minister and President of France: "Have some," she said, "have some, it gives energy."

One of Madame's favorite tricks, in order to assess what she called "important people," was to show them her collections. Their reactions invariably told her almost all she wanted to know about them— even the extent of their wealth. "Most people can't help showing off," she would wink. "I soon know what they have if they compare their stuff to mine and that, that tells me how rich they are!"

Mr. Pompidou didn't seem to own a thing.

But he knew about everything.

"He's what I call a real connoisseur!" Madame nudged me. "I'll let him have that apartment as soon as we have discussed the key money."

(In France as in many countries where rents, if compared to the United States, may seem minimal, there is a subtle Gallic dodge known as "key money." The owner of a property, particularly an apartment, may charge a premium before the prospective tenant receives the lease or . . . the key. As Madame admitted, "It's a racket. But how else can poor landlords like myself make a profit?" Poor landlords, indeed. . . .

Key money could involve considerable sums. This depended on size, condition, and location—and 24 Quai de Bethune, Madame's building, was looked upon as a splendid address where, as she put it, "Only the best people live.")

"I'll ask him for plenty," Madame confided. "After all, he's worked for the Rothschilds; he was recommended by a friend of yours *who is* a Rothschild; and if he's Prime Minister one day, he'll make a packet."

"Not in France, Madame. Most Prime Ministers die poor," I interjected.

"Rubbish!"

"What about the key money—the *pas-de-porte?*" Madame inquired of Mr. Pompidou as he seemed ready to leave. Her voice was that of Oliver Twist asking for an extra helping of gruel. It was barely audible.

"It's for you to decide."

"No. You're the banker. Now tell me, before I tell you, how much should it be?"

"Eight million." Mr. Pompidou didn't hesitate.

"Did you say eighteen?" Madame cupped an ear.

"No, *chère* Madame. Eight."

"Make it ten. It's a lovely apartment."

"I know. My wife has set her heart on it."

"Then, surely, it's worth ten?"

Mr. Pompidou wasn't one to quibble. He nodded. Madame looked disappointed.

"Eleven?"

"No. Ten . . . *très chère* Madame."

"*Bon, comme vous voulez.*"

I was surprised Madame had let him off the hook that easily. Later she said, "Nice man. I should have insisted on twelve. But you, *you!*" She almost snarled. "It was *your job* to see that I didn't weaken!" These attacks always numbed me. What was I to do? So I said: "But Madame, he may be helpful to you if and when he's prime minister. Who knows?"

"Yes, I thought of that. Still, you were of no help!"

I suffered these brief attacks and fortunately forgot them. I knew that Madame didn't always mean them. She was still "educating" me.

The Pompidous, when they moved in, were exemplary tenants. Some months later, when he became prime minister, Madame took pride in the fact that she harbored such a distinguished couple; and that he seemed to favor living and sleeping in his new apartment, Quai de Bethune, rather than at the Palais Matignon, his official residence.

"He likes our place," she told the inquiring press. "It's quieter than that palace of his where he pays no rent."

Whenever in Paris Madame enjoyed looking down, peeking, at the Pompidous. From the small dining room of her apartment there was a clear view of Madame Pompidou's bedroom and her husband's dressing room, three floors below.

"Let us see what they're up to!" She would urge me by her side, particularly in the mornings, when all of the windows were open and a maid dusted, vacuumed, and aired the Pompidous' beds.

Madame Pompidou's conventionally feminine bedroom was tastefully paneled in gray *boiserie*, while Mr. Pompidou's dressing room might have been a stage set for the bachelor quarters of an English squire—one whose solid taste hearkened back to turn-of-the-century music halls.

Over a mahogany day bed, set in an alcove, there hung the full-length portrait of a nude wood nymph. From a distance, the space of three floors and a hundred yards of separating courtyard, it looked like a Bouguereau.

"Who's Bouguereau?" Madame asked me.

"A nineteenth-century academic painter who liked the human form," I answered.

"I can see that! Valuable?"

"No. Interesting."

"I can also see that!"

Always curious, she longed to know what the rest of the Pompidous' apartment looked like and was saddened, as their landlady, not to have been invited down "for a visit."

The concierge furnished cursory details. It was *"très moderne, très correcte, très comme il faut."*

Mr. and Mrs. Pompidou, when we met them in the elevator, were also *"très correctes, très comme il faut."* He bowed, she smiled.

"What a dull pair!" Madame couldn't help voicing her final disappointment.

But she discovered that the prime minister was a man of punctual habits. He always left his apartment and her building at ten to nine, on the dot, in an official Citroën. It was flanked by two outriders on motorcycles and followed by a police car.

Madame's aged Chrysler had finally collapsed. She was reduced, much to her relief to being transported back and forth between her home and her office in taxis. These were hard to find until the variety summoned by radio came into being.

"Very useful. They cost a bit more but they're still cheaper than a lousy car and a lazy chauffeur."

Now aware that Mr. Pompidou left at ten to nine, she had me call a radio taxi, ordering it to wait for her at a quarter to nine.

"We'll follow his car!" Madame announced.

"Why?"

"*Nudnik!* It doesn't stop for anything. It gets to Quai d'Orsay in ten minutes. We would take twenty."

So we roared to work behind the prime minister's cavalcade, oblivious of traffic lights, policemen, pedestrians.

"See?" Madame leaned forward and looked at the meter. "That saves at least a hundred francs."

"Twenty-five cents," I murmured.

"A hundred francs in France is much more than twenty-five cents in America!" She shook a finger under my nose. "Will you ever learn? *Small sums make big ones.*"

In her tenth decade saving taxi money became an obsession with Madame—one that had grown steadily since first we met—as was turning out lights and watching my alcohol consumption.

"You drink too much, just like Roy."

"Maybe we both have to?"

She was again silent but began measuring bottles in the pantry behind my back. She would attack, retreat, and retrench—only to attack again when I least suspected it. This nagging continued in various subtle ways. In the spring of 1963 we were enjoying a respite from travel in New York when my mother, whom I adored and who would do her utmost to soothe me when life with Madame became too difficult, broke her hip. She fell on a street corner but still managed to call me at the office. As I rushed out, Madame intercepted me.

"It's only three. Where are you going to?"

"My mother's had an accident."

"People have accidents every day."

I must have raised my voice, such was my anguish, because Madame recoiled. She fiddled with her purse and produced a dollar bill.

"Here, go. For your taxi . . ."

I rushed by her.

Madame was unable to encompass human anxiety or grief. When President Kennedy was assassinated she complained bitterly that her offices should be closed. It was the same thing with my mother.

A week later as I was by my mother's bedside, visiting her, she suddenly stared at me strangely, plucked her sheets, and then reached for the bell hanging by her side. Before her hand could press the buzzer to summon a nurse, an intense pain must have welled in her left breast. She fell back on the pillows. I now grabbed the bell, pressed it repeatedly, before rushing out in the corridor for help. It was too late. In a matter of seconds my mother had died of a massive embolism. As is the case with many single men, compulsive bachelors, I worshipped my mother and my grief was sincere. Still, much of it also stemmed from misguided feelings of guilt, as it always does. Had I been a "good" son? Should I have been absent, all of those years, traveling with Madame? Had I been sufficiently attentive? These thoughts, and many more, plagued me.

After the funeral I returned to work where Madame greeted me abruptly. She had carefully assessed the situation. What I needed was a change.

"We'll both go to Europe, as soon as possible. There's work to be done in Switzerland, Germany, France . . . Aii! If you only knew."

She was again—as when the Prince and Horace had died—creating "a diversion." My crisis had given her the energy she craved for. It had stimulated her. The only therapy for bereavement, in her mind, was movement and work.

Off we went to Europe. Whenever my eyes grew vacant, whether it was in Germany or Switzerland, Madame piled more and more work on me. My only satisfaction was that I wore out a typewriter and she had to buy me a new one. I was badgered and bullied but in no shape to fight back because the full impact of my mother's death was gradually undermining my health. I couldn't eat, slept fitfully, often dis-

"I like to pay cash!" Madame with Van Dongen after
having "paid cash" for one of his paintings.

"He's a nice man, but I don't always like his taste!" Madame and Cecil Beaton, 1959. (*Photo William Connors*)

"Anyone interested in money must study the stock exchange. . . ." Madame did so daily, in bed, wearing a four-dollar cotton nightdress, 1964. (*Photo Max Scheler, Magnum*)

charged my duties as might a sleepwalker. This enraged Madame: "You must pull yourself together!" She shook a warning finger under my nose, to no avail. Although Madame was right, her methods were wrong. We reached Paris as a flu epidemic broke out. I was one of the first victims.

Sickness, particularly among the members of her staff, but specifically in her own household, was anathema to Madame. For the first few days, as I lay sweating and comatose in the Prince's small bedroom, she contained her anger and ignored me. Her way of hastening my recovery was to send me, along with a sustaining cup of broth, folders of documents on which I was to note my opinions and state my recommendations.

"Eugénie! Tell her I can't even see straight."

"I know, Monsieur, but she misses you."

As my flu abated, complete lethargy took over. I was limp, apathetic and sad.

"Six days in bed!" Madame hadn't come near me but she complained to Eugénie who, always ready to pour fuel on any fire burning in the household, was only too pleased to quote Madame's displeasure as she delivered the notes the latter bombarded me with. Most of these were accusations of self-indulgence. Finally, hearing that I was no longer feverish, she summoned me, one evening, to her presence.

Madame had a sense of the dramatic. She had carefully staged our interview. Her room looked as if a typhoon had hurled hundreds of letters and papers onto every available piece of furniture and square inch of floor. In this setting she sat, her chignon unraveled, her make-up askew, scribbling away at a bridge table which had been specially set up for her labors.

"See, no one to help me!"

I stood mute before her, as if about to be court-martialed. This produced a holocaust of words.

"As God is my witness I swear, I swear you're useless to yourself *and to me*! Look at the work I have to do alone while you sleep all day. At your age. I call you weak. You're nothing, *nothing but a no-good bum*!"

I bowed acquiescence and slowly walked out. It was then I was aware that tears blurred my eyesight. When I reached my room, alone and unseen, uncontrollable sobs wracked me with a ferocity I had not experienced since childhood.

". . . no-good bum!" Madame's invective kept echoing in my mind. My palms were moist again; sweat poured down my shirt front; I trembled uncontrollably. It was then I decided I had to see a doctor but, at eight in the evening, most doctors in Paris are sitting down to dinner. Only extreme or unavoidable emergencies will budge them.

I took a taxi to the American Hospital in Neuilly after advising Eugénie: "If I'm not back in a couple of hours, please tell Madame. But only do so in the morning . . ."

An intern received me. He felt my pulse, examined my eyes, studied the thermometer he had placed in my mouth and then whistled.

It read 104°!

"But I've just had flu!" I told him.

"You're in for a relapse and, besides, there are other symptoms."

"What?"

"Have you been under a great strain, recently?"

I briefly told him about the stress of the past few weeks—my mother's death and my life with Madame. Tears again rolled down my cheeks.

"Your other symptoms," he said gently, "are what the French call '*Une crise nerveuse.*' You've been having a nervous breakdown. Now, off to bed!"

"What about my pajamas?"

"Don't worry, we'll call your home in the morning and have everything you need sent over. What's more, if I have a chance to talk to that old lady . . . I'll tell her a thing or two!"

For a week, sedated and somnolent, I gradually recovered—awakening only for meals and a brief gossip with the staff. It was the best therapy.

"Guess what?" a giggling nurse confided. "The Aly Khan is in the room next to you. It's a double. He's having *his* nervous breakdown with a lady!"

Madame didn't telephone or even have a member of her staff inquire for my news. My resentment against her slowly grew to boiling point. "The selfish old bag!" I remembered thinking of her when the

Prince died. She was . . . she was utterly heartless. And yet? I was always one to hesitate or as Madame was fond of saying: "Give others the benefit of the doubt."

What I didn't know, and only learned later, she was distressed and anxious on my behalf but, as I had seen time and again, unable to voice her sentiments.

The doctor insisted on further rest when I had recovered and was about to be discharged.

"Don't go home, it will only happen again!"

I now wrote a short note to Madame telling her I was going away. I didn't specify where, but planned to fly to Marrakech. It was the only place I could think of, in March, where sun and a serene atmosphere were assured. Then, and only then, did I realize I had no money to speak of.

Jean Dessès, the dress designer, came to my rescue. Few friends could have been kinder. Without a moment's hesitation, when I told him of my plight, he drove over to the hospital, took me to the airport, and then pressed an envelope in my hand. It contained a thousand dollars.

"Less than one of my dresses," he laughed. "Travel now and pay later."

He had always called Madame his "fiancée," even to her face. She adored such attentions. "The Greek . . . the Greek's a real nice man —a gentleman! I only hope he's not serious?" Madame's sense of humor failed to encompass such elegant banter.

"I'll call up my fiancée," were Dessès's parting words to me, "and tell her that if she keeps on giving you nervous breakdowns I'll break off our engagement!"

As I flew off to Morocco waves of guilt, coupled with the jitters, hit me, for I realized, belatedly, that it would have been courteous had I called Madame and informed her where I was going. But such a confrontation was beyond me. I took the easy way out.

A dilapidated taxi drove me to the Mamounia Hotel. It was here I proposed to "hole in." Arab courtesy and French luxury soon soothed me. The view from my bedroom window of snow-capped mountains, of tropical gardens, of a vast swimming pool filled with the clearest water I have ever seen soon made me forget my troubles—both real and imaginary.

For two days I never budged but slept, ate ravenously, and gradually recovered my health, and my optimism. On my way to the dining room, for my first meal outside of the protective confines of my bedroom, I encountered Nina Mdivani and her husband Tony Harewood. It was she who had first said, years previously, when I questioned her about Prince Gourielli: "Darlink! In Russian Georgia, to be a Prince, all you have to have are six sheep."

No one knew better. Nina Mdivani had been born a Georgian Princess. Her life, from the time she fled Russia accompanied by several lusty brothers and a vague mother, read like a novel. At least so Madame Rubinstein liked to tell me. They were also old friends.

"Nina's the salt of the earth!"

Over the years, Nina married first an American millionaire, next one of Conan Doyle's sons (whose father invented Sherlock Holmes) and, finally, the young man who was now with her and who had been her second husband's secretary. He was dark, skeletal. Seen together they were an "odd" couple—just like Madame and myself—for Nina, besides being some years older, was enormous and practically blind due to a glandular defect.

While her brothers had also all married sensationally—one of them to Barbara Hutton—the whole extraordinary family was plagued by bad luck. The "marrying Mdivanis," as they were called, were invariably divorced by their rich spouses and then killed in a series of strange accidents.

Nina, however, endured. She tiptoed, gracefully, from one grand hotel to the next, sightless, weighing more than the late Aga Khan, but blessed with an inexhaustible supply of charm and sweetness.

On the sensational clothes created for her by Balenciaga, Dior, and Saint Laurent she wore huge pieces of equally extraordinary jewelry. One day encircling her powdered neck there would be massive necklaces of cameos of every Roman emperor after the Decline; the next, equally large turquoises, set in diamonds. Like Edith Sitwell, who was taller than the average basketball player, Nina firmly believed that clothes and accessories should be "statements"—daring and dramatic. Only her slender legs, and tiny feet, suggested she had once been slim and beautiful.

"Darlink, you look so sick!" Nina brushed her cheeks on mine: "What you doing here?"

I explained I had had flu but, with a second cocktail, told her the truth and described "my breakdown."

"So, finally, 'The Computer,' she did you in?"

Nina always gave Madame a series of evocative nicknames—"*La Reine de la Crème,*" "*La Machine Infernal,*" and, now, "The Computer!"

"I send her telegram. Tell her you're in my care. Not to worry, not to bother . . . "

But Nina's telegram had the opposite effect. It activated Madame. Almost daily, until I eventually returned to Paris two weeks later— cured, rested, and strangely at peace—I received a handwritten letter from her. Even so, during my first carefree days in Marrakech, I had decided to resign from my job and leave Madame's employment. As she had often said, during our grueling travels: "Who needs this?" Life was too short. I had worked too hard for her, and while my love and admiration had not yet soured I wanted "Out!" Madame had gone too far, asked too much, showed too little sympathy. During the dozen years of our association my private life had been nonexistent and my holidays, as I had often complained, were few and far between.

"Your life is one long holiday!" Madame quipped when I wanted to go on a cruise of the Greek Islands, invited by Elsa Maxwell. Stavros Niarchos, the Greek shipowner, had organized it.

"I need you here, with me . . ." she said.

I capitulated.

But I now realized, finally, although life with Madame had been fascinating . . . it would have been anyway—even without her. She was the instigator—self-centered and selfish—but I was the catalyst. And yet I learned much from her. Still, was I in her debt; or was she in mine?

These thoughts, and many others, haunted me while I tried to make my mind up in Marrakech: a good life of servitude versus a free one? A free one . . . that meant uncertainty! What finally brought me back to heel, to her side, were Madame's letters.

"My dear Patrick," the first one read, "I was astonished not to have seen you before you left. The maid, Marguerite, just came in. I honestly nearly dropped dead when she told me I had been unkind to you. I swear, on the memory of your dead mother, I care more for your well-being than anyone living. I can't show it because all of my life I have been alone. It is impossible for me to be demonstrative . . ."

Her writing was almost illegible. There was a P.S.

"I wanted to send you five hundred dollars. But since you are not here to open my safe I cannot!"

Madame's letters kept on appearing. They were confused but affectionate. She was unwell. She was home, resting. For Madame, evidently affected by empathy (or subtle diplomacy?) succumbed to a breakdown of her own. I answered her letters politely if vaguely.

"My dear Patrick," her second letter read, "I am ill myself but hope that the rest and sun are doing you much good. I was so very upset that you should have felt bad concerning me. I'm still trying to send you five hundred dollars but, without you, who's to do it?" Her letter finished, "I plan to go to Cannes where I shall hopefully recover."

From Cannes, where she had fled to, Madame continued to write.

". . . I want to forget our differences. I hope you know that I love you, *as a mother*. The mother you lost!" There was no mention of the five hundred dollars but another P.S. rounded off this missive. "Give my love to Nina and her husband. Tell them that I love them very much!"

I showed this letter, as I had all of the others, to Nina.

"Darlink! 'The Computer,' she feels guilty, because of me. *I am witness*. Has she sent money?"

"No."

"All this love to Nina and lovely Tony . . . just window dressing. Don't move until she send money!"

But, by then, I had completely recovered and now realized that it was impossible for me to leave Madame. I couldn't escape from her. What's more, her letters had touched me and I longed to be by her side.

Nina kept urging me to stay. She soon gave up. "You're fool, darlink! But nice fool. I see you off and then write to 'Computer.' Tell her that Irish, like Russian, very sensitive—must be treated *delicately*."

I returned to Paris on the day before Madame flew in from Cannes.

"Ah, Monsieur!" Both Eugénie and Marguerite greeted me. "Madame . . . Madame was in a terrible state. She really loves you. Who else does she have to love? But you are young and she is old. It's for you to make peace! . . . besides, *she needs you!*"

On the following day I met Madame at the airport. Her arms cradled a huge bunch of carnations—those with small blooms that grow wild, come spring, in the hills of Provence.

"Here!" Madame nipped a carnation and tucked it in my lapel, "For luck, for us . . ."

She held up a small gloved hand. It was to prevent me from expressing the feelings I longed to pour out. We never discussed "our" breakdowns, mine and hers, and our relationship, until her death two years later, was that of a devoted son and a demanding mother. Demanding? No more, probably, than the average employer. But, by then, I had surely replaced Horace—Horace, the principal love of her life. Horace, her dead son.

Madame now went out of her way to seek my advice. She watched over me. She was kindness itself.

"Eat more than less. Drink less than more. Get lots of rest! Air . . . what you need is air. Come and visit me, in the country, next week end. You'll get lots of air and, besides, we'll be able to talk shop. *It will do us both good.*"

I went, willingly.

I was again at her beck and call.

She had finally won.

# "You Can Kill Me.
# But I Won't Let You Rob Me!"

❦ ❦

E arly on the morning of May 21, 1964, Madame's secretary called me at home in New York.

"She's been robbed!"

"Who?"

"Who else? Madame! Madame's been robbed, tied to a chair, and attacked," Nancy Goldburgh repeated on the telephone. Few people had a keener taste for drama, or a sharper voice, than Madame's "Number One Little Girl." I thought she must be joking.

I was stupefied. It seemed inconceivable, for all her millions, that anyone would try to rob Madame, in her home, in broad daylight, early in the morning. Why, it was as if Cardinal Spellman had been held up on the front steps of Saint Patrick's Cathedral. Then I remembered that Lady Diana Cooper had just had a similar experience in London. Three gunmen, wearing masks, had pranced into her bedroom as she was getting dressed for dinner. She fell on her knees and started praying. "What are you doing?" one of her assailants queried: "I'm praying for you!" I wondered if Madame had had the same fortitude. Then the words "tied to a chair and attacked" sank in.

"Is she all right?" I asked.

"Of course, you clunk! Better come quick! Everyone else is here. The police, press, TV." She made it all sound like a glamorous cocktail party—and barely refrained from suggesting I was a fool to be missing all the fun. I hurried over.

Police cars and television trucks still ringed Madame's apartment building when I arrived there half an hour later.

"Where are you goin', Mac?" A large Irish cop stopped me.

"To Madame Rubinstein's apartment."

"Any identification?"

I pointed to the doorman, another Irishman, and winked. "Pat will tell you. I'm her stepson."

The three thieves, I later discovered, had been far more inventive. They gained access into the triplex by pretending they were delivering a table arrangement of red roses.

Two city detectives now opened the front door. Nancy Goldburgh again exercised her powerful lungs. She screamed out from behind them, "Guess what? Madame's the only one who isn't hysterical!"

"Who's this guy?" one of the detectives asked her.

"He's the Irish help . . . ," I heard her say as I edged my way down a flight of stairs to Madame's bedroom.

Madame always disliked an orderly bedroom. But this time it looked as if it had been struck by a tornado. Piles of clothes covered the floor like the crazy flagstones of an English rock garden. The mattress on her lucite bed had been ripped apart, the telephones torn out of their wall sockets, the drawers and closets thrown open and emptied.

"Hallo!" Madame greeted me softly. "Nice mess?" She was still seated on the curved, transparent lucite chair to which she had been bound and gagged with her own bed sheets. She looked pale but composed and even now was knotting her chignon back into place.

"Fancy, they seemed to be such nice boys. I wonder what drove them to do such a thing?"

"Profit!" I mumbled.

"But all they got was a hundred dollars!"

"How did it happen?"

"I was having breakfast. Albert came in again some minutes after he had given me my tray. This time there were three men behind him. I thought they were the lawyers. But I couldn't see their faces. Then, then one of them came up to me. He held something black, shiny,

:[ 272 ]:

and cold close to my head. I was sort of befuddled and didn't realize it was . . . it was a gun."

While Madame had first been incoherent when interviewed by the police right after the robbery (claiming later that their questions were boring), she now felt chatty and assured me that she hadn't been frightened—merely inconvenienced, because she wanted to go to the toilet.

We were joined by Albert, Madame's nurse, and Nancy. Some minutes later, Madame's daughter-in-law, Nieuta Titus, and Mala Rubinstein rounded off the audience.

"Albert! Tell us how they got in!" Madame was now in full, magnificent control of herself. But Albert, having also been bound and knocked down by the thieves, was still suffering from shock.

"With flowers!" he answered, rubbing his elbows pensively.

"What sort of flowers?"

"Roses. . . ."

"Nice roses? Where are they?"

"In the pantry."

"Good! Put them later in the icebox in case we have company for lunch!"

Albert now told us, in an indistinct singsong, how he had opened the back door and been faced with three men each holding a gun. Their faces were covered with silk stockings. These were later found in the service elevator.

"Take us to Princess Gourielli!" he recalled one of them saying.

"See, they knew me by my good name," Madame nodded with satisfaction.

More than five hundred yards separated the service entrance of the huge triplex from Madame Rubinstein's bedroom. The thieves were out of breath and nervous when they finally reached their victim's presence. Moreover, they hadn't expected to find her still curled up in bed, munching a piece of toast, partially shielded by *The New York Times*. It was only when her maid Mathilda walked into the room— some minutes after the thieves' appearance at eight-thirty A.M.— screamed and fainted, that Madame finally fully registered what was happening around her.

"What do you want?" she remembered asking them.

:[ 273 ]:

"Give us the keys of your safe or we'll kill you," one of them ordered.

"I'm an old woman," Madame snapped back. "You can kill me. But I'm not going to let you rob me. Now get out." She pretended to resume her reading until she suddenly realized that the keys she had just been asked for were in her purse and her purse was by her side— hidden, fortunately, by masses of papers. While the thieves were busy emptying drawers and disconnecting the telephones, Madame some- how managed to pluck them out.

"Think if I had walked in!" Nancy Goldburgh injected breath- lessly. "Good thing I was late."

"You always are!"

Madame now admitted to us where she had hidden the keys. She pointed archly to the cleavage of her bosom and went on to say how one of the thieves had then spied her purse. He emptied its contents in her lap.

Two enormous diamond earrings rolled out on the counterpane with handfulls of paper, a compact, and several twenty-dollar bills. The thief grabbed the money. It amounted to a hundred dollars. The earrings were worth forty thousand dollars, but Madame had managed to cover them with a Kleenex, as they rolled on her bed. The two other thieves now reappeared. They had just tested the door lead- ing to Madame's treasure trove. It was solid oak and armed with a pair of strong locks. Nothing, nothing but the required keys or a jimmy could have opened it.

Time was running out. The thieves must have known that at nine on the dot, even if Madame's secretary failed to appear, others would.

It was twenty-five minutes before nine.

They again surrounded the lucite bed. Madame admitted to "feel- ing good." These were the words she used to describe her victory. The keys were safe. The safe was safe . . . and so were the earrings. She not only felt "good," but "cheeky."

"Your friend took a hundred dollars out of my purse. See to it that both of you get your share!"

Huddled in bed, Madame pointed to her assailant. He reacted by tearing the covers off the tiny, defiant body, yanking her to her feet, and then tying her to a chair. She began to scream. For such a small woman, one well over ninety years of age, Madame's lungs, as we all knew, were still powerful. She must have sounded like the sirens on the police cars which appeared shortly after the intruders had left. Albert had managed to break free and call for help.

"Fancy! They ripped my good sheets to tie me up before running out with only a hundred dollars . . . ," Madame chuckled, "minus about forty for roses." Yes, she had won the day.

"But they could have taken a Picasso drawing or that Braque gouache hanging by your fireplace," I said.

"Yes. But they didn't have your taste for art!"

"They could have taken some of those gold boxes and jewels in the vitrine of your bedroom," it was Nancy Goldburgh's turn.

"Yes. But they didn't have your sharp eyes!"

"They could have taken your sables from the cupboard in the bathroom," Madame's daughter-in-law suggested.

"So, so furs are what *you* like?"

For the next hour, Madame continued sitting on the lucite chair talking away to us while she tried to fathom who had robbed her and why.

"Such nice boys," she kept repeating.

"How could you know?" I asked.

"Their voices were refined. They had clean hands, well-manicured nails. But, I swear, I swear they were amateurs. You all want to know something?"

Everyone leaned forward.

"I think they must have known me from somewhere. I think they were people I knew, too. Like. . . ."

"Like what?"

"Like people who work for me!"

She eyed us all suspiciously.

There was a knock at the door. We all jumped involuntarily. But it was only Ann Walsh, the new director of publicity, who informed Madame that every network television company had a truck standing by on Park Avenue, with a crew waiting to interview her.

"Quick, quick! I must get ready. . . . Order me a car. One of those big, black, shiny things that cost only fifteen dollars an hour!"

Madame now dressed with infinite care. She applied her own make-up and then spent some minutes selecting her most important pearls in the cupboard the thieves had failed to enter. Later, when I thought about these careful preparations and recalled Madame's appearance before the television cameras, I couldn't but help remembering the last scene of *Sunset Boulevard*. While Gloria Swanson had been wild and demented, Madame behaved with an almost mystic calm. She tottered forward, like some exotic deity, flaunting the jewelry that hadn't been stolen. Her bowler hat was of scarlet velvet. On it an enormous clip of baroque pearls shimmered in the spring sunlight. More pearls encircled or rather froze her neck into place and poured down the front of a magenta suit.

"Miss Rubinstein! Madame Rubinstein! Princess. . . ."

Microphones were thrust under her nose. It was a jungle of hands, wires, and anxious faces waiting for a statement.

"Princess! Madame! Miss! . . . , say something!"

"So, so I was robbed. It can happen to the best people."

"More! More!"

"They took a hundred dollars. I'll make it up at bridge tonight."

She slowly heaved herself into "the big, black, shiny thing"—a Carey limousine—and waved vaguely at the crowd.

"Where is she going to?" someone asked.

"Long Island. . . ."

Madame, sitting regally with her nurse by her side—so small that only her hat and eyes could be seen—ordered the car to drive slowly around the block, to the service entrance of her building; the same entrance the thieves had used to break into and then escape from her apartment.

She rested for a few hours before going to Long Island and trying to resume her normal activities.

But she was never fully able to do so again. Belated symptoms of fear plagued her. She complained of hearing strange noises in the middle of the night. The apartment was too large. Every lock had to be changed, an intricate antiburglar system installed. "I'm afraid! I'm afraid!"

:[ 276 ]:

The thieves were never apprehended nor was any clue discovered as to their identity.

"Why are you afraid?"

"They might come back. Or others. . . . And I know that I wouldn't be as lucky . . . the second time!"

# "I Know How Much
# You'll Miss the Old Girl"

❦ ❦

"The second time. . . ." This was much on Madame's mind as she kept repeating: "I don't feel so good. . . . I'm not going to the office today. . . . I don't think I'll have the strength to go to Europe this summer. Aii! I'm afraid."

For Madame, who never admitted to a single weakness, these complaints were a bad sign. She felt herself to be slipping; but who, who could help her?

For months after the robbery, she would lie in bed, hour after hour, not in the now dreaded lucite bed from which she had been forcibly evicted by the thieves, but in a special hospital cot equipped with an oxygen tent. Madame's heart, her circulation, many of the vital functions of her body were, as she put it, "conking out."

I tried, we who were close to her all tried, to find new ways of entertaining her, of amusing her, of stimulating interests that seemed to flutter, uncertainly, as did her heart.

Magazines, newspapers, books—even the precious financial statements—no longer interested her. While awake, in the hospital cot, she slowly worked her way through the two hundred typed pages of a black, leather-covered book. This was her will—"My testament."

It had been bound specially for easier study and looked like a huge Puritan's bible with, studding the outer margin, a line of bright red letters—the letters of the alphabet. Madame would vaguely flip from one to the next, asking me: "What's the name of that nice woman in Boston whom I've known forever? She writes for a newspaper. Grace . . . Grace?"

"Grace Davidson."

"Yes, I must remember her. . . . And then there's the advertising man in Paris. You know, the real clever one who was always having trouble with his . . . his kidneys!"

"Capdeville?"

"That's him. We should never have let him go. I must remember him, too."

The lawyer was called in. Codicils were inserted. The big black book grew fatter and, instead of sleeping with her purse, as she had done in the past, Madame now cradled her will.

New York's summer heat made her suffer. The air-conditioning units in her apartment were old and wheezing: "Why buy new ones? I may not be alive next summer. Better we go to Europe . . . on a boat. What I need is good, clean air. Sea air."

So, with her nurse and myself in protective attendance, we set sail on the *France*. I was again alarmed at the enormous responsibility. Her doctor did little to reassure me. "She can die any time and anywhere. So why hold her back?"

Madame's small cabin faced the bridge. It was on the top deck. Here, she could lie in her narrow bunk, propped up with pillows, and scan the horizon.

"I used to love to walk on deck. Can't now. . . ."

Paris depressed her. She didn't want any new clothes; and her office on the Faubourg no longer held the magic of expectancy, of a good fight, of problems resolved, that it once had. Even her favorite restaurants—La Méditerranée, La Cremaillère, Le Grand Véfour—left her disenchanted.

"Why spend the money?"

It still amused her to see a few old friends, particularly women, whom she called "intellectual women."

"Let's go out with Janet. You know, the one with the monocle who writes for *The New Yorker*."

Janet Flanner had just written a piece on Madame in *L'Oeil* magazine. She was portrayed as a great collector. This had pleased her.

"Why does she say my voice is 'plum rich'?"

"It's a figure of speech."

"Nice."

The summer wore on. By August there was no one left in Paris and the office, that she had shunned, was closed.

"I swear. They all take too long for their holidays!"

"Why shouldn't we have one?" I now suggested. "Together. . . ."

"Where will we go? Cures are no good for me. I don't like fancy places. I need air . . . sea air," she repeated.

It was then I reminded Madame that her friend, and mine, Nina Mdivani was in Tangiers staying at the Minzah Hotel.

"But that's a place for bums."

"Barbara Hutton has a house there."

"So?"

In desperation I added that it was by the sea and therefore cool. Madame finally agreed to go: "Two weeks won't kill me unless I die before. . . ."


Tangiers suited Madame as it did me. Sleazy, freewheeling—prettier than Casablanca, but without Marrakech's Islamic elegance—the rich lived there cheek-by-jowl with the down-and-out.

"Darlink, you've made peace with 'The Computer,'" Nina welcomed me, thrusting her cheeks in the air and waiting for my lips to brush them. "Helena, my love, you're finally having a honeymoon with Patrick!"

Madame prodded the vast but elegant haunches with a finger. She could have been a shy teen-ager being ragged by her best friend.

"I already feel better," Madame admitted on the second day of our stay. Her airy room had a terrace, facing the sea, and every evening I arranged a bridge marathon for her entertainment. There were few available players—most of them antiquities. Eugenia Bankhead, Tallulah's little sister, was one of the faithful. It was she who, after a particularly heated game, declared: "If you add up the ages around this table we're back in the sixteenth century."

"Don't. . . . ," Madame cautioned, "until you've paid the ten francs you owe me!"

All of Tangiers was buzzing with extravagant rumors concerning a party Barbara Hutton planned to give. She was going to import five hundred "Blue Men"—members of a nomadic Sahara tribe who, from protecting their faces and bodies against the desert wind with blue-black djellabahs, were permanently blue of skin, like ancient Britons. She had lured a new English group called the Rolling Stones. Plane-loads of celebrities were reported to be flying in from all over Europe. The Blue Men were to guard her palace, in the Casbah, against would-be gate-crashers. What confused tightly-knit and competitive Tangerine society was that few among them had received invitations to attend the party. Even Nina, who was Miss Hutton's ex-sister-in-law, seemed to have been overlooked—a difficult feat.

Intrigue, due to boredom, was then one of Tangiers' undisputed avocations. As with the Montagues and the Capulets of ancient Verona, there were two rival factions—not Arabs, but Englishmen—lording it, socially, over the shifting and sometimes shiftless crowds of summer visitors.

David Edge—a burly, crusty, paternal figure—ruled over the international and artistic members of Tangerine society from a tasteful palace in the Casbah. It had once been the royal harem. Like an eighteenth-century autocrat, he presided over a mini-court, sometimes receiving his guests while sprawled on a canopied bed which had reputedly belonged to Catherine the Great. On these occasions he wore a jeweled caftan and looked not unlike an Anglican Bishop dressed by Dior. His receptions were magnificent, as was the exotic food he served on a grandly theatrical terrace strewn with brightly hued carpets. David Herbert, his archenemy, lived in a suburban district of Tangiers known as La Montagne, where he welcomed his guests as might an English nanny, on Christmas Day, in the nursery. He was toothy but humorous. His home, although he maintained a private zoo for damaged animals, could easily have been transplanted to the Sussex Downs where the flowered chintzes, Regency furniture, and faded family portraits would have passed muster unnoticed. But in Tangiers they caused a stir. *"Très Anglais."* Moreover, Princess Alexandra of Kent had spent a fragment of her honeymoon there. This

added luster, in the smoldering eyes of Tangerines, to "Lord Herbert."
He wasn't a lord, but an Honourable. The residents of Tangiers have
always been prone to exaggeration. His father, and now his older
brother, was the Earl of Pembroke. Few Englishmen could boast of
bluer blood, greater lineage.

The feud between the "two Davids," as they were called locally,
was probably sparked by the fact that one longed to be a great noble-
man, while the other itched to be a refined host. Each was inordinately
jealous of the other.

"They should merge forces! Two are always better than one . . . ,"
Madame quipped—although she favored Mr. Edge, whose opulence
and theatrical behavior amused her. She found Mr. Herbert "nice,
but ordinary. . . ." It then came out that Mr. Herbert was making all
of the arrangements for Miss Hutton's party. He had completely ex-
cluded all of Mr. Edge's circle.

"What was it like?" Madame asked one of the rare but lucky guests
after the party. "Was she drunk?"

"Who?"

"The rich girl."

"She wasn't even there."

"What did I tell you, she was drunk . . . poor thing."

On this anticlimactic note, we left Tangiers and again, as if sensing
this was to be her last visit to France, Madame decided that, in quick
succession, we should visit "a few nice places"—places she had loved
or which evoked a few happy memories. And what an odd choice they
turned out to be! There was the Flea Market outside Paris: "This is
where I bought some of my best bargains!" Next came Honfleur, an
enchanting little port on the Channel coast of Normandy: "This is
where I made up with Titus after our first big fight!" And lastly we
repaired to her first French factory, near Saint-Cloud, where a ruined,
sprawling building—more of a country house than a cosmetics plant—
still stood. "This is where I was always happiest . . . working in my
kitchen, my laboratory!"

Christmas and the New Year of 1964–1965 came and went; by
then we had been back in New York three months. Madame seemed
to be living as if in a dream, a disinterested dream. She did not give a

family dinner as she had done in the past, saying, "It's time someone else did the entertaining." But when her son Roy invited her to his home she refused. Her complaints were now aimed at the weather, at the intense winter cold.

"What do you think of death?" Madame asked me one morning as we waited for a meeting to convene around her bed. How could I have guessed she had only twenty-four hours to live?

"Inevitable," I shrugged.

"Don't be funny. I want a serious answer."

"As a Catholic, I was raised to believe in the afterlife. But somehow I don't see myself sitting on a cloud with a harp."

"Nor do I."

"I would like to believe in reincarnation."

Madame slowly raised herself on an elbow.

"So would I."

"Are you afraid of death?" I asked, as two members of her staff sat down on their accustomed chairs by Madame's bed. I could hear their breathing accelerate. "Not in the least, now. I was. But I've waited too long. It should be . . . an interesting experience." Madame gave me a sly wink. She was again playing for the gallery. She would obviously be eternal!

But later that morning, following a brief appearance in her office, Madame suffered a slight stroke. She was taken home by her doctor. Oxygen revived her as did several of the pills she gulped down regularly, those which had once helped to increase her fortune when she bought Abbott Laboratories stock. She started reaching for the telephones. After months of disinterest in her affairs (was it a strange premonition?) Madame again wished to be involved, to be informed, to control.

Her doctor, Doctor Nachtigall, thought it advisable to have her moved to a hospital. For a second time in the day, she was ushered into a waiting ambulance, but, this time, she screamed out. And tried to resist, to no avail.

On the following morning—April 1, 1965—my telephone rang. It was barely seven o'clock. Force of habit, as I picked it up, made me think that Madame was summoning me.

Mala's voice—cool, musical, informal—said: "Madame's dead!"

In the hospital Madame had had another stroke, followed by a massive blood clot. She died—no, I like to think she drifted, painlessly, into a long sleep leading, possibly, to a swift reincarnation.

Only her doctor was by her side.

I sat on the edge of the bed and stared, through the open window, at the early morning sunshine brightening the empty streets. There were tears in my eyes. Madame wouldn't see the sunshine and I wouldn't hear her voice again: "Remember, I'm your friend. . . . Are you learning? Are you getting strong? . . . So what's new?" It was the end of an era. The phone rang again, some minutes later, and Roy's wife, Nieuta Titus, repeated the news. She hoped, as did Roy, I would attend a family council later that morning to discuss the funeral arrangements.

The meeting "to discuss Madame's funeral arrangements" lacked a leader—one who would reach and implement the proper decisions. It was Madame's job, of course. It had always been her job. But she was no longer there to jostle, to coerce, to bully her family into reaching decisions—her decisions.

Finally, Harold Weill led Roy Titus out of the room where we all sat glumly toying with cups of coffee.

"Where are you going?" Roy's wife called after him.

"To Campbell's. We plan on a very simple affair." I felt my palms moisten. The one "affair" that Madame would not have wanted to be "simple" was her own funeral. Mala looked at me. She had read my thoughts and between the two of us we saw to it that even Madame would have been pleased with the final results.

We selected her clothes, her jewels, with care and love, as if she were going to attend one of the parties she loved to give. The dress, the first to be designed for her by Yves Saint Laurent, was a heavily embroidered tunic glittering with an intricate constellation of rhinestones. The jewels were her "best" pearls and, on her tiny hands, she would wear matching cameos of rubies and emeralds.

"I still think we should go and look at her . . . ," Mala suggested, "in the casket, before others do so."

We met at Campbell's funeral parlor early on the following morning.

The obituaries were already out. Madame would have been happy.

:[ 285 ]:

Her death was front-page news in all of the newspapers and *The New York Times*, in a glowing panegyric, gave her four full columns.

I have always hated the anonymity of funeral parlors and during the conference in Roy's apartment wanly opted that the service be held in Madame's own apartment. I was overruled.

"But that's what she would have liked . . . as would those who loved her, coming to say a final good-by, in her home, her own home."

Madame was not "resting"—to use the odd language of funeral parlors—in the main chapel. In fact, she was secreted on the fourth floor of the establishment, in what looked like the comfortable bed-sitting room of a Miami Beach hotel. The only thing lacking was a television set. There were large plastic upholstered armchairs set about an alcove in which, on a catafalque, I could just discern the outlines of Madame's profile. Two bunches of American Beauty roses, set on twin pedestals, rounded out the sparse decorations. Tears again blurred my vision. It was such a sordid last setting for "The Empress of Beauty."

"We plan on a very simple affair," Mr. Weill had said.

Fortunately, Mala took charge.

"Isn't Madame beautiful?" she said. "Others must share our joy, and our sorrow. . . ." She turned, regally, to an attendant, "Have Madame Rubinstein moved—let her 'rest' in your best chapel!"

"It will cost a thousand dollars a day," he murmured. Mala's imperious glance suddenly reminded me of her aunt. She didn't say "yes" or "no," but bowed, slightly, and pointed to the door.

"Patrick," she said softly, "see to it that the flowers are those Madame loved. Lots of them!"

I ran to her favorite florist and in an orgy of love, or rage, ordered four thousand dollars worth of flowers to replace the two bouquets of American Beauty roses.

(Later Madame's lawyers called me and questioned the bill. But I had previously informed myself. It had already been paid for by "The Estate of Helena Rubinstein Gourielli"—as had everything else to the tune of some ten thousand dollars.)

The funeral proper was to take only an hour, but the lying-in-state lasted for three days. Six thousand people filed by Madame's casket, signed the guest books, were thrilled or saddened.

In death, she seemed to have shrunk from her diminutive four feet, ten inches, to the size of a small doll—one that was Mexican in its opulence and beauty. It was said that a great part of Madame's huge success with the American public—particularly with Jewish women who were some of her principal customers—was due to the fact that she was so small, dumpy, old. They felt safe observing her dictates, buying and using her products. But now, seeing her, they must also have felt, as I did, that their investment was justified.

In this, her final repose, Madame looked, as Mala had said, "beautiful." The flowers I had ordered rose about her like Titania's bower. She was all but smothered in an extravagant trellis of carnations, delphiniums, and peonies. But what I shall never forget—although her darting eyes were closed—was the nobility of her features. The jaw, the nose, the cheekbones were strong, firm, and powdered in the most exquisite shade of violet I have ever seen. Her skin glowed, her hair shimmered, she was virtually unlined; while the blue veins at her temples seemed to have been drawn by an artist of consummate skill.

Until noon on that first day, the mourners were mostly strangers. I sat, in a room near the chapel, quietly nipping on a flask of whisky as if attending an Irish wake. Madame's friends appeared after lunch, having first fortified themselves, no doubt, with a cocktail or two. By then, Roy Titus and most of the family were present, lined up as if on a parade ground, exchanging futile words with the curious, the sincere, and Madame's devoted staff.

As at all funerals, and the deathwatch that precedes them, there were moments of hilarity counterpointing those of sadness. Three of Madame's favorite newspaper ladies blew in, so to speak, on the last night, to pay their "respects." A twenty-four-hour taxi strike had paralyzed the city. After a long day in their offices, Nancy White, Eugenia Sheppard, and Sally Kirkland decided to join forces to soften their ordeal. They had to take a bus up Madison Avenue, obviously a new experience for them. The bus stopped frequently and they got out equally frequently, unsure of where they were. At each stop a friendly bar helped them to quench their thirst and they then proceeded. It took them two hours to cover a distance of forty city blocks. When they finally arrived, around eight in the evening, I was the only person present. We all kissed and even laughed, exchanging anecdotes concerning Madame. I then led them into the chapel and, as if they had memorized a new litany, each murmured, "Hallo, Madame. My, but you look beautiful. Good-by, Madame. . . ."

The funeral service played, as it were, to standing room only. By now, Madame's casket had been closed. It was smothered in a blanket of spring flowers. There was no altar, no candles, and no other religious trappings. Again, I was reminded of a set for *A Midsummer Night's Dream*—but where was Titania?

"Good-by, Mother!" Madame's son, Roy, roared out as he led the family procession—a strange crocodile that included his current and previous wife—past the bier. A rabbi, who might well once have been billed at the Palace, officiated. He delivered a lengthy oration. The words "cosmetics" and "money" seemed to take precedence over the usual sentiments expressed at funerals. I anticipated, when he finished, a burst of applause. None came. When it was all over, I expected to be asked to attend the burial service at a cemetery in New Jersey where Prince Gourielli had been interred ten years previously. No invitation came. It was then I realized with a pang that my life with Madame—the corporate Madame—had come to an end with hers.

The will, "my testament," listed several hundred beneficiaries. They received sums varying from a quarter of a million to five hundred dollars. The brilliant businesswoman, even after death, continued to exercise her greatest power—that of manipulating money—wisely. Her total assets were said to exceed a hundred million dollars. Some even claimed it was a hundred and thirty million dollars. What difference? There was real estate, there were stocks and bonds. There were jewels, art, furniture, and quantities of cash scattered over three continents.

Then, finally, there was *the business*, which—besides employing more than thirty thousand people—owned factories, salons, and real estate in fifteen different countries; had millions in cash reserves; but, also boasted of several thousand beauty formulas for the skin, the hair, the body, of perfumes, deodorants, depilatories, and . . . there was what Madame valued most: the good will of faithful, satisfied customers.

"When I die," she often told me, *"buy our stock!"* (It was never "my stock.")

"Why?"

"It will go up ten points until people know what's in my will. . . ." It did. Inquiries poured in: "Is Rubinstein for sale?" L'Oréal, M.C.A., Lever Brothers, even "The Nail Man"—Revlon—were interested. But the business was not for sale. Although a public corporation in America, it was owned by Madame in all of the other countries where she was represented and where her cosmetics were sold, with the exception of England that belonged to the Helena Rubinstein Foundation. This foundation, by the terms of her will, inherited all of her own shares—the voting majority.

Madame's will was a brilliant exercise in financial manipulation and foresight.

Some said she might have been more generous to faithful servants, devoted friends, loyal employees. And yet she left no more, no less, than what she felt was their just due. Albert, the Filipino butler who had served her well—albeit sometimes erratically—for so many years received five hundred dollars per annum for life.

In Madame's curious mind, this was a large bequest. On it, in the Philippines, so she must have thought, he could retire. Madame had a very hazy idea of the cost of life, even in the Philippines. But Albert did not want to live in the Philippines. He was furious and voiced his rage by saying to anyone who would listen to him: "She left me a dollar and thirty cents a day . . . until I join her."

Mala Rubinstein, in addition to some important pieces of jewelry and two unimportant paintings, was given a yearly income of five thousand dollars—a trivial sum for a niece, for an heir apparent! And yet again . . . If Mala was to continue in Madame's footsteps, she would be paid accordingly. Madame wanted her to continue in her footsteps and had she left her a princely sum—equal to the four million dollars Elizabeth Arden, who died a year later, is reputed to have left to her own niece—who knows? Mala might have retired.

Madame was much against anyone retiring—particularly members of her own family.

As for me, I received five thousand dollars in cash plus a yearly bequest of two thousand dollars until I died. Madame even mentioned to Harold Weill, when she added this codicil in my favor, "It's so he won't starve!"

Here again, irrespective of the odd footnote—". . . so he won't starve . . ."—I was treated with generosity. After all, I wasn't a "relative" and I had worked for her only fourteen years. A yearly income of two thousand dollars for life, should I manage to live twenty years, represented a capital outlay of sixty to eighty thousand dollars.

But would it not have been more munificent and generous to have left me half that sum outright? This thought coursed my mind until I recalled Madame asking me, "If I was to leave you twenty-five thousand dollars in cash, what would you do with it?"

"Have a lovely holiday! Spend it . . . ," I answered.

"That's what I thought." She nodded.

So Madame played it safe.

There were few really important capital sums among her many bequests left to anyone, even to members of her own family. Oscar Kolin, her nephew, reputedly received a quarter of a million. This, he claimed, was a debt. Madame had promised it: "For services rendered." Her promise was honored.

As in life, the monumental will she made veered between small tips (for "little girls" or "secretaries") to larger tips. The "little girls" received a basic five hundred dollars, the "bigger girls," such as Sara Fox, were left ten thousand dollars. Albeit retired, "Fox"—as Madame called her—had started her career with Rubinstein as a secretary and risen through the ranks until she handled advertising and sales promotion for the American corporation. "She's rich . . . ," Madame often said.

What was odd, in a will of such size and importance, were the few "personal or intimate bequests" of paintings, furniture, and jewelry. "If you give to one," Madame claimed when alive, "you have to give to the other." Hence she stipulated, rather heartlessly it seemed, that all of her belongings, with the exception of clothes and furs, were to be auctioned off to help pay death duties. These were rumored to be more than ten million dollars—irrespective of the foundation to which the bulk of her wealth was designated.

Madame's furs—the sables she adored to huddle in; the "best," the "good," and the "second best" mink coats; the chinchilla cloaks; even the strange karakul *tailleur* made for her at the cost of twelve thousand dollars by Maximilian were all divided between her daughter-in-law, Nieuta Titus, and her niece, Mala.

I often visualized the two ladies flipping a coin in their efforts to be fair.

As for the closets full of elaborately embroidered dresses, some dating back more than forty years and designed by Poiret, they were given to museums, though a few found their way to poor relatives and friends.

Less than a year after her death, New York's Parke-Bernet Galleries, "By Order of the Executors," first auctioned off Madame Rubinstein's jewelry. This sale realized only a fraction of what it was hoped it would—well under half a million dollars.

It was a glittering event, carefully reviewed in *The New York Times,* and attended by a mixture of rich socialites (who bought little), shrewd jewelers (who pounced on bargains), and the curious (who bought nothing). In less than five hours, some three hundred separate items—including the unmounted precious stones of which Madame always kept a large supply in plastic pill bottles—were disposed of.

Her "best" pearls, those eight rows of irregular, glossy lumps she had worn for the last time dead, in her casket, only fetched eleven thousand dollars. They had once been insured for a hundred and fifty thousand and the first string, the first fatal string, had been bought by Madame Rubinstein upon her discovery that Edward Titus was unfaithful to her.

"Whenever I was really unhappy, I bought pearls . . . ," Madame was prone to say.

Her "good" rings—a huge, square-cut yellow diamond, an equally large sapphire the color of lagoons fringing the coast of Ceylon from whence it came, an emerald the size of a bottle cap—yielded little more. Their settings were overly elaborate. Their size frightened the average woman. Or else, possibly, as Madame was the first to admit, "Modern costume jewelry looks just as good!"

Several of Madame Rubinstein's old friends, particularly beauty editors, bought what she might have dismissed as "trinkets."

An enamel bracelet that she often claimed belonged to her mother (although it was obviously made in the early twenties) went to Sara Lee, the editor of *House Beautiful*; while Amy Green of *Glamour* magazine fought a winning battle with her husband, who, unknown to her, was sitting in another part of the room, bidding for her, and captured a single string of polished rubies for a mere five hundred dollars.

The jewelers came from afar to seize their loot. Phillips' of Bond Street purchased back an antique necklace of rose-cut topazes which they had sold to Madame thirty years previously—for a third of what she had paid. They fared even better with a massive pair of pear-shaped diamond earrings. These had cost five thousand pounds in 1932, when the pound stood at five dollars. They were sold for six thousand dollars!

Exactly a year after Madame's death, on April 1, 1966, I resigned from the Helena Rubinstein Company. Why? Was it disenchantment due to my own volatile spirits? Life just wasn't the same (nor was the work I was given to do), without Madame's imperious ways, her rages, her tantrums, and the sound of her husky voice ringing me up early in the morning: "What's new?"

I went off to Europe, to seek, to mull, to formulate the course of my uncertain future. I was always a free spirit and it could only have taken Madame's block-busting personality to tie me down, to hold me by her side for fourteen years.

While I was away, the vast accumulation of art, furniture, bibelots, and miscellaneous antiquities—the Helena Rubinstein "collections" —went before the block. These had been gathered from her homes in France, England, and America. Parke-Bernet's brilliant auctioneer John Marion, who had once been likened to "a wizard run by an adding machine," again officiated in a marathon that lasted ten days and reaped close to five million dollars. This sale, carefully catalogued in five massive books, included paintings and sculpture, drawings and prints, French furniture and decorations, African and Oceanic art.

Did Madame really want her property to be dispersed? I often wondered. Or was it that she couldn't bear the thought of anyone, any one of her heirs or beneficiaries, so easily acquiring what had taken so long for her to collect? Madame Rubinstein finally left only money. The money not claimed by taxes went to her foundation—the Helena Rubinstein Foundation—which tactfully operates out of two small rooms in an office building on Madison Avenue. This foundation, as many before it, is family oriented; and while it succors a wide but vague spectrum of charities whose principal beneficiaries, according to the terms of Madame's will, are "Women and Children," little has been heard of any major grants.

In any event, such grants could not be made until all of Madame Rubinstein's vast property was sold. The apartment building in Paris, Quai de Bethune, went first. Madame's flat—where I had spent so many joyful and difficult years—was acquired by a French champagne magnate who soon regretted buying it. "Only three bedrooms linked by twelve useless salons . . . ," he is reported to have sighed. The apartment in London, maintained by company funds (as were all of Madame's homes), endured until Mrs. Cooper, who occupied it, died of a heart attack some eighteen months after Madame's own demise.

The Park Avenue building was the last of her major properties to go. It fetched more than six times what it had originally cost her: "Good real estate!" Madame would have nodded warm approval. But the final irony came when her own triplex in the building went to Charles Revson of Revlon—"The Nail Man"—her archenemy. As if Madame, from the grave, had watched over this transaction, the acquisition wasn't entirely painless for Mr. Revson.

It took him two years to modernize, to rewire, to redecorate his new home—her old one—before he could move in. Mr. Revson is a perfectionist. But the decorations he finally elected upon would have made Madame chuckle with glee. "Such a waste!" she might have said. "So *nouveau riche*, so . . . Hollywood."

Only the marble in the hallway, the eighteenth-century paneling in the dining room, and the Gothic ceiling in the drawing room remain, and strange to tell, in all of this elaborate and expensive wilderness there isn't one certified antique, one beautiful painting or precious object, to which the eye can react. " 'The Nail Man' has very ordinary taste . . . but, then, that's why he's so successful!"

Madame's final posthumous appearance occurred with the sale of her collections at Parke-Bernet. It was a widely heralded, generously advertised, well-publicized event. Day after day, more than a thousand people packed every seat and corner of the sumptuous main gallery which was linked by TV projectors, such was the crowd, with a series of outer chambers.

The bidding, like surf on a beach, rose and fell as each lot was displayed. Prints and drawings by Picasso, Matisse, and Braque fetched astronomical sums—particularly if compared to the few hundreds of francs Madame had once paid for them. African sculptures, of which there were several hundred, next caused a stir. A single Senufo mask went for twenty-four thousand dollars.

But this was but a mere curtain-raiser, a polite introduction, to what was in store.

Brancusi's majestic brass statue, "Bird in Flight" (of which there were several existing castings) fetched a hundred and forty thousand dollars, while the large, pastoral Bonnard that had hung in Madame's Paris hallway was captured for eighty thousand dollars by an English dealer who then sold it, a few months later, for a hundred and twenty thousand dollars. It had cost Madame ten and, as was her custom, a good lunch for the hungry artist!

A few paintings had to be removed from the sale. "My little mistakes . . ." Madame would have called them. They were fakes. This included a gigantic Picasso portrait of the French poet Guillaume Apollinaire.

(Picasso, when he heard Madame had bought it, expressed doubts as to its authenticity. "Send me a photograph," he told her. She did. It was soon returned with the bold word *Faux* scrawled upon it, and a cross, but no signature.)

Only Madame's lucite bed failed to meet the five-hundred-dollar reserve it had been appraised for. It was first stored and then given away—hopefully to a poor relative, some of whom had been overlooked in her will.

With the sale of Madame Rubinstein's last possessions there remained only her name—the business and the products which bore her name. This was her final legacy.

"I want the business to last three hundred years!"

Will it? One wonders . . . For beyond her niece, Mala; her nephew, Oscar; and her son, Roy—who albeit still active are perilously close

:[ 294 ]:

to the legal age of retirement—the supply of available relatives is nearly exhausted. Her two grandchildren by Horace, Toby and Barry Titus, are both married and went their separate ways armed with the legacies she left them. Roy's daughter, Helena, is still a small child. Will she, some day, have the imagination, the drive, the energy required to head a vast cosmetics empire? Or will it by then, as is the case with Elizabeth Arden's company, have been sold to a conglomerate?

For nearly seven decades, Madame Rubinstein not only created and built up her business, but guided its destinies, sacrificed, struggled, nursed it along. In the process she helped to create an industry. Cosmetics and the sale of cosmetics—until her appearance in Australia more than seventy years ago—were virtually unknown, sold secretly, formulated haphazardly, and used only by what she called "fast women."

The twelve jars of "Crème Valaze" proliferated. But for them to have done so, it required vision, inventiveness and guts for a single woman without money, with but a hazy knowledge of English, of chemistry, of business procedures, to expand a single face cream into a cosmetics line which today includes more than five hundred items and which grosses nearly a hundred million dollars a year throughout the world.

Madame was an opportunist. She was also a visionary, an adapter; sometimes, even, an inventor. Not only did she help to invent an industry, she also helped to stimulate related industries. Without her, department stores and drugstores, whose greatest income is derived from the sale of cosmetics, might not have grown into huge chains. The world of fashion, also, must smile approval upon her far-reaching influence—for what are a woman's clothes without the proper skin care, make-up, hair styles?

Advertising agencies, magazines, newspapers, television, all benefited from Madame's genius as a merchant. And, finally, her own industry—the cosmetics industry—which is, incredible as it may seem, one of the top ten in America, owes much of its extraordinary growth to Madame—to Helena Rubinstein.

"If I hadn't done it, someone else would. . . ."

Madame was a strange combination of paradoxes. She could exude sophistication and then be a child. She could be a calculating tycoon, a benevolent empress, a greedy peasant.

When Madame died at ninety-four—although some claim she was ninety-nine—the first telegram I received read: "How sad! I know how much you'll miss 'the old girl.' "

It was signed Diana Vreeland—*Vogue* magazine's fiery editor-in-chief.

Yes. Not only have I missed her—I always will.

*New York, November 1970.*